THE DIRECTOR'S CUT

FINDING *God's* SCREENPLAY

ON THE CUTTING ROOM FLOOR

Erik L. Strandness, MD, MATh

WESTBOW°
PRESS
A DIVISION OF THOMAS NELSON
& ZONDERVAN

Scripture quotations are from The Holy Bible, English Standard Version (ESV), copyright 2001 by Crossway, a publishing ministry of Good News Publishers. Used by permission. All rights reserved.

WestBow Press books may be ordered through booksellers or by contacting:

WestBow Press
A Division of Thomas Nelson
1663 Liberty Drive
Bloomington, IN 47403
www.westbowpress.com
1 (866) 928-1240

ISBN: 978-1-4908-2317-1 (sc)
ISBN: 978-1-4908-2318-8 (hc)
ISBN: 978-1-4908-2316-4 (e)

Library of Congress Control Number: 2014900901

Printed in the United States of America.

WestBow Press rev. date: 03/10/2014

Contents

Dedication...vii

Preface ix

Acknowledgments xv

Introduction xvii

1. Christian Couture 1
2. To the Unknown God...32
3. Improvisation Or Masterpiece Theater?..............60
4. All The World's a Stage 86
5. Propped Up 115
6. Meet the Cast 130
7. Houston, We Have a Problem............................160
8. Pathology Report...199
9. Conflict Resolution..222
10. Cruci"fix" 253
11. The Cast Party 288
12. Lingua Dei..325

Notes 351

Dedication

THIS BOOK IS DEDICATED TO my dad, who taught me integrity, hard work, and a love of learning. I wish he had been alive to see the profound changes in my life. I love you, Dad.

For what can be known about God is plain to them, because God has shown it to them. For his invisible attributes, namely, his eternal power and divine nature, have been clearly perceived, ever since the creation of the world, in the things that have been made. So they are without excuse.

—Romans 1:19–20

Preface

THE BOOK YOU HOLD IN your hands represents a journey of biblical proportions, not because it rises to the level of monumental, earth-shattering literature, but because it chronicles an expedition into the wilderness of life, where, as it turned out, the only reliable navigation tool I could find was the Bible.

I was raised in a Christian home, I attended church regularly, and I accepted most doctrine without hesitation. I had lived in a Christian state of mind, which inappropriately had seceded from my "united state" of life. Instead of being one nation under God, my existence was split in two by a sacred-secular divide. I had become so enamored with my personal Christian "state" that I never bothered to see if it had anything to say about the vast country outside its borders.

One particularly sunny day as I strolled through town, admiring my mental Christian iconography, I was met by a first-time visitor to my own "private Idaho." He commented on the beautiful scenery and the interesting historical monuments, but then he did the unthinkable; he asked me to explain why I bothered to live in this sparsely populated spiritual state in the first place. I had no answer! Here I was, living in the Christian Gem State, and all I could offer him was potatoes. I had become so content living in the urban Eden of my theoretical Christian knowledge that I neglected to consider what difference that knowledge made to my friends who lived in the boonies.

At that moment, I decided to take a road trip and carefully map the world outside my Christian happy place. I hooked up my spiritual Airstream and toured the countryside of life, not knowing exactly where I was going or even how I would get there, but what I found was astounding!

I discovered that every historical sight, natural wonder, and small community I encountered had already been described in detail by a several-thousand-year-old biblical atlas.

I wrote this book because I have many friends who also live in this great Christian state, but because the transit system is so good, they don't own cars and never venture beyond the state border. In light of my experience, I knew that sooner or later their comfortable routine of walking dogs, frequenting cafes, and taking buses to work would be interrupted by out-of-towners who would not only want to know where the bathrooms were but who would have very touristy questions about the state they were visiting. "Who's the Governor? Why does the state tree have a man hanging on it?" And most important, "Why would I want to relocate my family here?"

I want my friends to be knowledgeable about the state in which they live so that they will be qualified to give guided tours, make a case for relocation, and hand out spiritual souvenirs to the visitors to take back to their families who live in the Badlands.

It all began in the summer of 1997; there I was, happily minding my own business, building my career as a neonatologist, when God grabbed me by the scruff of the neck and set me on a path I would never have chosen or thought possible.

My wife, daughter, and I had recently moved to Spokane to begin building my medical career after I completed my specialty training at Stanford University. I couldn't have asked for a better job. I had the opportunity to work with an outstanding group of physicians and nurses in the perfect-sized city, small enough to avoid long commutes and large crowds but medically sophisticated enough to meet my technology-dependent intensive-care interests.

We quickly found a church, which was unlike any I had encountered before. I'd been raised a Lutheran, nourished on a steady diet of fruit-infused, spiritual Jell-O, but this church offered me a more nutritious Holy Spirit diet of meat and potatoes. For most of my life, I had successfully kept Jesus locked away in my personal safe room because I feared if I let Him out, He might make me do something crazy, like sway to a praise song or raise my hands during a service. This new church, however, freed me from my stoic Scandinavian shackles, and my religiously mummified body began to show signs of life.

This church frequently took me out of my comfort zone. Small groups were popping up all over the place, and one of my friends recruited me to be a small group leader. I accepted the job with great fear and trepidation because I recognized the limits of my Christian knowledge. I began leading discussions, organizing Bible studies, and finding interesting Christian literature to discuss. This was a bit of challenge since I had previously considered all Christian literature to be mindless fluff that gave readers a pleasant religious sugar high but in the end left them with more spiritual cavities than nutrition.

This all changed, however, when my dad gave me the book *Soul Survivor* by Philip Yancey. Yancey introduced me to a disparate cast of primarily Christian writers who were brilliant, insightful, and witty. Men and women who had done the hard work of intellectually engaging their Christian faith.

> Always being prepared to make a defense to anyone who asks you for a reason for the hope that is in you; yet do it with gentleness and respect. (1 Pet 3:15–16)

About the same time, my agnostic brother-in-law asked me about my faith. He had noticed that I thought and behaved as if I were a citizen of another kingdom prompting him to inquire about my King. I was completely unprepared for such basic questions. I felt like a complete idiot because I couldn't adequately explain my Christian faith to him. I wanted to speak to him with "gentleness and respect" but couldn't find the words to give him "a reason for the hope that [was] in [me]." I found this situation intellectually intolerable because it was at odds with the way I practiced medicine. Every day, I would prescribe medications and employ medical technologies based on time-tested, peer-reviewed scientific literature, but here I was, practicing my faith based on personal anecdotes and untested theories. How could I in good conscience prescribe Christianity to others without first carefully testing it in the laboratory of life?

I knew if my faith was real, I should be able to logically, reasonably, and articulately walk someone through the process of becoming a Christian, from the existence of God to the necessity of Jesus as Savior. I began to devour books on theology, history, and philosophy, which was quite remarkable for a guy who just a few years earlier had thought a good time was a cup of coffee and a good scientific journal article.

The excitement I experienced with every new insight was soon crushed by a double whammy of despair; my father died of pulmonary fibrosis, and I was named, for the first time, in a malpractice lawsuit with several other physicians. These two events sunk me into a sea of desolation in which it seemed the only air I could breathe was laced with the toxic fumes of pain and misery.

I remember one distinct moment during this time that I wouldn't completely understand until years later. I was on my knees, earnestly praying that God would take away my pain, and then, for the first time, I told God I would do whatever He wanted with my life. It was the only time I had surrendered with absolute sincerity, no strings attached, to the will of God. I didn't receive instant relief from my suffering or obtain clarity about my life, but things slowly started to improve. I was dropped from the lawsuit, and the sadness over my father's death became manageable. Despite this time of intense emotional suffering, my desire to completely understand my faith continued.

This book began as a simple collection of quotes from some of my favorite authors, but over time, it took on more structure and began to feel more like a Sunday school class. As I started to organize the material into a somewhat coherent curriculum, I heard a still, small voice suggesting that it might be better as a book.

Once this idea entered my head, I became obsessed with completing the manuscript. During this process, my passion for neonatal medicine began to wane and was replaced by a profound, new interest in all things Christian. It reached a point that I began to resent medicine because it was taking me away from my new love, theology, and so, in 2009, I decided to leave neonatology and go back to school to get a master of arts degree in theology, which I completed in 2011. My desire to better understand the Christian worldview then inspired me to participate in the yearlong Centurions program established by the late Chuck Colson, graduating in 2013.

So where am I now? I have always loved teaching, so it seemed natural to combine my interests and find a school in which I could teach theology and science. I found the perfect opportunity at my children's Christian school. So now, when not writing books, I teach high school theology, history, and biology.

Remember that moment when I promised God I would do whatever He wanted with my life? Well, that moment has arrived. This book and my new occupation are evidence that God will take your sincere surrender seriously. It may not happen immediately, but God always makes good on His promises.

Many people have told me how much they admire my courage for dramatically changing jobs to follow my passion. While these changes may seem dramatic, I can assure you that in my mind, the transition seemed a natural progression over which I had little control. God was with me at all times, gradually preparing me for each step. The path I took is not a testament to my courage but a demonstration of the overpowering but comforting work of the Holy Spirit. Once I surrendered to God, His will left me no choice, but this was not forced labor; it was always a gift, a gift that was too good to be true and could not be left unwrapped.

I have written this book with a bottom-up apologetic approach in mind. I have found that many worldview books tend to approach their subjects from the top down, basing their arguments on doctrinal and philosophical speculation, which I find quite interesting but suspect most lay people find a bit tedious.

I recognized that if Christianity was true, it had to be relevant, easily understood, and capable of explaining the world around us. If it didn't satisfy these three criteria, it was just one more exclusive club of like-minded individuals with secret handshakes, fancy hats, and weekly meetings.

The most powerful truth I uncovered during this decade-long process was that I lived in God's world—He didn't live in mine. While this may seem quite intellectually obvious, I found it practically difficult. I had foolishly tried to build a cute bungalow on my personal property for the almighty God of the universe to dwell when in reality, I was just lucky to live in a mud hut in His kingdom. I realized if it was God's world, the evidence should be everywhere. He built it and sustains it, so the problem wasn't a lack of evidence but rather my inability to adequately perceive it.

I suggest that everyone of any religious background subconsciously recognizes this evidence. They hear what Philip Yancey would describe as "rumors from another world" but can't figure out where they've seen that "world" before. If this is true, we are not at odds with non-Christians but are fellow travelers on this earthly expedition. We need to congratulate them for filling their life glasses half full with God's truth but then ask them why they had stopped midpour. We can confidently say with St. Paul that "they are without excuse," but we must also call ourselves to task and recognize our present ignorance is also unacceptable because "we [also] are without excuse."

> For what can be known about God is plain to them, because God has shown it to them. For his invisible attributes, namely, his eternal power and divine nature, have been clearly perceived, ever since the creation of the world, in the things that have been made. *So they are without excuse.* (Rom. 1:19–20 emphasis added)

Acknowledgments

IF YOU HAD KNOWN ME fifteen years ago, you would realize just how unlikely this book is. I didn't read much, I was only a fair writer, and my primary interest in life was medicine. I, therefore, need to begin by thanking God for taking my unconditional surrender seriously and inspiring me to do things I would never have thought possible.

I now have great respect for anyone who tries to write a book. It is time- and thought-consuming and frequently distracts us from our roles as parents, spouses, and friends. So beyond my divine thanks, I begin by honoring my beautiful wife, Kim, and our amazing children, Haley, Jordan, and Kjersti. They have sacrificed a great deal for the changes that have occurred in my life, and despite not being able to hear the voice in my head, they faithfully accompanied me on a journey they often didn't understand and were frequently unprepared to take.

Thank you, Larry, for visiting my Christian "state" and asking me questions I couldn't answer; you set me on a glorious path of discovery. I want to thank everyone who read my manuscript as it was being formulated, Kim, Rob, Bruce, Larry, Olivia and my kids. I want to give a special note of thanks to Christian Overman and his lovely wife, Kathy, for their encouragement, because it was their interest that validated all my years of work and gave me the courage to publish my book.

I also want to honor the men in my Bible study, Paul, Jeff, Arn, Matt, and Amir, who encouraged me during this process and helped shape many of my ideas. I want to thank the men at the

Union Gospel Mission who helped me realize that lofty theological ideas are valid only when they meet the needs of the person on the street. You have inspired me through your commitment to sobriety and the hard work necessary to achieve and maintain it.

Finally, I need to thank a whole series of people who have touched my life in profound ways—all the physicians, nurses, and patients I have had the honor of working with over the years, the outstanding professors in the Whitworth theology department, and my fellow classmates in the master's program. Every one of you has been an important character in my life drama, and I look forward to one day seeing you all at the cast party. Thank you!

Introduction

"WELL, THAT'S JUST GREAT, DR. Strandness, but all I really got out of your preface was that God created everything. I think I already read that on a bumper sticker just last week. Is that all you have to show for your many years of higher education? Why would I bother reading your book when I could just drive around the block and pick up some other life advice from a fender?"

"A-ha," I say. "You didn't let me finish; God did create everything, but this idea is more than just a Christian motto. It has been thoroughly tested in the laboratory of life, and the results have been published in every major life journal. I'm not just going to tell you that God is the Creator; I'm going to help you gather all the evidence by pooling all these individual studies into one comprehensive, statistically powerful, meta-analysis that will leave you without any excuse."

It's fine to say God made everything and the evidence for His existence can be found everywhere. It may satisfy the average Christian, but the skeptic and seeker know it's not that easy. They have already beaten their heads against the enormous wall of human experience in the hope of finding the answer to life, the universe, and everything and come away bloodied and bruised, sporting a whopping, transcendent headache.

If we Christians want to be relevant to those who desperately need Jesus in their lives, we need to help them piece together all this evidence in a rational and compassionate way. We can't just ridicule the rickety worldview they have cobbled together because when we do, we deny the deep emotional investment they have already put into such a massive undertaking. A better approach is to compliment them on the occasionally well-placed nail or two-by-four of God's truth they have subconsciously used in their own worldview construction projects but show them how they can take those particular pieces and begin holy remodeling projects based on a sound, time-tested set of preexisting blueprints.

What does this blueprint look like? How do we take all this divine raw material and build a structurally sound Christian worldview? I began this book by telling you a story, a story about the sequence of events that led to the transformation of my faith and career. All humans tell stories; in fact, stories are the basic medium by which we transmit information. A story may be as simple as describing the time someone unwittingly wore a new shirt all day long and neglected to take off the sales tag, or as complex as explaining the political, social, philosophical, and religious intricacies of the Holocaust.

To begin, we must consider one important fact: if you remove human beings from the planet, you remove the possibility of story and are left with nothing but grazing sheep. You have to conclude, therefore, that there is something unique about mankind that allows him to understand and generate stories.

In light of this important observation, it seemed to me that the best way to organize all God's evidence was to structure it around the key elements of any good story, including the setting, the props, the characters, the conflict, and the resolution. If your worldview doesn't adequately explain each individual component or is incapable of seamlessly integrating them, it becomes nothing but the incoherent ramblings of a Unabomber manifesto and not the nuanced, timeless prose of classic literature.

Our worldview discussion begins by describing the evangelical limitations of an ill-equipped Christian laity that is intimidated by the cacophony of criticism blaring from the cultural bleachers. We then examine how St. Paul successfully navigated similar cultural waters during his encounter with the Athenian philosophers on Mars Hill. Paul directed the spiritual thirst of the Athenians to the spring of the one true God, a spring which had been bubbling under their feet for centuries.

His task, however, wasn't easy, because he had to make a case for the God of Abraham, Isaac, and Jacob and completely reorient their philosophical mind-sets. Just as Paul had to make his way through the philosophical eddies of Epicurean and Stoic thinking, we must also navigate two prominent philosophical rivers of thought meandering through our own cultural valley, modernism and postmodernism.

Modernism declares that man is just a highly evolved animal, while postmodernism declares that there are no universal, overarching explanations for the world around us. The combination of these two poisons, if swallowed, ultimately leads to the death of man and the death of story. The good news, however, is that despite the influence of these two philosophies, mankind still thinks and behaves as if he's pretty neat and hasn't diminished his obsession with "big picture" stories.

We will then discuss the major story components and their real-world counterparts, practically assessing the ability of each competing worldview to adequately explain all these narrative categories. When you begin to carefully look at the world around you, you begin to realize that our stories are performed on a glorious, meticulously crafted, and well-planned set made up of land, sea, and sky. This set is littered with a host of fascinating plant and animal props that enhance our human story.

While the set and props provide an extraordinary backdrop, the drama doesn't begin until the human characters step on stage. This profound difference between man and animal, character and prop, cannot be adequately explained in evolutionary terms and is understood only when one accepts the fact that man was created in the image of God.

As with any good story, there has to be a plot conflict, and our human drama is no different. The world's plot tension seems to be characterized by a universal unhappiness, and this collective discontent, when carefully analyzed, seems to originate in man. We humans, however, not wanting to look in the mirror and see the ugly truth, try to put the blame elsewhere, invoking incompetent government, repressive religion, and even sugary Twinkies.

Despite the fact that man is the problem, we also recognize he is good, and we are left with a unique creature that seems to be a conflicted mess of good and evil. It sounds eerily biblical, as if we were created good but then in our hunger for the divine, we bit off a bit more knowledge than we could chew and ended up making evil real. Since there is this universal unhappiness in the world, it's no surprise that over thousands of years there have been countless attempts to remedy it. It is this obsessive need to resolve this conflict that drives every worldview.

If man is, at his core, a good creation that has since taken on some bad baggage, it would seem silly to scrap him and start over again. It would seem that the proper remedy would look more like a restoration, reclamation, or dare I say, a redemption project. It's quite fascinating to see that the default mechanism the world uses to deal with pain and suffering is redemption. Why, that even sounds a bit New Testamenty, don't you think? Maybe considering the life, death, and resurrection of Jesus as the only appropriate answer to our dilemma isn't so far-fetched after all.

Finally, if life were in fact one big theatrical performance, wouldn't it make sense that after it had run its course, there would be a cast party, a chance to meet the Director and reminisce with fellow actors? The fact that we are part of a grand drama and yet have time-limited earthly performances raises important questions about death and the afterlife to come.

Ultimately, all this storytelling is a *lingua Dei;* a common language established by God that we all understand but have long since forgotten. Yet, despite our linguistic lassitude, God continues to wash us in the rhetorical splendor of the life-giving water of the words He spoke into creation long ago.

God's story has been reworked, revised, and rejected by many an alternative worldview, and we are called to review their manuscripts to see if they have engaged in mere poetic license or have committed narrative high treason. My goal is to engage the most popular alternatives to Christianity—atheism, Buddhism, Hinduism, pantheism, and New Age religion. I recognize that even within these worldview groupings there is still quite a bit of diversity, so I will focus on the major tenets of each belief system. In addition, we need to remember that none of them is an immovable island in the middle of the cultural ocean. They all, like flotsam and jetsam, float uncontrollably on the currents of modern and postmodern philosophical thought.

It is so easy to get caught up in the intricacies of life and fail to see the larger God story being performed all around us, but this is our task. We are characters in a story so good that it must be shared, but before we can get others interested in it, we must first carefully read it ourselves. I hope you find this book entertaining. I hope you will laugh and cry, but most of all, I hope you will become comfortable in your Christian skin, release Jesus from your spiritual happy place, and sit at His feet and listen to *The Greatest Story Ever Told*.

Chapter 1

CHRISTIAN COUTURE

Lady Gaga and the Amazing Technicolor Meat Dress

TWO THOUSAND AND TEN WAS an amazing year for Lady Gaga; her CD, *The Fame Monster,* became a huge best seller that garnered nominations for best single, video, and CD of the year. She became the first artist to have her YouTube site experience over one billion hits. Her typically outrageous personal comments and fashion statements were taken to dizzying heights, reaching the pinnacle of absurdity at the 2010 MTV Video Music Awards show when she stepped on stage to receive the Video of the Year Award in a dress made entirely of meat. Yes, you heard me, meat!

When asked by a reporter what statement she was trying to make with her fashion choice, she replied, "It has many interpretations, but for me this evening, if we don't stand up for what we believe in and if we don't fight for our rights, pretty soon we're going to have as much rights as the meat on our own bones. And I am not a piece of meat."[1]

While her ladyship and I would probably agree on very little, I do have to admire her for being exceedingly bold. How many people do you know who could have pulled that off? She had the confidence to express what she believed no matter how ridiculous it looked to everyone else. How was she rewarded for her efforts, you might ask? Well, *Time* magazine awarded her with the distinction of making the number-one fashion statement of the year, and on

June 16, 2011, the dress was placed in the Women Who Rock: Vision, Passion, Power exhibit at the Rock and Roll Hall of Fame in Cleveland. (If you thought the smell of Lazarus after four days was bad, just wait for the yearly cleaning of that display.)

I think we as Christians could learn quite a bit from Ms. Gaga's boldness; read once again her comments: "If we don't stand up for what we believe in and if we don't fight for our rights, pretty soon we're going to have as much rights as the meat on our own bones." Don't you think it makes us Christians look bad when something as bizarre as wearing a dress made of animal flesh is admired and rewarded as a bold fashion statement and yet the gospel, which actually has some meat to it—pardon the pun—appears more like a fashion mistake? If people are not asking us about our Christian clothing, then perhaps we look like everyone else. The gospel is the only hope for mankind! Does it get any more important than that? (I do have a question, though—when her dress gets dirty, does she go to a dry cleaner or a butcher shop?)

> Most of us dress our Christian faith in an ill-fitting discipleship that, like a cheap suit, leaves us uncomfortable most of our lives.[2]
>
> —Calvin Miller

History is full of examples of seemingly inappropriate fashion choices becoming bold cultural statements, James Dean's rebel look, the mop tops of the Beatles, Madonna's mix of secular and sacred, and the sagging pants of hip-hop to name but a few. How were they able to make personal statements and establish fashion trends? Each of these pioneers radiated the unshakeable confidence that what they were doing was meaningful despite its initially absurd appearance. Unlike these celebrities, however, most Christians seem to lack confidence in the power of the gospel message, so when they wear their faith in public, they end up looking more like fashion emergencies than bold fashion statements.

As we all know, these fads have their fifteen minutes of fame and then flicker away as the flame of celebrity quickly burns out, but we Christians need to remember we possess the flame of truth that cannot be extinguished, a cultural fashion statement that will never go out of style. If this is true, why are we so timid about walking down the cultural fashion runway in our stylish Christian chic?

Do you feel uncomfortable in your Christian attire? Do you examine yourself in your bathroom mirror, privately feeling quite elegant, but then worry about the fashion statement you will make in public? Do you think your Christian outfit makes you look too fat, too old, too young, too out of date, or too intolerant? Your discomfort prevents the Christian good news from being taken off the hanger; it remains hidden in your closet to be worn only at home or in church like a fez at a Shriner's convention. How can we confidently wear our Christian clothing not just in the hope of being accepted as one of the world's many religious style alternatives but as a fashion trend that will change the world?

> The religious marketplace is full of spiritualities that can costume us in fancy dress. All or any of this may be therapeutic, but therapy is not the purpose of religion.[3]
> —Kathleen Norris

I suggest that our discomfort with PDAs, public displays of apostleship, is rooted in our inability to articulate the relevance of the Christian message to the world. I don't just mean knowing Bible stories or reciting verses of Scripture but also helping others to see that the world around them makes sense only when they recognize that it's God's world in which they live and not theirs. Thankfully, we have a Christian fashion icon from whom we can gain encouragement and advice; a guide steeped in the spiritual fashion industry of his time yet who understood the emptiness of all these religious fads.

Our mentor, the apostle Paul, was viewed as a cultural fashion mistake: "We preach Christ crucified, a stumbling block to Jews and folly to Gentiles" (1 Cor. 1:22–23). Nonetheless, he proudly proclaimed the gospel: "I am not ashamed of the gospel, for it is the power of God for salvation to everyone who believes" (Rom.

1:16). He carried on despite the ridicule he received because he was supremely confident in the cultural relevance of the gospel message. His assurance was anchored in the unshakeable knowledge that the one true God and His plan of salvation was evident to everyone no matter what ethnic, educational, or religious background he or she came from.

In the first chapter of his Letter to the Romans, Paul proudly displayed his Christian garb by explaining to his readers that the gospel was not some body of esoteric knowledge accessible only to supermodels, academicians, theologians, and mystics; rather, it was available to everyone.

Paul knew the evidence for the truth of the gospel message was right in front of their faces; they just needed someone to point it out to them. Since the gospel message was universally relevant and easily accessible, Paul was called to preach it to everyone. "I am under obligation both to Greeks and to barbarians, both to the wise and to the foolish" (Rom. 1:14).

The early Christian church followed Paul's example by boldly proclaiming this unfashionable countercultural Christian message despite ridicule and persecution from the surrounding pagan culture and the Roman state. In spite of overwhelming odds, the church grew! This was not accomplished through clever apologetic arguments but through the confident public display of the lived-out gospel. Athenagoras, one of the early church fathers who wrote in the middle of the second century, described this Christian behavior in a letter to Emperor Marcus Aurelius.

> With us, on the contrary, you will find unlettered people, tradesmen and old women, who though unable to express in words the advantages of our teaching, demonstrate by acts the value of their principles. For they do not rehearse speeches, but evidence good deeds. When struck they do not strike back; when robbed, they do not sue; to those who ask, they give, and they love their neighbors as themselves. If we did not think that a God ruled over the human race, would we live in such purity? The idea is impossible. But since we are persuaded that we must

give an account of all our life here to God who made us and the world, we adopt a temperate, generous, and despised way of life.[4]

Is our current culture that much different from Rome's? The Roman state knew that if it gave people an illusory sense of power by allowing them to import any religious belief they wanted, the masses would be much easier to govern. The only caveat was that the emperor had to be acknowledged as the head curator of the state's cultural and spiritual museum. The Roman state gladly allowed people to hang religious art in the divine gallery as long as they didn't declare theirs to be the only original masterpiece and intolerantly accuse others of being cheap forgeries. It believed that a government policy of enforced religious tolerance was an adequate infrastructure upon which to build Roman society.

The emperors foolishly watched from above as the cracks began to form in their cultural foundation, and instead of being alarmed, they looked on with admiration at the unique patterns those cracks created in the infrastructure until it collapsed under the weight of its own excess. Our government is no different; it also increasingly protects the display of any cause or spiritual movement in the name of tolerance but quickly cracks down on those who claim they possess ultimate truth.

History reveals that no kingdom or government can be successfully built from the top down; it must always be built from the bottom up.[5] "The kingdom of God does not come with your careful observation, nor will people say, 'Here it is,' or 'There it is,' because the kingdom of God is within you" (Luke 17:20–21).

Jesus made it clear that the kingdom was composed of the poor, meek, peacemakers, merciful, hungry, sorrowful, and persecuted, which hardly sounds like the governments we encounter today. To be part of God's kingdom building, we need to take Athenagoras's description of Christian power to heart and begin construction with a "temperate, generous, and despised way of life."

True Confessions

> But when God is present in our lives only as a still small
> voice, we prefer to use a still smaller voice in response.
> Is it any wonder, then, that we often act less like we are
> spreading the good news than like we are spreading the
> good secret?[6]
>
> —Martin B. Copenhaver

So what's your excuse? For most of my life, I excused myself
from being a bold witness for Christ because I didn't want to
appear too aggressive and offend anyone. I hoped the way I lived
my life served as my Christian testimony, a very nice sentiment, but
in reality, the way I spoke and acted wasn't all that much different
from the way people around me spoke and acted. The real source of
my anxiety was in my inability to come up with material evidence
for what I knew to be spiritually true; instead of doing the hard
work of trying to find that link, I chose to live in two worlds, a
spiritual and secular one.

I was afraid of living the Christian witness because it might
prompt someone to ask me about my most treasured possession,
My faith was based on the belief that Jesus Christ was my Lord
and Savior. I hoped it was occasionally evident to others, but I
found myself woefully unprepared to logically explain and defend
it. How could I describe my hope to someone when I couldn't
explain it to myself?

> I was no good at arguing the matter with him [an atheist
> friend] and avoided it whenever I could, partly because
> I wasn't knowledgeable enough to refute his caricatures
> and partly because *I was squeamish about putting up
> for debate anything in which my emotional investment
> was so great.*[7]
>
> —Frederick Buechner (emphasis added)

I was afraid to subject my emotionally invested faith to scrutiny
and ridicule. I treated my faith as if it were built on sand instead

6

of Rock. If we are not confident that under the floorboards of our Christian faith is solid rock, we will be content showing people Polaroids of our spiritual home but never inviting them over for tea in fear it may collapse under the weight of our shared human experience.

Home Is Where the Heart Is

Despite having been raised in a Christian home, I never felt I was adequately equipped to explain my faith to those around me. My insecurity caused me to live in what Francis Schaeffer, the famous Christian apologist, described as a two-story existence, an upper spiritual story and a lower, material, "rest of my life" story. Conveniently, there was no interior staircase between the two levels of my home. The upper spiritual level was like a mother-in-law's quarters with its own entrance. I was forced to go outside as I left one story and entered the other. I recognized they were both levels in my personal home, but what happened in one story stayed in that story.

In my case, Jesus lived upstairs while I resided downstairs. When life got hard and the heat went out on the main floor, I'd hurry outside, climb the stairs, and sheepishly knock on Jesus' door. At His invitation, I'd step inside and warm myself beside His fire. Uncomfortable in His presence, I would nervously wait to hear the sound of my main floor furnace come back on and quickly but politely thank Him for his hospitality and leave Him with the vague promise of a return visit. As I descended the stairs, I often turned and looked back only to see His sad face pressed against the window, tears streaming down His cheeks, fearful this was my last visit. Jesus wept.

> Yet Jesus Christ is standing at the door of our lives, waiting. Notice that He is standing at the door, not pushing it; speaking to us, not shouting. This is the more remarkable when we reflect that the house is His in any case. He is the architect; He designed it. He is the builder; He made it. He is the landlord; He bought it with His life-blood. So it is His by right of plan, construction and purchase.

> We are only tenants in a house which does not belong to us … He will not force entry into anybody's life.[8]
>
> —John R. Stott

My pleasant, two-story existence began to crumble after two friends questioned me about my faith. The first was a nurse who asked me if I really believed Jesus was God's Son, and the second was my brother-in-law who periodically noticed my home had an upper story and inquired as to what it looked like inside. In both cases, I felt completely inadequate to give a satisfactory answer.

I realized I had to do the hard work of constructing an internal stairway between the two levels of my home so I could comfortably move between them. As it turned out, however, I inadvertently allowed Jesus unfettered access to my entire home, and He didn't like what He saw. He pulled out His whip, overturned tables, drove out the moneychangers, and declared my home to be a den of robbers. Be warned! Once you allow Jesus to roam through every room of your home, your dwelling will be transformed from a house into a temple, and your former den of thieves and robbers will be transformed into a house of prayer. In the words of the beavers describing Aslan in *The Lion, Witch and the Wardrobe,* "Course he isn't safe. But he's good."[9] You can be assured of Jesus' goodness, but He will make your comfortable existence dangerously demanding and exciting.

> Do you not know that you are God's temple and that God's Spirit dwells in you? If anyone destroys God's temple, God will destroy him. For God's temple is holy, and you are that temple. (1 Cor. 3:16–17)

> I am a temple in which God dwells. I sense the sanctity in my soul. I see the beautiful paintings and statues depicting my Savior and God. I feel his presence in the Holy of Holies, yet I am restless. Why? Sadly, if you look closely at my temple, you will see the damage I have inflicted, the spray-painted graffiti on the murals, the untended sanctuary full of garbage, and the stained glass

windows covered in dirt. I have desecrated the temple
and I am ashamed. I realize I alone cannot maintain my
temple. I hear Jesus say, "I forgive you for the desecration,
but it is time for temple restoration, and since I know you
cannot do it alone, I have sent a helper, the Holy Spirit. If
you let Him in, the sun will shine through the windows,
the choir will sing, the beauty will be restored, and your
temple will be called a house of worship and not a den
of robbers." (Confessions of the author)

I recognized that building a staircase between floors was not
enough. I also had to knock down walls, remove toxic asbestos
and black mold, and paint the outside. I was forced to critically
think through the renovation of my temple. As I looked around,
it became clear to me that I was not alone, that there were houses
everywhere just like mine, hoping to become little human temples.
We all lived in the same housing tract, Mr. God's Neighborhood,
and were all built upon the same detailed architectural "image of
God" plan, but the problem was that most of the temples lacked
curb appeal.

Sadly, we frequently take the architecturally sound image of
God and make it unrecognizable through our imaginative but
engineeringly unsound remodeling projects. Or, lacking that
creative energy, we allow our homes to fall into disrepair and
become obscured by overgrown weeds of neglect. Our houses
begin to look like either the Winchester Mystery House, in which
stairways ascend nowhere and doors open to brick walls, or
eyesores where trash, broken refrigerators, and dilapidated cars
accumulate and decay in our front yards.

Regrettably, this two-story existence has become the default
position for the majority of us. Stephen Jay Gould, a famous
evolutionary biologist, furthered this cause by putting his
scientific seal of approval on the architectural soundness of a
split-level existence. He tipped his scientific hat to the spiritual
side of life by introducing the postmodern philosophical concept
of NOMA, or non-overlapping magisteria, which grants science
and religion individual domains, and neither is qualified to

comment on the thoughts or actions of the other. It is a nice, tolerant sentiment but ultimately just an excuse to have a disconnected two-story home.

On this point, I have to agree with the atheist Richard Dawkins, who felt that NOMA was intellectually corrupt.

> Gould carried the art of bending over backwards to positively supine lengths in one of his less admired books, Rocks of Ages. There he coined the acronym NOMA ... This sounds terrific— right up until you give it a moment's thought. What are these ultimate questions in whose presence religion is an honoured guest and science must respectfully slink away?[10]

I would, however, append Dawkins's argument by asking, what are these questions that make science the honored guest and force religion to slink away?

Francis Schaeffer recognized that these two separate domains have become quite firmly entrenched in our minds: "The line between the upper and lower stories has become a concrete horizon, ten thousand feet thick, with highly charged barbed wire fixed in the concrete."[11] While he recognized that the ever-changing cultural landscape significantly contributed to this bunker mentality, he acknowledged that the Christian church had to shoulder a significant amount of responsibility by failing to diligently engage each new cultural movement. We as followers of Christ are commissioned with the daunting task of personally and culturally breaching this ever-expanding barricade.

In addition to my inability to externally justify the foolishness of my two-level home, I was also convicted internally by the contrast between my faith and my medical practice. My medical training taught me to utilize treatment strategies based on their experimentally demonstrated efficacy; did the data support the use of a certain drug or technology? I was troubled by my inability to present the supporting physical data for my spiritual truth. Where was the peer-reviewed literature for my religious conclusions? Why did I feel like a fashion freak? I became a little angry, because despite all my academic training in the scientific method, I was never encouraged to think critically about the rest of my life. I could analyze a medical research paper, find its flaws, and discern its clinical relevance, but when it came to my faith, I left my critical-thinking skills at the hospital.

Thankfully, as I began to construct the stairway between my spiritual and material floors, I began to realize that the world is one enormous laboratory and that history is one thoroughly peer-reviewed journal; I just needed to take the time to seriously analyze it. If we are going to hypothesize that God is the Creator of the universe, the data must be everywhere, leaving us without any excuse for not critically evaluating it.

Hell Hath No Fury Like an Atheist Scorned

> As I wrote these words, and as you read them, people of faith are in their different ways planning your and my destruction, and the destruction of all the hard-won human attainments that I have touched upon. Religion poisons everything.[12]
>
> —Christopher Hitchens

> It is fashionable to wax apocalyptic about the threat to humanity posed by the AIDS virus, "mad cow" disease, and many others but I think a case can be made that faith is one of the world's great evils, comparable to the smallpox virus but harder to eradicate.[13]
>
> —Richard Dawkins

Our efforts will be met with resistance. Modern atheist writers such as Richard Dawkins, Daniel Dennett, Christopher Hitchens, and Samuel Harris have, just like in the movie *Spinal Tap*, turned up the volume of their rhetorical amplifiers to eleven, which as we all know is just the same volume but with attitude. Their argument is always the same, but the delivery is more caustic. They reserve their most fierce attacks for the three great monotheistic faiths, Judaism, Islam, and Christianity because these traditions just happen to worship a God of consequence, a deity who has something to say about how we should live our lives. Most Christians, however, are too intimidated to engage these critics and instead embarrassingly retreat to the emotional safety of their Christian nurseries.

Things, however, are changing! The ominous banging of our critics at the door is shattering the peace and quiet we once enjoyed in our Christian hideaways. We're left with a choice: curl up in the fetal position, cover our heads with our blankies, and suck ever more vigorously on our bottles, or grow up, put away the spiritual milk, and break out the forks and knives for the meat of the gospel.

> For everyone who lives on milk is unskilled in the word of righteousness, since he is a child. But solid food is for the mature, for those who have their powers of discernment trained by constant practice to distinguish good from evil. (Heb. 5:13–14)

Polls consistently show that 85 to 95 percent of all Americans believe in God. In light of these numbers, it is surprising to see that the believing majority is the one always being put on the hot seat and fielding questions from the angry atheist minority. It seems to me that a set of beliefs clearly in the minority should require the most scrutiny. If you are an atheist with integrity, you cannot attend a Christian press conference and heckle the press secretary; you must also be willing to stand at the podium and field the same tough questions, explaining the cultural and personal benefits of atheism.

Everyone should have a voice, but the debate must be fair. It's very telling that many atheists ironically attack the character of the very God they say doesn't exist. Why would they waste their critical breath on an issue that is a problem only for the believer? You get the sense that deep down they do recognize the existence of God but feel He needs a good tongue-lashing.

Sadly, most Christians are very uncomfortable asking other worldviews to explain themselves and end up looking like pummeled fighters with faces bruised, swollen, and bleeding, leaning against the ropes in the hope they'll be standing when the bell rings. We need to take a page out of the Muhammad Ali fighting textbook and embrace the rope-a-dope strategy he employed in his epic 1974 "Rumble in the Jungle" battle with George Foreman. During that fight, Ali carefully protected his body while allowing Foreman to throw countless ineffectual punches until he was thoroughly exhausted, and then, while Foreman was at his weakest, Ali went on the offensive.

We need to remember that we've seen every atheist punch before, and they have long since lost their sting. Our problem is that we've been so preoccupied protecting ourselves from their blows that we've forgotten how tired and exhausted their arguments have become and never question their ability to defend themselves from the same punches. We need to go on the offensive and have them explain the difficult issues of pain, suffering, purpose, and the uniqueness of man.

The good news is that despite the world's amusement with this ongoing worldview battle, we all continue to live our lives as if a God does exist. Our culture tips its hat to the atheist intellect but wisely lives in a way that makes sense with the data it encounters every day.

> But the masses just ignore such gloating, intellectual posturing because they are well aware that these "experts" are woefully unable to force-fit life's mental furniture by restructuring reality.[14]
>
> —Ravi Zacharias

Much to the chagrin of our atheist brothers and sisters, the majority of people in this world think God is still a pretty good idea. Sam Harris laments this reality in his *Letter to a Christian Nation*.

> This letter is the product of failure—the failure of the many brilliant attacks upon religion that preceded it, the failure of our schools to announce the death of God in a way that each generation can understand, the failure of the media to criticize the abject religious certainties

of our public figures—failures great and small that have kept almost every society on this earth muddling over God and despising those who muddle differently.[15]

—Sam Harris

Unfortunately for our atheist friends, millions of years of evolutionary pressure have been unable to eradicate the blight of religion. Confronted with this inconvenient truth, they are forced to somehow explain belief in God as a beneficial evolutionary trait that promotes tribal survival. The problem is that by their own reasoning, they have inadvertently made themselves evolutionary dead ends by denying themselves the very religious trait they recognize as beneficial. Maybe, just maybe, God is real, and everybody but the small vocal atheist minority knows it to be true.

The Church of Our Lady of Public Broadcasting

Instead of shrinking away from criticism, we need to embrace the challenge. The fact you have been singled out in this debate is the ultimate compliment. It implies that your belief has serious implications, not just for you personally but also for the world in general. Ask yourself why it is that Christianity is being assaulted and yet New Age religion is given a free pass. Why are there efforts to remove the Ten Commandments from courthouses but New Age gurus such as Wayne Dyer and Deepak Chopra are used to generate money for public broadcasting? The "religion police" know the New Age movement doesn't pose a threat to anybody because it's theologically empty, optional, and ultimately irrelevant to the culture in which it's allowed to exist.

You could argue that the New Age movement has exerted significantly more influence on our culture than has traditional religion, so why don't atheists spill more ink on these movements? Simply put, atheists are too smart a bunch to waste their time engaging a movement devoid of any intellectual substance or consequence.

Christianity, on the other hand, presents real intellectual, spiritual, and historical challenges, making it extremely dangerous to their atheist position. I think most Christians are perplexed that their faith encounters such fierce opposition when all they see is a rather benign bunch of people just trying to find their way in the world and help others in the process. Maybe atheists don't like the fact that Christianity has been holding a mirror up to the world and has revealed that the cultural emperor has no clothes. As we endure the slings and arrows of criticism, we need to remember that Jesus already warned us about the frosty cultural reception we would receive.

> If the world hates you, know that it has hated me before it hated you. If you were of the world, the world would love you as its own; but because you are not of the world, but I chose you out of the world, therefore the world hates you. (John 15:18–19)

Dirty Phones and Good Haircuts

It's sad that these critics often fail to see the consequences of their own arrogance. The late writer Douglas Adams, himself an atheist, illustrated this danger in his book, *The Restaurant at the End of the Universe*, in which he related the story of the inhabitants of the planet Golgafrincham. He tells the story of the descendants of the great circling poets of Arium who had invented spurious tales about the impending destruction of the planet and had passed them down from generation to generation. The planet's cultural elite appropriated these myths of doom to rid themselves of the useless third of their populace, primarily the middlemen, hairdressers, and telephone sanitizers. They spread the word that the planet must be evacuated and proposed sequentially launching three spaceships, or arks, each containing one of the designated cultural third. Ark A would contain the brilliant leaders, scientists, and great artists. Ark B would house the undesirable middlemen, and Ark C would consist of those who did all the work.

15

To accomplish their plan, they designated the B Ark, consisting of the useless third, as the first spaceship to colonize a new planet. The leader of this ark was told "very nicely ... that it was very important for morale to feel that they [the other two arks] would be arriving on a planet where they could be sure of a good haircut and where the phones were clean."[16] After the B Ark left, the "useful" cultural two-thirds felt like their planet had become a better place, and they "lived full, rich, and happy lives until they were suddenly wiped out by a virulent disease contracted from a dirty telephone."[17]

If your philosophy doesn't work for the average man, the telephone sanitizer, then you had best abandon it, because your indignation at the lower caste may spell your doom. The "useless third" may be the ones who possess the truth, the ultimate answer to life, the universe, and everything.

> Only mystics, clowns and artists, in my experience, speak the truth, which, as Blake was always insisting, is perceptible to the imagination rather than the mind. Thus an animist groveling naked in the African bush before a painted stone may well be nearer to the heart of things than any Einstein or Bertrand Russell, and a painted clown riding a bicycle round and round a circus ring more attuned to the reality of life than a Talleyrand or a Bismarck can hope to be. Jesus was making the same point when He insisted that God has revealed to the foolish what is hidden from the wise.[18]
>
> —Malcolm Muggeridge

Atheists, in an effort to bolster their position, frequently characterize believers as gullible and superstitious, deluded by mindless adherence to holy books and ritual. Michael Shermer, an agnostic, wrote about the correlation between personality traits and religious beliefs in his book *How We Believe*. He pointed out that most polls reveal the more educated you are, the less likely you are to believe in God. These findings are frequently used to support the notion that religion is merely superstition held by the less educated. The problem with these findings is that they are measuring intellect by the number of years of schooling, which says nothing about whether these people have seriously investigated the evidence for the existence of God.

I am a prime example of this; despite all my medical education, nobody encouraged me to think about these larger philosophical, religious, and cultural issues. Most institutions of higher learning don't even allow the questions to be raised. Much to our chagrin, higher education has all too often built indoctrination camps rather than centers of critical thinking. Why has the question that has undoubtedly generated the most academic literary output in history been deemed educationally irrelevant?

In my educational experience, the best instructors I have had were those who began their lectures by saying, "I'm no rocket scientist, but ..." They were great teachers because they simplified the complex and made us look at the big picture. All too frequently, those immersed in academia are drowning in vast amounts of detailed information and cannot see the forest for the trees. The scientist studying the tree proclaims he has found truth in the sap without stepping back and seeing the greater ecosystem that allows the tree to survive in the first place. As C. S. Lewis, a brilliant academician, remarked, unless a complicated argument could be simplified to appeal to the average person, the chances were that the one doing the explaining didn't understand it either.[19]

Leap of Faith

Christians are frequently criticized for promoting a view of the world that relies on faith, an ignorant leap into the unknown. I want to clarify this notion because it brings up two very important Christian concepts, consequence and destination. First of all, when it is described as a leap, it means we must be jumping over something, implying consequences if we fail to reach the other side. Our leap is frequently described as one of ignorance, but I counter that it's ignorance we are leaping over to obtain knowledge. Since

God created the universe, we know if we want to understand the world around us, we must seek the mind of the Creator.

Second, leaping implies there are two sides, a leaping point and a landing point, the physical world and the spiritual world. History has shown that the question of how to link the two has been a perpetual dilemma for mankind. The scientific world pays lip service to the spiritual and tries to create a physical bridge alone, designating neurotransmitters and cerebral pleasure centers as the "spiritual" side of the chasm. Most people, however, recognize that the spiritual realm is not merely a physical illusion but also a distinct reality that cannot be ignored. They know it's impossible to anchor a bridge to a spiritual cliff with material stakes. The chasm can be spanned only if we secure the other end with spiritual stakes.

> Aim at Heaven and you will get earth thrown in. Aim at earth and you get neither.[20]
>
> —C. S. Lewis

This debate is being fought on different battlefields, a spiritual and a material one. It's similar to the abortion debate, in which we have a women's-choice battlefield and a human-life battlefield. The question cannot be resolved unless the two battlefields are merged. I think this is one reason why that debate has become important to me; as a physician, I fight my battles on a spiritual and physical or a religious and scientific battlefield. When science fails me and a baby dies, I am confronted with a new dynamic. Questions of purpose, God's will, heaven and hell, guilt, and compassion arise. I have never had a mother and father attribute the death of their baby to evolutionary unfitness; that just doesn't happen. On the flip side, if I encounter a baby with a treatable condition and all the parents want to do is pray about it, I have to put my foot down and intervene. We need to discard this illusory separation between the spiritual and material because nobody truly lives that way.

Our unhappiness stems from the fact that an artificial wedge has been driven between our material and spiritual unity. Mankind will continue to be unhappy until these two worlds resume their proper integrated place in our lives. Christianity has the perfect answer, Jesus, the God/man, uniting the physical and spiritual.

Tagged by God

Gray hair is God's graffiti.[21]

—Bill Cosby

Sadly, intimidated by these cultural stereotypes, most lay Christians defer the question of God's existence to the intellectuals and retreat into their isolated, spiritual upper story, where nobody presses them for a reason for the hope they have. The problem is that they have confused intelligence with wisdom. They need to remember that accumulation of large amounts of data has nothing to say about its proper use. Do you want the surgical resident, whose book knowledge is most likely at its peak, to perform an appendectomy, or the surgeon who has been out of training for decades but has done a thousand such procedures?

This medical truth was brought home to me during my neonatal fellowship. I tend to look younger than my age; I'm a Doogie Howser type if you will, which is a blessing now but was more of a curse during my early medical training. One afternoon, I was asked to explain to a woman who was in premature labor the morbidity and mortality associated with a baby of her gestational age. As I entered her room, her first words were, "My God, he looks like my paper boy!" Her comment was all in good fun, but I suspect she would have liked to have heard from someone who had been tagged with a little more of God's graffiti.

Faith does not conform itself to ideology but to experience.[22]

—Kathleen Norris

Wisdom is not measured by level of education, SAT scores, academic awards, or publications but by the number of wrinkles and gray hairs we have accumulated on our life journeys. Wisdom is found in someone whose life has been a series of personal experiments conducted under the frequently harsh conditions of the world's laboratory and whose findings are not just theories but actual data.

Wisdom is frequently acquired at a life price higher than any college tuition. We frequently seek out wise people to help us see things our limited experience cannot comprehend. We can't learn to hit a sand wedge from someone who has never played out of a sand trap before. Wisdom is not Republican or Democrat, liberal or conservative; it's God's truth rescued from each camp.

A wise person allows the worldview of others enough breathing room to resuscitate pieces of God's truth but also recognizes the wheezing of worldview inconsistency. You will never be able to get others to consider the proposition that they live in God's world if you reject the emotional investment they have already put into their worldviews. I'm asking you to be wise by taking all the information you encounter and test it in the laboratory of life. Like any good scientist, you will need to check your preconceived notions at the lab door and go where the evidence takes you. In the Bible, wisdom is associated with God's creative endeavor, so it follows that the created order is infused with God's wisdom.

> *(Wisdom is speaking)* The Lord possessed me at the beginning of his work, the first of his acts of old. Ages ago I was set up, at the first, before the beginning of the earth. When there were no depths I was brought forth, when there were no springs abounding with water. Before the mountains had been shaped, before the hills, I was brought forth, before he had made the earth with its fields, or the first of the dust of the world. When he established the heavens, I was there; when he drew a circle on the face of the deep, when he made firm the skies above, when he established the fountains of the deep, when he assigned to the sea its limit, so that the waters might not transgress his command, when he marked out the foundations of the earth, then I was beside him, like a master workman, and I was daily his delight, rejoicing before him always, rejoicing in his

inhabited world and delighting in the children of man. (Prov. 8:22–31, my addition)

Proverbs tells us that wisdom was with God when He created the world. Through our life journeys, we have stubbed our toes on the nuggets of God's truth and the blood and pain we have experienced has become the seeds of personal wisdom.

> The Lord by wisdom founded the earth; by understanding he established the heavens; by his knowledge the deeps broke open, and the clouds drop down the dew. My son, do not lose sight of these—keep sound wisdom and discretion, and they will be life for your soul and adornment for your neck. Then you will walk on your way securely, and your foot will not stumble. (Prov. 3:19–23)

Your seat in the balcony of wisdom will provide you with the big-picture perspective necessary to make sense of it all. You must first put the fruit of knowledge into the blender of existence and then be able to describe the taste of real-life smoothie to others. We—believer and unbeliever, academician and layperson—need to heed the warning of the great Greek philosopher Socrates, who warned that "an unexamined life is not worth living."

> Men stumble over the truth from time to time, but most pick themselves up and hurry off as if nothing happened.[23]
>
> —Winston Churchill

Religion of Tolerance

Despite the harsh voices of the New Atheists, our culture seems to be softening to the spiritual claims of religion. It is fashionable to tell people that you are a "spiritual person." The problem is that just saying you're spiritual does nothing but identify you as one more confused human being trying to find the ever-elusive material-spiritual link. In the process, our culture has deified the search at the expense of the answer, even going so far as to suggest that if we find the answer, we are intolerant heretics.

If spiritual searching is our new God, then tolerance is the new mode of worship. We pay respect to our God by singing the hymns of liturgical tolerance, but in the process redefine what tolerance actually means. Tolerance is the amount of deviation allowed before something becomes nonfunctional or unrecognizable. Machine parts are allowed a certain amount of tolerance in shape or size beyond which they become useless. In pediatrics, we use growth charts to evaluate whether the weight, height, or head circumference of a child is within acceptable parameters. Any measurement outside of the range of tolerance suggests that something is wrong.

With this in mind, we must reevaluate the meaning of religious tolerance. If a religious practice or doctrine doesn't meet basic criteria, it is inadequate, and the best way to test it is to place it in the machine and see if it works. This is not intolerance; this is basic common sense! If we don't measure the degree of deviation in others' spiritual theories, we are cruelly looking on as their religious wheels continue to spin but go nowhere. Our neighbors' spiritual journeys become cars on blocks in their front yards; we compliment them on the fact they have a car but never ask them why it isn't going anywhere.

At its core, then, tolerance is quite disrespectful of the deeply held spiritual beliefs of our fellow man. Tolerance will never unite us; it will only continue to fracture us into billions of personal spiritualities that are ultimately irrelevant. I have suffered enough at the hands of my own spiritual innovations. Why would you encourage me to sharpen my personally created spirituality when it's almost certain I'd cut off my finger in the process? I need a greater, wiser, universal spiritual truth because I'm far too dangerous to others and myself.

You Want Freedom? I'll Give You Freedom!

Our everyday lives are full of decisions of varying degrees of importance, but we rarely have the thrill and responsibility of making life-or-death decisions. Christianity, however, pays us all the ultimate compliment by asking us to participate in the most important decision we will ever make, one that has consequences for all our personal destinies. What an honor, but also what a scary proposition!

> I call heaven and earth to witness against you today, that I have set before you life and death, blessing and curse. *Therefore choose* life, that you and your offspring may live, loving the Lord your God, obeying his voice and holding fast to him, for he is your life and length of days, that you may dwell in the land that the Lord swore to your fathers, to Abraham, to Isaac, and to Jacob, to give them. (Deut. 30:19–20, emphasis added)

Faith traditions other than the three monotheistic faiths are all irrelevant because they are optional; they have no bearing on anyone's ultimate destiny. Most of them offer a cosmic mulligan, a chance to do it all over again. If you miss out on being absorbed by Brahman or can't quite extinguish your personhood in nirvana, at least you can come back as a toad or cosmic-dust leftovers and be reincorporated into Mother Earth. If God is real, we are talking about soul surgery and not just Band-Aids for our psychic pains.

> And he said, "I will do this: I will tear down my barns and build larger ones, and there I will store all my grain and my goods. And I will say to my soul, Soul, you have ample goods laid up for many years; relax, eat, drink, be merry." It is for those who are in fear of hearing God say, *"Fool! This night your soul is required of you,* and the things you have prepared, whose will they be?" So is the one who lays up treasure for himself and is not rich toward God." (Luke 12:18–21, emphasis added)

The World According to God

A worldview should be a comprehensive and coherent understanding of the world around us. It must be able to universally integrate every aspect of our lives into a seamless whole. If it fails in this task then it is merely a world opinion, which may be individually satisfying, but is corporately meaningless. What we really need is a view of the world that comports with reality and is universally relevant.

It's becoming popular to speak of a worldview war raging all around us. We frequently get so caught up in the heat of battle that we fail to see we're actually fighting it on a particular battlefield. In our haste to maneuver our worldview artillery around hills and rivers, we neglect to ask ourselves where the hills and rivers came from in the first place.

Maybe we're doing battle on God's own turf. The word *worldview* can be problematic because it suggests there are many options as to how we view the world, but in the end, we all know there can be only one reality. Therefore, let's not waste any more time fashioning rose-colored glasses so we can see the world the way we want; instead, let's make a trip to the optometrist and get some prescription spectacles so we can see the world the way it really is. The world already has a view, and it's God's, not yours, so we need to stop skirmishing with our fellow man over our mental constructs and look at the world the way it is.

You live in God's world; God doesn't live in yours! You may want to construct a nice guest room on your property for God, but you'll soon see that the God who created the universe is far too big for it. Once you realize the futility of trying to mold an omnipotent, holy, loving, and just God into your image, once the clay relinquishes control of itself to the potter, it will find freedom. You can relieve yourself of having to continually construct fake Hollywood sets to keep your personal worldview illusions alive and allow yourself the freedom to admire the handiwork of a far superior carpenter. Is it really that bad to be the *David* to God's Michelangelo, the Narnia to God's C. S.

Lewis, *The Last Supper* to God's da Vinci, a remarkable creation
to its Creator?

> How much larger would your life be if your self could
> become smaller in it.[24]
>
> —G. K. Chesterton

Puzzle Pieces

Correctly constructing a worldview is like putting together a
jigsaw puzzle. The box contains all the pieces you need, but until
you begin putting them together, you cannot be assured it will
match the picture on the cover. The battle between the various
world opinions ultimately comes down to disagreements over what
the picture on the puzzle box looks like, an argument that can be
easily settled by just putting the puzzle together. Every piece must
be accounted for and properly positioned. If you have pieces left
over or find yourself forcing them to fit together, anyone looking
at your work will quickly notice the discrepancy.

Most Christians seem content to admire the picture on the
box, faithfully believing that all the pieces inside will fit together
nicely if they just had time to assemble them. Our ability to
successfully evangelize others will ultimately come down to the
question of whether what we say is believable; does the puzzle
match the picture? Did we do the hard work of putting it together
for ourselves?

> Every questioner has a worldview. If you do not appeal
> to the legitimacy or the illegitimacy of the worldview,
> you will never give satisfactory answers to the skeptic.
> In short, apologetics may begin in specifics but inevitably
> moves to the general, which then explains the specifics.[25]
>
> —Ravi Zacharias

While there is certainly a component of faith to this discussion,
God has also given us physical evidence, the picture on the box,

and we are obligated to demonstrate it to others. If God thought it was important enough to empty Himself, become physically human, and live in our world, His fingerprints and footprints should be found everywhere. God, by creating the material world, made Himself universally relevant and universally discernable. We need to remember that the subliminal glory of God's created order and the people made in His image are relentlessly evangelizing believer and nonbeliever alike every day.

When confronted by skeptics or seekers, do we retreat to our upper story and warm ourselves next to Jesus' fireplace, or do we do the hard work of cracking open the box, putting the puzzle pieces together, and showing them that the puzzle matches the box top exactly?

The good news is that the picture on the box is accessible to everyone, and we Christians have the unique privilege and awesome responsibility of helping others to see it. We are called to make sure that the deaf and blind are able to hear and see this overwhelming torrent of evidence.

Are You on Drugs?

The secular world will accuse us of being delusional junkies strung out on the opiate of the masses. They will suggest that the picture on the cover of the box is merely a Christian happy place that doesn't exist. How should we respond? If Christianity is the opiate of the masses, it's quite a bitter pill to swallow because it calls us to admit our sinful nature and accept the fact that we cannot save ourselves. I don't believe that meets the criterion for a religious drug high. I argue that it's the other traditions such as Buddhism, Hinduism, and New Age religion that offer drug holidays. They have set up a spiritual needle exchange program that allows people to shoot up for a religious high without the risk of acquiring the disease of consequence, but they avoid discussing the real-world withdrawal that sets in when the effects of their holy hallucinogens wear off.

Tongue-Tied

Well, that was a great motivational speech, but how can I, a mere mortal, be expected to put this enormous puzzle together? There are so many people smarter and more articulate than me. How could I possibly explain life to them?

> Most Christians are tongue tied and most communists are articulate—that is the most serious fact in our world. If faith is real to us, we should be able to make it real to others.[26]
>
> —Samuel Shoemaker

Although writing during the aftermath of the two world wars and the beginning of the Cold War, Samuel Shoemaker's statement continues to ring true. In the "Truth Project," an excellent apologetic video series put out by Focus on the Family, the host, Del Tackett, puts it like this: "Do you believe that what you believe is really real? Because if you really believe that what you believe is real, then Christians will change the world." If we Christians truly believe we have truth on our side, we have no choice but to confidently preach the gospel through word and action. This confidence, however, can be obtained only when we understand our faith is the only one capable of explaining the world around us. We must first make our faith relevant to ourselves; only then can we effectively convey it to others.

The Dignity of Divinity

Since God created the world and fashioned human beings in His image, pieces of His truth will inevitably be found everywhere. We need to congratulate others for divining some of these truths but with gentleness and respect show them how each piece fits in God's world. We are often too quick to point out the deficits in the worldviews of others and neglect the powerful evangelistic strategy of acknowledging their successful contributions.

27

The worldview of others is not half empty but half full; any worldview that doesn't have at least some nuggets of God's truth isn't believable, so we need to congratulate others for finding pieces of it but then show them the way to the mother-lode Don't you think it's more effective to begin a conversation by helping people recognize they are created in the image of God rather than alienating them by telling them how evil they are? We need to be sensitive to the fact that a worldview is a deeply cherished thing that forms the infrastructure, however rickety, of many a lifestyle. When we challenge others' worldviews, we may be challenging the very foundation of their existence, a foundation that they have devoted a significant portion of their lives building, and to cruelly mock it would touch a conversation-ending nerve.

We need to honor their effort to construct worldviews but then be willing to point out the structural irregularities that could cause them to collapse. If they do recognize that their worldview edifice is not up to code, and choose to seek shelter elsewhere, we cannot leave them standing outside in the cold; we must be prepared to help them build a secure, God-certified worldview capable of weathering every cultural storm.

"Your mission Jim, should you decide to accept it ..."

God did all the work. His spoken word echoes throughout the world. We don't have to be experts in Christian doctrine or come up with clever apologetic arguments. God handed us the evidence, and all we have to do is point people toward it. The picture has been painted, the novel written, the symphony scored. Our task is simply to open the eyes and ears of our fellow man so they can hear God's voice over the din of the deafening cultural white noise.

Conclusion

While I'm intrigued by the academia of theology, I'm too old to write a book concerning theological mental gymnastics. This will most likely be the only book I will write, so I won't waste my time or yours on theories that may be interesting but ultimately irrelevant. I am interested in conveying to you only what I had been denied most of my life, the realization that my Christian faith is real and consequential.

Our culture has reduced the concept of God to a spiritual happy place where we can escape from the trials and tribulations of the world, but if that's the case, God becomes an irrelevant, optional, personal convenience. I don't want to waste my time dancing with fairies in my happy place; I want to stand in front of God's throne and ask Him what He demands of my life. God by definition cannot be optional. He is or He isn't, so let's find the God who is, and put aside our silly efforts to transform God into who we want Him to be.

I want this book to be dangerous where choices matter, where life is serious business, and consequences exist for ignoring the truth. I want you to ask, "Is my worldview convenient or true?" I think God would be disappointed if follower and critic didn't truly look at all the data He has revealed and test that data in the laboratory of life.

Perhaps one of the best definitions for truth may be "that which if not accepted has consequences." If something is true, then neglecting, disregarding, or deriding it has consequences. If we don't accept the law of gravity as true, our defiant dive off of a building will be met with the concrete of consequence.

> One can never wrestle enough with God if one does so out of pure regard for the truth. Christ likes us to prefer truth to him because, before being Christ, he is truth. If one turns aside from Him to go toward the truth, one will not go far before falling into His arms.[27]
>
> —Simone Weil

If you are a believer, I hope this book will bolster your confidence in the realization that you are living in God's world. If you are a nonbeliever, I hope it encourages you to take an honest look at your worldview and test it to see if it makes sense. This book is designed to take you on a stroll and point out crucial pieces of evidence you may have taken for granted.

Once you have swallowed your pride and acknowledged that the world is God's, not yours, you must take the next step and ask yourself, "Am I living in a way consistent with that knowledge?"

It should be reassuring to know you're not alone on this journey. Throughout history, Christians and non-Christians have already blazed these trails and have left comprehensive journals of their travels, excerpts of which I have interspersed throughout this book. I have also tried to use many current cultural examples to illustrate my points, many of which will date my writing but never date the problem. If you come across an illustration that seems particularly out of date, feel free to insert your own contemporary example, because the sins of man are unoriginal and seem to unfailingly repeat themselves.

We need to bring sanity to the whole worldview discussion by encouraging others to quit wasting time with the erratic combatants who ignorantly try to stick victory flags in soil that was never theirs in the first place and instead help people look at the unchanging terrain upon which this illusory battle is fought. I encourage you to walk the battlefield and carefully listen for the echoes of the worldview that was spoken into existence long ago, the one with the "very good" housekeeping seal upon it.

We cannot continue to put it off until tomorrow; we need to begin to understand God's world today! We need to take a step back, gather all this fractured information, and organize it into a whole so it makes sense. Christian apologetics has become very good at pointing out the logical flaws and inconsistencies in the worldviews of others, but has it done a good job of explaining the overwhelming explanatory power of its own Christian worldview? That's my task.

While I will continue to point out the flaws of other worldview philosophies, I hope I present a solid case for the truth and coherence of the Christian worldview. You have all the data you need; you just don't realize you do. God's existence is already evident to 85 to

95 percent of the population, so don't let the other 5 to 15 percent intimidate you and discourage you from your task. It is with this confidence that we are called to dress in our Christian finery and proudly walk the red carpet of our lives in view of millions, immune to any fashion criticism that may get thrown our way, and boldly proclaim the gospel to the world. So what's your excuse?

> Rome is burning, Jesus says. Drop your fiddle, change your life, and come to me, Let go of nostalgia and mourning for the good old days that never were anyway. A Sunday school in which you never participated, traditional virtues you never practiced, legalistic obedience you never honored, and sterile orthodoxy you never accepted. The old era is done. The decisive in break of God has happened.[28]
>
> —Brennan Manning

Chapter Two

TO THE UNKNOWN GOD

I N THE LAST CHAPTER, I lifted up the apostle Paul as perhaps the most prominent first-century Christian fashion icon. I explained that his boldness was due to his unshakeable confidence in the evidence for God's existence and his certainty about God's plan of salvation for everyone. Paul's audience, however, was very skeptical and considered all his talk about Christ to be a "stumbling block" and "folly." Given such a tough crowd, how did Paul convince the skeptics and plant the seeds of Christianity throughout the ancient Near East? In this chapter, we will use Paul's first-century evangelistic experience as a model for our own lay Christian witness.

Life on Mars

It appears that we Christians spend most of our time hiding Jesus away in our own spiritual lock box, safe from criticism by the secular world. We mistakenly feel like a small regiment trapped behind enemy lines in a raging worldview battle when in reality, our critics are the ones hemmed in by the artillery of God's evidence.

I suspect that our intentions are noble; we just want to protect our cherished faith from being toppled by outside arguments, but with that line of reasoning, we greatly underestimate our God. We need to remember God chose to create this world and establish a relationship with mankind. Through His actions, God put His physical stamp on the world, inviting us to question and investigate everything we see around us. Paul understood this and used it to his advantage as he evangelized the Athenians on Mars Hill as recorded in Acts.

> So Paul, standing in the midst of the Areopagus, said: "Men of Athens, I perceive that in every way you are very religious. For as I passed along and observed the objects of your worship, I found also an altar with this inscription, 'To the unknown god.'" (Acts 17:22–23)

Paul began by appealing to the religious nature of his audience, a shared spiritual restlessness that compelled them to seek God. He pointed out, however, that their once-earnest search had come to a dead end. They had clearly grown weary of their previously sincere efforts to find the divine and lazily ended up covering all their spiritual bases by building an altar to the unknown god, a god they didn't know but felt compelled to acknowledge.

Paul applauded their spirituality but made it clear they were hedging their deistic bets. For the Athenians, the beauty of the unknown god was that it gave them a false sense of divine security by fostering the belief that they had covered all possible god alternatives while creating a deity so conveniently vague that they didn't have to worry about any theological baggage or obligation.

Our current religious climate is no different from that of the Athenians; our hillsides are strewn with multiple altars to anemic, New Age deities trying to lay claim to the title of the unknown god. Despite fresh coats of paint applied by a never-ending series of New Age prophets, these idols are the same deistic pretenders from Paul's day.

New Age religion could be considered the first truly green religious movement because it's so good at recycling old pieces of junk. If you take a close look, you will see these gurus are just trying to cash in on our shared religious nature by rebuilding the Athenian altar to the unknown god, temporarily filling our spiritual hole without any tangible obligation. Like Paul, we should be encouraged by the religious nature of our audience but concerned that they don't know what they worship. As humans, we know deep down there are no free lunches, the piper must be paid, and religion without obligation is just deceptive self-worship.

Unfortunately, I think we often confuse our mode of worship with the idols themselves. We talk about worshipping the idols of money, power, or sex and treat them like overpowering little gods, but I think if we look closely, we will see that what we call idols are in fact acts of self-worship. We as individuals are actually the gods, and greed, tyranny, and pornography are nothing but the acts of self-worship. We like to blame the overpowering allure of these idols to distract us from the sobering truth that we are in reality worshipping ourselves.

The next time you read about the latest New Age movement, whether it's *The Secret*, *The Power of Now*, or the *Power of Intention*, ask yourself who is really being worshipped here, you or some other power. Paul gets the Athenians to consider this question by asking them to ponder whether or not what they worship is truly divine or a mere creation of man.

> "In him we live and move and have our being"; as even some of your own poets have said, "For we are indeed his offspring." Being then God's offspring, we ought not to think that the divine being is like gold or silver or stone, an image formed by the art and imagination of man. (Acts 17:28–29)

Paul praised the Athenians for finding pieces of God's truth even in their poetic literature but cautioned them to think carefully about how that little truth fit together in God's big picture. Paul offered a solution to their god problem.

> What therefore you worship as unknown, this I proclaim to you. The God who made the world and everything in it, being Lord of heaven and earth, does not live in

temples made by man, nor is he served by human hands, as though he needed anything, since he himself gives to all mankind life and breath and everything. (Acts 17:23–25)

He told them about the one true God who is in charge of everything. He said in essence, "You can travel all over town, shopping at every dollar store for cheap religious knock-offs to fulfill your spiritual needs, or you can go to the megastore and get the genuine stuff in one trip."

And He has made from one blood every nation of men to dwell on all the face of the earth, and has determined their pre-appointed times and the boundaries of their dwellings, *so that they should seek the Lord, in the hope that they might grope for Him and find Him, though He is not far from each one of us*; for in Him we live and move and have our being. (Acts 17:26–28, emphasis added)

As Paul pointed out, the one true God made his presence physically known to the world through His creative acts. He purposely created the world and stepped into time to personally walk with the pinnacle of His creative effort, mankind. Paul encouraged them to seek and grope for this God themselves, because he knew that the evidence was everywhere and that once they discovered it, they would be without excuse.

The times of ignorance God overlooked, but now he commands all people everywhere to repent, because he has fixed a day on which he will judge the world in righteousness by a man whom he has appointed; and of this he has given assurance to all by raising him from the dead. (Acts 17:30–31)

Paul provided a theological unity to their diverse spiritual longings and offered true salvation with true obligation. Paul, in short order, deftly walked the Athenians, a group that had no Judeo-Christian background, through the Christian story. He identified the one true God, linked Him with the physical world, pointed out mankind's problem, and revealed Jesus as the solution.

42

Paul knew the answer to their God dilemma, but the Athenians didn't seem to know what the question was. Instead of trying to link the question and the answer, they took the easy way out and built an altar to a vague, unknown god that didn't provide any answers to any questions. They knew all their little gods were somehow important, but they didn't know why.

Douglas Adams, in *The Hitchhiker's Guide to the Galaxy* series, once again gives us some amusing insight. Arthur Dent, the main human character, is saved from Earth's destruction by hitchhiking on an alien spacecraft. In his travels, he discovers that earlier in the history of the universe, a hyperintelligent race had built a supercomputer, Deep Thought, to run a seven-and-a-half-million-year program to find the answer to life, the universe, and everything. The result turned out to be the number 42, which greatly upset this hyperintelligent race because it seemed like such a meaningless answer.

> Forty two! Is that all you have to show for seven and one half million years work?" Deep thought responded, "I checked it very thoroughly … and that quite definitely is the answer. I think the problem, to be quite honest with you, is that you've never actually known what the question is.[29]

Therefore, a new, more powerful supercomputer was designed by Deep Thought to find out what the question was. They knew that once the question was clearly revealed, the answer would make perfect sense. Surprisingly, Adams describes this new computer with biblical imagery reminiscent of John the Baptist's words about Jesus: "I speak of none but the computer that is to come after me … a computer whose merest operational parameters I am not worthy to calculate."[30] The new computer turned out to be Earth itself.

The spiritual seeker, just like this hyperintelligent race, needs to understand the question before the answers will be meaningful. I suggest that the biggest question most people have is, "How do I coherently explain the world around me?"

To be fair to Douglas Adams, his later books revealed that the question once discovered still didn't make any sense, and he had God apologize for all the confusion. However, despite Adams's frequently brilliant work mining pieces of God's truth, he sadly "exchanged the truth for a lie" and missed that which was "evident to everyone."

In our zealous desire to tell people about Jesus, the ultimate answer, we must not forget to seriously consider the questions our seeker friends may be asking. Paul, unlike the hyperintelligent race, recognized that linking the questions and answers did not require a supercomputer but rather just ordinary human beings willing to take a hard look at the world around them and once again see it for the first time.

> And in the end of all our exploring
> Will be to arrive where we started
> And know the place for the first time.[31]
>
> —T. S. Eliot

Life on Earth

Our religious milieu is no different from Paul's. Day after day we pass by just as many altars to the gods of our culture. Our audience is also largely religious. As I pointed out earlier, polls consistently show that 85 to 95 percent of all Americans believe in God. Every day we are confronted with the religious thoughts and practices of our fellow man. Most of these religious discussions ebb and flow around unique ecological, political, and cultural events such as natural disasters, terrorist attacks, political campaigns, book releases, and movie premieres, but despite seeming variations in intensity, religion remains a part of our everyday lives.

Every couple of years, our country makes its way through another political season in which speeches, debates, and commentaries dominate every news cycle. Every campaign speech uniformly closes with the phrase, "God bless America." Beyond the candidates' economic and foreign policy lurks questions about their theology. In 2008, it was about Barack Obama's controversial pastor Jeremiah Wright, Mitt Romney's Mormon faith, and George Bush's evangelical beliefs. Many of these issues resurfaced in the 2012 election. Polls continue to show that atheists are the least likely people to be elected president. While their support appears to be increasing, they continue to lag behind every other subgroup. Why do we care about the sincerity and content of our political candidates' religious beliefs?

> Regardless of what one thinks of a politician's religion, the mere fact that he has one offers the voter essential information about where his moral and ethical lines are theoretically drawn ... In the case of the atheist politician, however, the voter not only has no information, he has no easy means of obtaining that information.[32]
>
> —Vox Day

Doesn't it seem odd to hear about the struggle to separate church and state; to remove the words *In God We Trust* from our currency; to stop prayer in schools; to remove the Ten Commandments from our courthouses; to take crosses down from our hillsides; and to have our politicians ask for prayers for the victims of hurricanes, floods, and famine? Why are we perpetually embroiled in religious controversies stirred up by the artistic community such as *The Da Vinci Code* by Dan Brown and *The Lost Tomb of Jesus* documentary by James Cameron, and movies such as *Religulous* by Bill Maher and *Expelled* by Ben Stein? Who cares?

In spite of the overwhelming evidence for mankind's inherently religious nature, a small but vocal group of atheists continue to tell us there is no God. I find it quite interesting that such a small atheist minority feels empowered to boldly call out the clearly religious majority. Once again, I offer the example of the pediatric growth chart as a diagnostic tool doctors utilize to assess the health of a newborn. If the growth parameters of a baby fall outside the normal distribution, which is defined as that range of measurements representing 90 to 95 percent of the population, it indicates something may be wrong.

Ironically, regarding the question of God's existence, this sound diagnostic concept has been turned on its head, and the atheist minority is demanding the religious majority justify its normal distribution instead of the religious majority asking the atheist minority why it is a statistical outlier. How can those who fall outside of the norm be allowed to dictate the ground rules for the debate while simultaneously failing to account for their own deficient "growth parameters"?

It appears that the Athenian unknown god continues to be the elephant in the room. The atheists tell us that it is merely an illusion and hold their noses as they point to its excrement. Agnostics periodically bump into this massive animal and find it quite difficult to comfortably stretch their legs without banging against it. Politicians feel its presence and understand that almost every voter acknowledges its existence, prompting them to at least pay it lip service. The majority of us feed it, groom it, ride it, and teach it to do tricks.

The problem with all these people is that they don't bother to ask why there is such an enormous elephant in the room in the first place. The sheer volume of rhetoric generated by the question of God's existence seems to suggest that the answer has profound implications for understanding the world in which we live. It is not just an interesting theoretical question; it is also one that touches on the core of life.

> The absence of God is not just an idea to conjure with, an emptiness for the preacher to try and furnish, like a house, with a chair and sofa, heat and light to make it livable. *The absence of God is just that which is not livable.*[33]
>
> —Frederick Buechner (emphasis added)

Unfortunately, the word *God* has been watered down to refer to anything that elicits spiritual feelings. We talk about God just as politicians carelessly speak of the electorate when they think the microphones are off. Unbeknownst to us, the microphone is always hot, and God hears every careless word we speak about Him.

> I tell you, on the day of judgment people will give account for every careless word they speak, for by your words you will be justified, and by your words you will be condemned. (Matt. 12:36–37)

When I refer to God, I am writing of something far greater than us, a Being who created the universe, informs the world around us, and whose existence has real implications for our lives. The vast majority of people believe in a God of some sort, therefore, the question is not whether God exists but rather who is this God that most of us believe in? It is intellectually acceptable to try to find the God who *is*, but it is unacceptable to merely search for the God we *want*. If God exists, He exists regardless of who we think He should be. If you find a god that suits your needs, you have done nothing but divinize yourself. Your god has become a mini you, a selfish clone dressed in divine clothing. Stop mirror gazing, admiring your illusory divine spark, and perilously seek the God who is.

Perhaps the best way to proceed is to ask yourself whether your God explains the world around you. Is he, she, or it relevant to your everyday life? All of our clever apologetic arguments will be nothing more than the sound of one hand clapping unless our audience first asks themselves if their personal gods are actually relevant. God is not some model sitting for a personal portrait, waiting to have His picture hung in mankind's art gallery of spiritual creations: He is either a being to be reckoned with or a nice spiritual word we use to put a "divine" stamp of approval on our personal lifestyles. If the latter is the case, that god is optional to the rest of us and ultimately irrelevant. If, however, He is the former, you'd better figure out who or what that God is because there will be consequences for your decision.

Make no mistake; if God is not relevant, we are not truly discussing God but rather a human construct designed to justify our personal preferences. It's dishonest to be the creator of a personal pantheon. You cannot affix God's name to your purely human spiritual project; God will have none of that. Don't dare claim a divine endorsement without first asking permission from the Almighty.

We need to seriously heed the warning of the *Peter Principle*, which suggests that we rise to our level of incompetence; it is a sober warning to anyone seeking to create God in his or her own image.

While I suspect that most of the people who will read this book will be Christians, I challenge everyone to put their gods to the test: does your deity have something to say about life, or is it a mute idol of stone, wood, money, or power? If your God is truly God, He will not be offended by your inquiry; He may question the wisdom of darkening His council, but He will not be offended.

In addition, as you pursue this divine truth, you need to be prepared for the sobering realization that in the process you may topple your flimsy but cherished deity. You cannot be like the shopkeeper in Monty Python's "Dead Parrot" sketch, insisting your caged dead God is a fierce Norwegian Blue who just happens to be pining for the fjords.

We're Not Worthy! We're Not Worthy!

"But I'm not Paul!" you say. "He was a really smart guy who looked quite dashing in his Christian finery. I could never be like him!" While it's true there will never be another Paul, we need to remember he gave us a glimmer of hope because, despite his academic credentials, he also struggled to articulate the gospel.

> For they say, "His letters are weighty and strong, but his bodily presence is weak, and his speech of no account. (2 Cor. 10:10)

Perhaps even more important than his lack of rhetorical charisma was the fact that he considered his accomplished educational background rubbish compared to the truth of the gospel message he promoted.

> If anyone else thinks he has reason for confidence in the flesh, I have more: circumcised on the eighth day, of the people of Israel, of the tribe of Benjamin, a Hebrew of Hebrews; as to the law, a Pharisee; as to zeal, a persecutor of the church; as to righteousness, under the law blameless. But whatever gain I had, I counted as loss for the sake of Christ. Indeed, I count everything as loss because of the surpassing worth of knowing Christ Jesus my Lord. For his sake I have suffered the loss of all things and count them as rubbish, in order that I may gain Christ. (Phil. 3:4–8)

The gospel message is far superior to any messenger. We don't need Armani suits, Rolex watches, or a James Earl Jones voice to get people to pay attention; all we need is a broken and contrite heart. We need to remember that Paul didn't have to invent intricate theological arguments; he merely needed to shine a light on the product of God's creative handiwork. He made it clear that the evidence for God's plan was everywhere and accessible to everyone; this left no excuses for not seeing it. Paul's job was to replace the darkness of human deception with the light of God's truth. Our confidence will therefore be found in the evidence God has left everywhere, not in our theological training or personal rhetorical ability.

> After all, it would not be anything special if God did super things with super people. There would be no miracle in that. But it takes the mysterious power of God to do super things with very ordinary people. With disciples chosen from humanity at its most common and flawed.[34]
>
> —Martin B. Copenhaver

Paul eradicated all our feeble human excuses for not being bold advocates for Christ but assured us that despite our limitations, we would never be alone; the power of the Holy Spirit would be there to help us proclaim the gospel.

> And I, when I came to you, brothers, did not come proclaiming to you the testimony of God with lofty speech or wisdom. For I decided to know nothing among you except Jesus Christ and him crucified. And I was with you in weakness and in fear and much trembling, and my speech and my message were not in plausible words of wisdom, but in demonstration of the Spirit and of power, that your faith might not rest in the wisdom of men but in the power of God. (1 Cor. 2:1–5)

I have frequently seen this truth displayed in the Christian witness of others. I remember attending a talk by a well-known Christian professional baseball player. He began by inarticulately amusing us with baseball stories, but as soon as he launched into a discussion about the transforming work of Christ in his life, he became articulate, and his words took on a power lacking in his opening monologue. The contrast was quite striking.

> For consider your calling, brothers: not many of you were wise according to worldly standards, not many were powerful, not many were of noble birth. But God chose what is foolish in the world to shame the wise; God chose what is weak in the world to shame the strong. (1 Cor. 1:26–27)

Paul was bold because he believed that what he believed was "really real." He saw the evidence for God's world everywhere and available to everyone. We also have the same data that Paul had therefore we have no excuse.

You will soon discover that even when you witness to nonbelievers, you're preaching to the choir, except that the members of this particular choir just don't know whose hymnal they're singing from.

People of faith stumble across God everywhere: in nature, in the Bible, in daily acts of providence. God seems amply evident. But the secular mind sees no such evidence, and wonders how it is even possible to find God in the maze of competing claims. Unless we truly understand that viewpoint, and speak in terms a faithless person can understand, our words will have the quaint and useless ring of a foreign language.[35]

—Philip Yancey

Worldview Warehouse

All competing worldviews can conveniently be broken down into several basic categories based on how they view the relationship between God and man. The first branching point in this religious discussion hinges on the question of whether God exists. For a small atheist minority, this is where the search ends, but for the vast majority of us, this is where the adventure begins.

While it seems the most heated public debates occur over the question of whether God exists, the question of greater relevance to the vast majority of people is who is this God in whom they believe. The attitudes and behavior of every religious worldview are ultimately dictated by the answer to that question.

We need to begin by asking if we are trying to find a god that suits our needs or trying to find the God who exists. If we are basing this search on what best fits our lifestyles, we are deceiving ourselves, we are worshipping a phantom of our creation, and in the end, our religion becomes nothing but a club of like-minded individuals who have sprinkled divine pixie dust on their personal preferences.

But if we are truly seeking the God who is, we must go where the evidence leads. Since mankind seems to have this insatiable desire to find God, we need to first ask if the God we seek even cares if he, or she, or it is found. Is our god personal or impersonal? Specific or vague? Concerned or indifferent? Necessary or optional? The vetting process must be thorough, and our god must be able to answer some very basic questions: Where did the physical world come from? Why is man unique? Why do we all have the sense that there's something wrong with the world? How can the problem be fixed?

Throughout this book, I will elude to each worldview by referring to its most common cultural manifestation, so let's begin with a brief overview of the deity or deities that form the focal points of the major religious worldviews.

It's All-Good

Pantheism is the belief that everything is God. There is no distinction between a rock, a slug, and a human. The sum total of all that exists embodies God. God is not an independent entity but rather the cumulative life spirit of the planet. Many spiritually infused environmental movements such as Mother Earth spirituality or Gaia worship fall into this category. It is a very attractive idea because it begins with the concept that the world is "very good," but it runs into the difficulty of having to call mankind "very bad" for screwing it up. The problem, as we shall see, is that it lacks any credible worldview foundation on which to build its attitudes and behavior.

Spill on Religious Aisle One!

Pan*en*theism is distinguished from pan*the*ism in that it recognizes a distinction between a god and the rest of the universe but considers its god to be an unknowable, indifferent entity that is the source of everything but that didn't purposely create it. The world is essentially the inevitable spilling over of the godness of this divine entity. The resulting universe contains bits and pieces of this celestial nature in the form of divine sparks. The ultimate goal is for mankind to recognize those sparks and work toward reunification with the divine. I will refer to this panentheistic idea as Hinduism because it embodies the precepts of the most common form, qualified, nondualistic Hinduism.

45

In this form of Hinduism, Brahman is the remote, unknowable, and unconcerned divine essence. The universe unintentionally but inevitably spilled out of the excess of Brahman's godness. Each piece of the universe that emanated from Brahman contained small divine sparks. Salvation therefore consists of finding the divine spark within and working to reunite it with its divine source by taking a spin on the reincarnation wheel of karma. The divine spark is the only reality, and our earthly life is merely an illusion. The many gods and goddesses in the Hindu pantheon are merely incomplete visions created by man to try to understand the unknowable Brahman. They are individually useful but imperfect guides on the innumerable legs of our *Tour de God* life-cycling race.

One and Done

Deism is the belief that God exists but that his contact with the world was limited to a divine act of jump-starting the universe and then sitting back and letting it run. A deist views God as a university professor who has delivered a dramatic one-time lecture but has no office hours. He is the powerful mind behind the universe but prefers not to entertain questions from pimple-faced freshmen. While not a major religious movement, it becomes a convenient escape hatch for those threatened by a God who hands out exams and expects a passing grade before conferring any afterlife degree.

Grand Delusion

Buddhism is a spin-off of Hinduism, but in its original form, it was more of an atheistic philosophy than a religion. Buddhism, as envisioned by the Buddha, begins with the recognition that there is suffering in this world due to our desire to create permanence in a world in which everything changes. We are miserable because we constantly try to make transient things permanent. We are deluded into thinking this physical world is important or relevant when in reality it's those thoughts that create our suffering. We search for significance in this life by trying to discover who we are, why we are here, and where we are going, when all those pursuits just continue to add to our desire problem. The Buddha offers hope that desire can be overcome by helping us walk down the noble eightfold pathway. Enlightenment becomes detachment from the desires of this world with the ultimate goal of extinguishing oneself into the impersonal nirvana.

Power to the People

New Age religion is a mixed bag of religious beliefs that recognizes God as a force mankind can harness. This power is variably described as being found in man, outside man, or infusing everything. It has been more recently described by the newest players in the ever-changing cast of New Age gurus as the *Power of Intention, the Power of Now*, and *The Secret*. The bottom line of this diverse religious movement is that it recognizes "god" as a force that may be made of pure love or pure joy but does nothing until it is manipulated by man. It treats God like a power grid but foolishly places the on-off switch in the hands of mankind, basically providing divine cover for the selfish aspirations of man.

Monotheism

The god systems I have discussed to this point are inconsequential. Adherence to their tenets may be attractive, but they are not compulsory. The salvation schemes they offer might appeal to your personal needs but are optional for the rest of us. Wouldn't you find it surprising if mankind's insatiable search for God ended with the conclusion that "god" is whatever makes you happy?

The three great monotheistic religious traditions—Islam, Judaism, and Christianity—are great because they recognize a single, consequential God, a God who is in charge and who makes certain demands on our lives. I sense that most of us feel beholden to something greater than us. The key word is *beholden*; it implies a God of relevance not just to us personally but also to the universe.

I will generally lump Judaism and Christianity together because I recognize Christianity as the culmination of God's work begun in His chosen people as chronicled in the Old Testament. My salvation is impossible without my Jewish brothers and sisters.

Islam, while admirably acknowledging one God of consequence, falls short because it fails to recognize that God is a God of intense relationship who is jealous for people created in His image. The Trinity is considered blasphemous polytheism to Islam, but I suggest that the Trinity is the very reason we search for a God of relationship. Allah represents a single entity that is not in His essence relational as is the Trinity but tends to be an unapproachable deity more concerned with obedience than love and forgiveness.

As we proceed, we will call each of these basic worldviews to task by asking them to explain the common, daily experiences faced by all human beings. If your worldview is incapable of explaining the basics, it may describe a world, but unfortunately, it will not be the one you live in.

Take a Hike

To proceed on this journey, we need to start at the trailhead. We will see beautiful sights along the way. We will run into forks in the road and be forced to choose a path, but if we look closely enough, we will see signs, often buried in the overgrowth, directing us to our goal. Our critics will say, "It doesn't matter which direction you go or what fork you take; just don't stir up the brush and upset the ecosystem!" They seem to think it's better to get lost and die somewhere along the trail than try to find your way to the lodge.

If you choose to proceed, stock your backpack with lots of food (curiosity), a reliable fishing pole (questions), and book on edible plants (discernment) so no matter how many twists and turns you take along the way, you will be healthy enough to make it to your destination. But be prepared to offer aid to your fellow travelers who didn't prepare adequately for this journey and are dying of hunger and thirst. You may be their last hope.

> Rescue those who are being taken away to death; hold back
> those who are stumbling to the slaughter. (Prov. 24:11)

Enjoy the journey! Stop and reflect on the sights along the way, read the historical markers, and take pictures.

I remember one particular hike with a high school friend between my first two years of medical school. We explored the beautiful alpine lakes on the eastern side of Washington's Cascade Mountain range. The hike was difficult, but with each successive lake, we were rewarded with vistas of increasing beauty.

My mind-set, however, was back in the restlessness of academia, and I had a hard time relaxing and enjoying the views. I felt the need to keep hiking and to get to the next lake because I felt uncomfortable at rest. That particular hike is only one of many examples of my failure to slow down and enjoy my life journey.

How sad! Life had become a series of career steps without Sabbath rest, no stopping at the summit to take in the view, just the voice of the next career mountain yelling at me to get off my butt and keep hiking.

Twin Peaks

The various religious worldviews I described earlier don't exist in isolation; they have also been deeply influenced by the reigning philosophical movements of the time. We therefore need to be keenly aware of not only the different views of the God-man relationship but also of the philosophical milieu in which they are practiced.

Christian hikers in the twenty-first century must scale two particularly treacherous mountains, the philosophical twin peaks of modernism and postmodernism. I don't want to get bogged down in philosophical minutiae, but these movements are particularly perilous for Christians as they navigate the terrain of our cultural wilderness.

The profound, historic changes that began in the Renaissance and were solidified during the Enlightenment ultimately created a modernist worldview that perceived knowledge in a new way. Knowledge went beyond its historical beginnings as a way to understand God's world and was transformed into a force for cultural change. Knowledge was understood as good, objective, and beneficial. As this movement grew, it divinized science and demoted God. Unfortunately, two world wars and the atomic bomb revealed the dark side of technology and tempered man's hope for a utopian world built on the back of science.

Despite these setbacks, modernism continues to thrive, primarily in the academic sciences, where it is most visibly seen in the promotion of evolutionary theory. Evolution takes center stage in this modernist drama because it is believed to scientifically account for the origin and diversity of life without having to import any supernatural explanation.

Evolution means different things to different people. It can be as simple as change over time, or as complicated as random genetic mutations conferring traits on an organism which give it a survival advantage when faced with the pressures of natural selection. It is the latter scientific definition, also called Neo-Darwinism, that I will be using when I speak of evolution.

Unfortunately, evolutionary theory has taken on a life of its own, going far beyond Darwin's original intent of just explaining the origin and diversity of life. It has been carelessly offered as the explanation for everything from anthropology to economics to psychology.

Modernism, however, has done the unthinkable; it has violated its own ground rules. It has created a new religion, a scientific Buddhism in which purpose, beauty, and design are considered mere illusions created by neurochemicals in our brains. True salvation becomes absorption in the great nirvanian nothingness of evolutionary insignificance.

Postmodernism arose as a response to the modernist claims that truth is determined scientifically and that life is just material substances. Postmodernism didn't like the idea of universal truth whether it was scientific, religious, or philosophical. It bristled at the thought of science as the new sheriff in town, especially since postmodernists thought they had already demoted the previous religious and government law enforcement agencies to mere cultural safety nets designed to catch those who partied too hard.

Postmodernism was also a bit peeved because science had reduced its cherished spirituality to isolated pieces of brain tissue and neurotransmitters. Unfortunately, postmodernism doesn't propose any new ideas or solutions; it finds its power deconstructing old ones, basically becoming skepticism on steroids.

The modernists claim that knowledge was good, objective, and beneficial was replaced by the postmodernist view of knowledge as good and bad, subjective and oppressive. Postmodernism, however, armed with the wrecking ball of deconstruction encountered a dilemma; how could it hold this crumbling cultural structure together while simultaneously trying to destroy it? Postmodernists' answer was the flimsy duct tape of tolerance, a concept that appears quite friendly and inviting on the surface but is practically speaking fraught with all sorts of difficulties.

Postmodernism has claimed that tolerance is our only salvation, and if we just invite every worldview to the cultural party, we can all have a good time together. Unfortunately, when we arrive, it soon becomes evident that this party is just a disparate gathering of people, some running around with lampshades on their heads yelling, "Toga! Toga!" while others are attempting to quietly read poetry to each other in the corner of the room. One group wonders why the other is so stiff and serious, while the other wishes that the partiers would grow up and stop acting like unsupervised children.

Tolerance merely forces us together and tells us it's better to hold our noses at the stench of our neighbors' beliefs than engage them in a discussion. Tolerance, if you carefully look at it, is selfish and disrespectful because it basically says to others, "I'm not going to do the hard work of understanding your view of the world. It's easier for me to just ignore your deeply held beliefs. I'll tolerate you, but I won't embrace you because your ideas are a major distraction from the real work of me."

While many people accept tolerance as a kinder, gentler way of behaving, they rarely think about the ramifications of such a philosophy. Tolerance allows everything except that which it considers intolerant to exist. Its own philosophy renders itself incapable of policing its adherents and finds itself inconveniently forced to turn to the government, which it dislikes, to make laws it finds oppressive in order to control the behavior of those who it is ironically quite intolerant of. The very things that postmodernists abhor—authority, rules, and intolerance—are exactly what they are forced to turn to in order to promote their agenda.

Postmodernism tries to give us the sense that it is inclusive, global, and capable of uniting us all, but what does the uniting? I suggest that it is amusement. It brings the bearded lady, the rollercoaster, and the fortune-teller into town and gives us the freedom to use our tickets to see whatever attraction we want.

The problem is that we fail to recognize that every circus has an owner who determines what we'll see and ride, collects the money, and signs the paychecks. The postmodern circus still needs to apply for a permit and submit to health and safety inspections. Strangely enough, the postmodern circus, which claims no supreme authority, is safe for us to play in only if some authority already exists to keep it in line. Every worldview, however vehemently it may deny it, has to acknowledge the man, someone or something that pulls the strings of their puppet-like philosophies. With this in mind, we need to constantly look up, follow the strings, and see the real force behind every person's worldview.

I remember my first exposure to moral relativism in a college philosophy class. I wrote a paper arguing against abortion but was downgraded because I took a stand instead of acknowledging that my opinion was just one of many valid viewpoints. I was frustrated because I felt that philosophy should be a rigorous search for truth and not an academic stamp of approval for any lifestyle we choose.

I find it ironic that we proceed through the developmental stages of childhood to reach the pinnacle of adulthood only to be told it's okay to behave like a selfish three-year old-who wants his or her own way and wants it now. I don't recall ever thinking I should ask my three-year-old whether he thought it was a good idea to share with his siblings or stick peas up his nose. My parents should be appalled that they paid good money just to have my philosophy teacher encourage the same self-centered, childish behavior they had spent years trying to eradicate at home.

Postmodernism is a confused, irrational worldview, but it remains quite influential. Its basic assumptions pull the rug out from any possible discussion, destroy the ground rules for debate, and leave a plethora of worldviews all scrambling to grab the worldview microphone and give voice to their own particular truths.

Unlike the widely publicized battle between Christianity and modernism, the battle against postmodernism is more like a battle against terrorists. They have infiltrated our ranks; they look just like us, go to our churches, and attend the same events, but they have hidden anti-intellectual explosives in their underwear, and we don't know that until an explosion rocks our sanctuary. We are being destroyed from the inside, not the outside. We can keep the modernists at bay, but we seem powerless to stop the postmodern cancer that grows within. We may wake up one day to find police cars surrounding the house next door, handcuffing our neighbor, and taking him downtown because as it turns out he was butchering the truth and burying it in his backyard. We never saw it coming; this man who "kept to himself and seemed to love dogs" was a serial truth killer, and we're overtaken by the uneasy feeling that he might have buried some of his victims under our own serenity garden.

Noxious Weeds

As modernity began clearing the cultural field of religious orthodoxy, the fallow ground left behind quickly became repopulated by the noxious weeds of New Age religion. It reminds me of the time when we built our house on a wheat field. Once the land was bulldozed and the house built, the nice uniformity of the wheat field was quickly replaced by fast-growing weeds. Nature abhors a vacuum, and the weeds of postmodern spirituality quickly filled the vacuum created by the modernist displacement of the Judeo-Christian God. New Age religion is a particularly noxious weed because it grows quickly in arid soil, frequently looks like other religions, but ultimately has no nutritive value.

> For the time is coming when people will not endure sound teaching, but having itching ears they will accumulate for themselves teachers to suit their own passions, and will turn away from listening to the truth and wander off into myths. As for you, always be sober-minded, endure suffering, do the work of an evangelist, fulfill your ministry. (2 Tim. 4:3–5)

Despite its limitations, postmodernism did reopen the door for the deities previously banished by modernism. True to form, however, postmodernism declares that all gods and spiritualities are welcome to the religious table but on the condition they not say anything mean to the other little gods. They have also demanded that the belligerent Judeo-Christian God sit quietly in the corner with an "Unknown God" sign around His neck.

It appears that each God needs to submit an agenda to the postmodern dogma clearinghouse to determine if it is suitable for widespread dissemination. However, a clearinghouse of tolerance sounds like intolerance to me, an abomination to postmodernism. The postmodernists hope that with enough counseling and the proper use of politically correct words, the lion will not only lie down with the lamb but will also eat a vegan meal, meditate, and crochet with the lamb. This sounds great until you recognize that every worldview clings to its own dogmatic truths that are incompatible with the others. So every time the worldview lion is forced to cohabitate with the worldview lamb, it doesn't see a courage-challenged sheep but rather lamb chops.

While the precepts of these two movements are frequently at odds with each other, they surprisingly coexist. The modernist claim that we are evolutionary accidents fits in quite nicely with the postmodern idea that we are not beholden to any supreme authority. It allows us to look really smart in our lab coats while simultaneously giving us permission to periodically take them off and dance around in our spiritual tie-dyed T-shirts.

The information superhighway is an interesting blend of these two philosophies. The technological computer chips and wiring of scientific modernity have brought the disparate ideas of postmodernity into our living rooms. This unprecedented access to information, not unlike the Renaissance and Enlightenment, has made us keenly aware of the diversity of opinions, lifestyles, and cultures. We see this diversity coexisting harmoniously on the Internet and are fooled into believing this electronic tolerance can be equated with cultural tolerance. It is one thing to admire diversity on a computer screen but quite another to live next door to it. The information revolution of the enlightenment, which stimulated the effort to find universal truth, has been replaced by an Internet information revolution, which now questions the ability to find universal truth at all.

The coexistence of these two contradictory worldviews presents a serious problem for most people because they want to live their unencumbered postmodern lifestyles but not at the expense of abandoning their reasonable modernist sensibilities. The angst generated by this irreconcilable tension creates a gospel-sized crack in our current cultural façade. As we solidify our understanding of our place in God's world, we need to be aware of how these philosophical undercurrents have shaped not only our own beliefs but also the beliefs of the culture around us.

We need not fear, however, because cultural change doesn't alter the gospel but rather brings it to its fullness by highlighting previously hidden strengths. As our worldview opponents rejoice at each Christian argument they have cut down, they look on in horror to see that they are messing with a Christian Hydra, and each apparently damaged argument is transformed into two new and more-powerful ones.

How Now Shall We Live?

The once-noble pursuit of discovering the unifying principles of life has deteriorated to half-hearted attempts to justify our absurd lifestyles. The pursuit of truth has become the pursuit of convenience. The good news is that worldviews of convenience have very shallow roots and are easily uprooted when the cultural weather changes, but the roots of God's truth run deep and cannot be shaken. It is within this cultural milieu that we as Christians are called to make our faith relevant to the world. The major cultural challenges presented by modernism and postmodernism can be distilled into two commonly held beliefs. First, there is the modern idea, fostered by evolutionary theory, that we are just the smartest monkeys, more highly evolved but inherently no different from any other animal. The second idea, fostered by postmodernism, is that all truth is relative and no unifying explanation for our world exists. Simply put, these ideas mark the death of man and the death of story.

So how do we navigate these philosophical minefields? How can we effectively communicate the truth of the gospel to a confused culture? We need to begin by remembering we're not trying to convince others of our particular Christian viewpoint but trying to show them they already live in God's world. As we turn our flashlight of human understanding on this world, we cannot forget that it's already glowing with the ambient light of God's creation, a radiance that most people sense one way or another.

How do we unite all this information into a coherent whole? We are bombarded with massive amounts of data and feel powerless to sort it all out. In fact, our culture gives us a free intellectual pass by telling us it's all relative anyway. Our ignorance is portrayed as an advantage to a fulfilled life. The ability to access information is put at a premium, while the coherence of that information is deemed irrelevant.

I want to build a worldview toolbox for you. I want you to be able to look under the hood of every worldview clunker out there so you will be an informed consumer. I want you to have access to the CarFax of every worldview so you can see how many times it's been totaled and how many times it's been rebuilt. We need to break the evidence that surrounds us into bite-sized pieces and ask ourselves if our worldview is capable of putting it back together.

Let's Begin

> You have heard that it was said, "You shall love your neighbor and hate your enemy." But I say to you, Love your enemies and pray for those who persecute you, so that you may be sons of your Father who is in heaven. *For he makes his sun rise on the evil and on the good, and sends rain on the just and on the unjust.* (Matt. 5:43–45, emphasis added)

Everybody recognizes and relies on God's common grace daily, yet they are surprisingly oblivious to its source. Our lives are played out on a planet that is remarkably kind to its inhabitants; so much so that we can take the stage for granted and concentrate on the drama of our everyday lives. Since this common grace is available to everyone, it would seem to be a good place to begin our discussion with others.

Every morning, humans step outside of their igloos, huts, and homes and are confronted with some very basic realities. We see a planet consisting of dirt, water, and air, dotted with plant life, and teeming with creatures. We strike up a conversation with a human, whether family or friend. We walk on the soil, breathe the air, and drink the water. We notice our lawn needs mowing, our garden weeding, and our leaves raking. We notice that once again the cat has missed the kitty litter, the dog is panting at the door expectantly, and the birds are singing. We organize our kids for school, kiss our spouses as they leave for work, and meet with friends at the coffee shop. It's as if every day we have stepped into a story. Some days it seems like community theater, while other days it seems like a glorious Broadway production, but either way, it strikes us as another scene in an ongoing drama.

We awaken from our slumber-story intermission every morning and watch as the curtain slowly rises on the next scene of our life. We once again step onto the beautiful set decorated with props— the peach tree in the backyard, the horse in the pasture—and we encounter another human, and the performance begins. We are struck by the fact that every character has his or her own story that has somehow been integrated into ours. We recognize that every good story has a conflict and a resolution, and we see this played out every day in the individual scenes of our lives, but we are also keenly aware that each of these smaller life chapters are bound into a larger book that is thematically tied together.

I suggest that the physical world consisting of dirt, rocks, water, wind, rain, and sunshine constitutes the set. The plants and animals are the props, and we humans are the characters in this story. As we look at the set, props, and characters, we need to ask ourselves a very basic question: are they good or bad? I suspect that most of us consider the set and props to be good or at least neutral. Even when the earth convulses with earthquakes, the wind becomes hurricanes, and the water becomes floods, I suspect that none of us would consider them evil. In addition, you wouldn't call amanita mushrooms evil if your pet ate one and died, and you don't call your cat evil because it deposits a dead mouse on your porch. I would bet, however, that as you contemplated the question of whether human beings were good or evil, you probably hesitated for a moment. Why would you hesitate? You may have flashed back to the betrayal of a friend, the rudeness of a store clerk, Mother Teresa, *The Undercover Millionaire*, or even the holocaust. It seems that with this very simple question we have uncovered a conflict in the world, a tension in our story—man is good and evil!

Man, it appears, is the only creature on this planet capable of simultaneously embodying good and bad, and it chafes at us like evil sand in the swimsuit of goodness; every movement, it rubs us rawer, and we can't take our mind off the pain. Sounds like a very interesting premise for a story, don't you think? How is it we don't consider the set and props evil but can easily find evidence of evil in mankind? It would seem to me that this is a question that cannot be ignored.

> The theory that everything was good had become an
> orgy of everything that was bad.[36]
>
> —G. K. Chesterton

If this is in fact the conflict in our human story, how does it get resolved? This is where it gets interesting; the rest of human history is about every political, cultural, legal, and religious effort to try to resolve this tension. Unfortunately, most of these efforts have been nothing more than mankind trying to write the final chapters to a book it didn't author.

The Original Sin of man brought up in Genesis 3 describes this conflict quite well—mankind trying to be like God, or in literary terms, the characters trying to be the author. It seems to me our lives would be a lot simpler if we accepted the fact that the Bible offers the best explanation for this larger story rather than trying to establish our own publishing houses and write prequels and sequels that were never sanctioned by the Writer.

When God created the universe, He began to tell us a story, "Once upon a *Time*," "In the *beginning*." Understanding our world as a great drama or story addresses the two main philosophical threats to the Christian gospel, the death of story and the death of man. Our task will be to break down this big story into its parts and see how they fit together. If any part of the story doesn't make sense, the whole story won't make sense. If the plot resolution doesn't address the conflict, it isn't a story.

I suspect many of you feel the power of your Christian faith but have a hard time understanding it in the context of your everyday lives. The chapters that follow will help you see your life as part of a larger God story. A story that seamlessly incorporates all the narrative components necessary to be entertaining and believable.

Chapter Three

IMPROVISATION OR MASTERPIECE THEATER?

Y OU CAN'T BELIEVE YOUR EARS! The television just announced that the most heralded Broadway show of all time is coming to your inconsequential little town. The national press has been fawning over it for months, unanimously giving it "two thumbs up," with one particularly tough critic going so far as to describe it as "Andrew Lloyd Webber on steroids." It is a story set in a faraway land of breathtaking beauty where the arid desert of desolation is a mere stone's throw from the tropical jungle of plenty. The plot of the story is familiar and exceedingly comforting; it's the tale of a kingdom threatened by menacing dragons and evil kings; despite seemingly endless brutal skirmishes, it continues to redraw its ever-expanding borders gloriously demarcated by the crimson ink of its bravest knights.

The entire range of human experience is flawlessly incorporated into the plot line: afflicted by tragedy, betrayal, and suffering, the heroes are redeemed through eternal love, compassion, and sacrifice. Tony Award– winning actors and actresses are slated to perform the roles of the main characters. The soundtrack went platinum months ago.

Thanks to speed-dial technology, you have scored front-row seats. The pregnancy of your anticipation has finally reached full term, and tonight you will experience the labor pains of theatrical delivery. Tonight is the night! Your dreary life of finding shelter and foraging for food has taken its toll, and you are almost completely drained by the apparent lack of meaning and purpose in your life. It's been a rough year since your father died, your divorce was finalized, and your company demoted you to a position for which you are overqualified and underpaid. You sense there should be more—every magazine advertisement and TV commercial tells you so—but where is it? Mercifully, this show is the biggest distraction you have been able to find in years, and you are hopeful it will give you at least three to four weeks of respite from your inner psychic pain.

You drive into town, park, and head to the theater. You are joined by thousands who are also seeking respite from their exceedingly tedious and dull lives. Like moths drawn to a porch light, you and your fellow pilgrims are inexplicably rescued from the dark recesses of the night and bathed in the emotional salvation of the brightly lit marquee.

You find your velvety soft seat and settle in. Your patience is finally rewarded as the house lights dim and the murmuring of the crowd fades. The curtain rises, and you are suddenly besieged by a visual tsunami of breathtaking beauty. You're struck by the contrast between the dull nightlight of the ordinary that ushered you in and the radiance of the extraordinary that now washes over you. You flash back to the awe you experienced as a child when Dorothy entered the land of Oz and the film transitioned from black and white to color. You marvel at the intricacy of the stage and props. The vibrant lighting enhances every detail of the set. The opening score swells, swaddling you in aural grandeur. It all seems so perfect.

Scene one, act one. You hold your breath and await the entrance of the actors. Suddenly, out of nowhere, your seemingly dim, indistinguishable face is bathed in a dazzling light as if veiled in divine radiance. One of the theater spotlights has been focused on you. Once again you feel drawn to the light, but this time it seems to be coaxing you onstage! You are exhilarated and yet have never

61

been more terrified. Palms sweating, you enter the story. You were hopeful the show would provide a temporary distraction from your dismal existence, but it appears that your seemingly insignificant life has become integral to this theatrical production. You make your way onto the stage, and as you step foot onto the set, you turn your head slightly to the side and catch a fleeting glimpse of the Director enthusiastically moving in the shadows offstage. You sense He is giving you directions, waving His hands, mouthing your lines, and pointing to your marks.

At first, it feels that you've been lured into some sort of candid camera prank; you get the sense you've been punk'd, but as you carefully take in your surroundings, it becomes obvious that this set is just too elaborate and complex and that there are far too many props and actors for this to be just a cruel joke. Somebody with a passion for grand theater must have spent a long time writing and planning this show. You look around and see that every character has a specific role seamlessly woven into the larger drama.

Intrigued by the harmonious integration of the set, props, and characters, you begin to contemplate what role you could possibly play in this astonishing production. You look into the wings, eyes still adjusting to the bright stage lights, and once again catch a glimpse of the Director as if through a glass darkly. His eyes seem to be passionately locked on you despite the intensity of the drama swirling about on stage. He seems exclusively interested in your performance, and with an encouraging smile, He begins to give you cues.

As the story unfolds, you begin to feel more comfortable in your character and recognize your role was not a late script revision but had been planned from the beginning. Curious, you look beyond the footlights and try to catch a glimpse of your former seat, but you find it impossible to distinguish the dullness of your past life in the presence of such intense stage lighting. You begin to ponder the immensity of the show, the multitude of characters, the perfectly placed props, and the intricate set. Your mind spins with questions. What will become of my character? What will the reviews of my performance look like? Will I get to meet the director? Will there be an encore when the curtain is again raised and the stage lights relit? What about a cast party?

Welcome to your story! Think about it. Your life reads like a story. You are born once upon a time and hope to live happily ever after. Our birth and death are the bookends to a remarkable drama. Our individual stories are embedded in a larger cosmic story; the universe begins with a bang, and scientists say it will end in a big freeze, heat death, or contraction back into a singularity. What transpires in between is gloriously improbable yet meticulously planned.

The reason that the concept of story is so important to us humans is because we were created to be in a story. The Genesis account essentially describes God's power to spin a yarn by speaking His story into existence, "And God said … and it was so."

I Never *Meta* Story I Didn't Like

While I will interchangeably refer to God's world as the Christian or biblical worldview, I want you to also be aware of the limitations of the term, *worldview*. When we imply that our Christianity is a view, we feed into the postmodern mind-set that it is merely one of many equally valid possibilities based on nothing more than our personal preferences. A worldview becomes merely an interesting way of looking at the world instead of a description of the way things are. When I refer to the Christian worldview, I use it to refer to reality, the way the world is, and not the way we want it to be. In my mind, the Christian worldview equals truth, which equals reality. We live in God's world, and we don't have a choice in the matter. If you don't accept this fact, your only option is to create an illusion and force-fit the square peg of your personal desire into the round hole of God's reality.

A worldview is also frequently referred to as a metanarrative, an overarching story that provides an explanation for the way the world is. Since every story must have an author, this terminology becomes a bit threatening to modern and postmodern sensibilities because it introduces the very sticky issue of who authored it. Modernists avoid this issue by replacing the creative mind with random chance and survival of the fittest and in the process reduce man to a deluded animal whose existence is driven by instinct rather than plot.

Postmodernists, on the other hand, because of their fear of oppressive, controlling narratives, deny the larger story and reduce our lives to billions of individually written and performed screenplays all vying for opportunities to perform on the world stage. Despite these critical voices, the vast majority of us live as if something bigger than us is going on, which strangely enough has the feel of a great theatrical production.

> When the storytelling is good, we are pulled into a world that is both truer and larger than the one we ordinarily occupy; but it is not an alien world ... Good storytelling involves us in what has been sitting right in front of us for years but we hadn't noticed or hadn't thought was important or hadn't had anything to do with us. And then we notice—the story wakes us up to what is there and has always been there. Without leaving the world in which we daily work and sleep and play, we find ourselves in a far larger world.[37]
>
> —Eugene Peterson

"On a scale of one to ten, what is the metaphysical certitude of ...?" Those of you who have seen the *McLaughlin Group* on PBS will recognize this as one of the questions frequently posed by the host, John McLaughlin, to his panel of political pundits. In essence, he is asking them if a particular political theory provides the overarching explanation for a particular event. Metaphysics is defined as the philosophical study of the ultimate causes and underlying nature of things. Guess what? We're all metaphysicians. We all participate in this noble venture, and whether we describe it with fancy philosophical terms, we're still looking for an explanation that will register a ten on McLaughlin's metaphysical certitude scale.

Medicine always tries to understand the bigger picture in its efforts to provide the most appropriate clinical care. Medical literature, however, is plagued with a plethora of clinical studies that look at very important questions but are too small to generate enough statistical power to provide significant conclusions. To try to answer these important questions, researchers employ a statistical method that combines multiple little studies into a larger, more powerful whole to gather enough data to make conclusive statements about a particular treatment strategy. A study like this is called a meta-analysis and is merely a scientific attempt to try to evaluate the universal applicability of a particular medical treatment from smaller inconclusive studies.

I remember when the announcement was made that there would be a twenty-four-hour news channel, CNN. I thought, *is there really enough news to entertain us for twenty-four hours a day?* In reality, I was right; there aren't enough news facts to warrant twenty-four hours of coverage, but what I failed to perceive was that there were not enough hours in a day to put those facts into a larger, more meaningful context. Twenty-four-hour news and sports channels present a few facts at the top of the hour and spend the rest of the time devoted to experts, pundits, and talking heads ruminating about how these tidbits fit into the big picture. Think about it; just before Hurricane Katrina hit, we heard from national weather specialists, dike specialists, disaster relief experts, Louisiana geography experts, and mental trauma specialists, all theorizing about the impact of the storm. They were trying to write the narrative before the event even occurred because they knew the audience wanted to see the bigger story.

When the tenth anniversary of 9/11 was observed, the majority of the media coverage was not about the details of the attack; the science of jet planes crashing into buildings is interesting, but we wanted to hear stories of lives forever changed. These were not just mininarratives of someone's isolated experience, they were stories played out on the world stage. Perhaps CNN should be called CMN, the Cable Metanarrative Network, because it seems to be obsessed with trying to understand the big picture. Whether you call it a metanarrative, big picture, overarching story, or worldview, it's not just the individual experience of you or me but also the global experience of *us*.

Whose Line Is It Anyway?

Postmodernism declares that all truth is relative, reducing God's grand theatrical production to mere improvisation. The vast created world around us is squeezed onto a small, poorly lit bar where humans become comics taking suggestions from the audience to create their personal realities. Have you ever seen the show *Whose Line Is It Anyway*? It is a very entertaining television program that showcases the talents of improvisational comics who are handed props or given suggestions from the audience and asked to create a skit or story revolving around those items and ideas. For improvisation to be successful, the stage must be bare so the comics can create any illusion they want. An elaborate set limits the ability to improvise; for example, pretending to be a man dying of thirst in a desert while standing in front of a waterfall in a rain forest just doesn't work.

Part of the reason that audiences enjoy improvisation is because it allows them to be in control of their own entertainment; they like being able to manipulate the behavior of the comics. One particularly entertaining segment of the show is called Newsflash; it consists of a comic standing in front of a giant green screen that looks just green to him, but video technology allows the producers to project a series of images visible only to the other comics and the audience. The comic in front of the screen plays the role of a news reporter covering the events being projected onto the screen behind him; the other comics enter into dialogue with him and try to give him clues about what's being shown on the green screen. What the audience sees is a total disconnect between what the comic is talking about and the images displayed.

All too often our fellow man chooses the role of the comic, foolishly improvising his life in front of the giant green screen of God's world. Their words and actions are incongruent with the grand drama being performed around them. Unfortunately for our postmodern friends, improvisation just becomes a theater of the absurd—amusing to watch but practically useless as a way to understand our world.

Though improvisational comedy is based on random suggestions, the comic's ability to create an organized, unifying story is what makes improv entertaining. The comic realizes that if he or she doesn't create some coherence around the props and suggestions, the audience will quickly lose interest. He or she then ends up cobbling together a narrative that can be amusing but when viewed in front of the green screen looks quite ridiculous. We, as Christians, need to avoid getting caught up in this bizarre postmodern charade, take a step back, and look at the big picture.

When you peer through your window in the morning, do you see a bare stage? Is your first thought of the day speculation about how you will improvise your own reality? Are you waiting to be handed props or respond to suggestions from the audience? No! You realize you are already standing on a very elaborate stage and the drama you put aside while you slept has once again resumed. It appears that today is another scene in the play, and the set, props, and characters are very familiar.

I suspect you'd find it quite strange if someone described your day as a series of animal instincts. Our days are not defined by the instinctual drudgery of foraging for food, finding shelter, and mating but rather by the dramatic plot conflicts of whether your spouse will find a job, your ailing father will make amends with your siblings, or your alcoholic sister will rid herself of her demons.

If we were to set up our own improvisational "life" theaters, we would soon discover our cherished little acts are always being performed in front of empty houses. The mere economics of this postmodern entertainment model make it impossible for you to perform for anyone but yourself, and you will ultimately be forced to close because of a lack of patronage; you can't pay your improvisational bills without an audience. In the end, you are left with nothing but a downtown full of clubs boarded up because of lack of interest. However, if you step outside your cold, dark theater where the power was turned off months ago, you will see a brightly lit marquee and people streaming in from everywhere to take in the greatest drama of all. You vaguely remember being handed free tickets, but you failed to redeem them. Maybe today is the day!

Toddlers and Tiaras

Why has reality TV become such a popular entertainment genre? We have shows about choosing a wedding dress, running a cake business, and driving large transport trucks over ice fields. If you'd told me twenty years ago that we'd be watching shows about the drama surrounding infants and children competing in beauty pageants, I would have said you were nuts! I obviously have had to rethink my ability to predict the future, but I think the reason these shows are so successful is because they highlight, although often to a ridiculous extreme, the fact that life is drama. We all understand there are stories swirling all around us, and we want to know how they fit together.

Humans are pattern-seeking animals, and the pattern we're most fond of seeking is that of a story. When you see a wreck on the side of the road, you crane your neck to look for pieces of evidence that will provide some sort of explanation. Are there bottles of alcohol strewn about? Is it a family? A lone teenager? I suggest we are not just morbid Lookie Lous but are detectives trying to piece together the data so when we get home, we can tell our spouse or family a story. We will eagerly turn on the news or scan the morning paper for more details so we can put the event into a larger context, to uncover the story we had just witnessed.

Bedtime Stories

Our society, whether it chooses to acknowledge it or not, cannot live without stories. When we are very young, we are captivated by stories of knights, princesses, castles, and dragons. Children seem to need stories to explain their little lives and prepare them to successfully navigate the world as adults. As we age, the fairy tales of our youth become stories built on more-concrete pillars but are no less magical or astounding. The dragons become Original Sin, the quest of the knight to rescue the princess becomes the work of sanctification, and slaying the dragon becomes redemption.

We utilize stories every day at our jobs. When I admitted a premature baby to the hospital, I began my work by obtaining information about the mother's medical and social condition. Each piece of data I obtained was integral to formulating the proper plan of medical care. My eldest daughter applied to college this last year, and it appeared that every school was interested in her story; they requested a personal statement. We take pictures of vacations and special events; we create scrapbooks and photo albums to earmark the important pages in our life story. Have you ever wondered why family reunions, school reunions, infantry reunions, all kinds of reunions, are so popular? They help connect our various stories to the larger story swirling around us. How did the star athlete at our school turn out? What about the cheerleader, nerd, or stoner? All of them are characters in our story but also characters in a larger drama.

At the wedding reception of my cousin's son, we were shown a slide-show montage of images of the bride and groom from birth to adulthood, each image subsequently building on the other to give us an overview of their personal stories. I saw pictures of my deceased grandma and aunt in the background, which would have been meaningless to the people who had never met them before, but they helped me recall my own stories. On the other hand, I saw pictures of people I didn't recognize, but they elicited stories from others. We all attended the same wedding, but the air was swirling with emotions, memories, and stories that were tangential to the event itself yet were linked in the same cosmic drama.

Special events periodically bring all our individual stories together in a symphony of narrative; if you listen closely enough, you will hear the unique melody of each instrument, but when taken as a whole, it becomes a grand symphony of story.

Microsoft employees Eric Horvitz and Jure Lescovec conducted a study based on 30 billion electronic conversations among 180 million people around the world. They found that any two people are separated from one another on average by only 6.6 degrees.[38] It appears that the popular folklore surrounding the six degrees of separation from Kevin Bacon is not so far-fetched after all. It is really quite amazing just how intricately interwoven our lives are both locally and globally. Could it be that we are in fact characters in a larger cosmic drama?

We all feel the power of this grand narrative from time to time, but sadly, we treat it like elevator music and fail to recognize how intricate it truly is. One of the most powerful aspects of a story is that it can be expressed in a variety of media, which honors our individuality while retaining its universal narrative power. We are free to view life as a Broadway show, a painting, a novel, or a song.

Dirty Laundry

Why are we so fascinated by the personal struggles of celebrities such as Lindsey Lohan, Brittney Spears, and Amy Winehouse? We have so many questions—was it their parents, their childhood, or their rapid rise to fame that caused them difficulties? We want to know their stories so we can understand why their personal trains came off the tracks. We voraciously read magazine articles and listen to expert psychiatrists and counselors attempting to give us the big-picture explanation for these troubled celebrity lives. We want to know the bigger story!

Recently, George Bush published his presidential memoirs. With today's technology, we already have enormous amounts of data about what was accomplished during his term, so why write a book? Why read it? We care because we want to know the bigger story behind his decisions. We want to know about his personal and interpersonal struggles as he tried to navigate the treacherous waters reserved for the most powerful man in the world. We want to know about his upbringing, his marriage, his children, and his faith. We want to know his story because only then can we put his presidency in the proper perspective, personally and globally. How did his performance fit into the larger drama played out on the world stage?

Why would we tell stories about our lives to others if we didn't think they could be universally understood? We relate stories about our lives because we want to entertain, inform, or create emotional connections. We want our stories to resonate with our listeners and are disappointed when they don't. Our stories yearn to be parables that convey the timeless lessons we've learned during our lives.

Parables are stories, general enough to invite others in but specific enough to address real-life issues. We invite readers or hearers to insert their names and faces into our stories and ask how they would respond. Why do you think Jesus taught in parables? The first reason is that humans learn and teach most effectively through stories. Second, the New Testament refers to Jesus as the "Creating Word of God." Jesus was the master storyteller of God's theodrama and as such, He frequently alluded to the natural world in His parables. Jesus moved the felt plants, animals, and humans around on the flannel board of His own creation to teach us the story of the kingdom of God. He wanted to show His audience how their personal little life "*word*" was written into God's larger "*Word*" story.

> Telling and listening to a story is the primary verbal way of accounting for life the way we live it in actual day-to-day reality. There are no (or few) abstractions in a story. A story is immediate, concrete, plotted, relational, personal. And so when we lose touch with our lives, with our souls—our moral, spiritual, embodying God-personal lives—story is the best way of getting us back in touch again. And that is why God's word is given for the most part in the form of story, this vast, overarching, all encompassing story, this meta-story.[39]
>
> —Eugene Peterson

We are exhilarated when we connect with another person and discover a shared plotline. This is frequently found in a favorite writer or musical artist. Todd Rundgren is one of my favorite musical artists. He has taken me on an emotional adventure with every album. His music fleshed out adolescent emotions I didn't understand and was incapable of conveying. I have vivid memories of sitting by the stereo, bulky 1970s headphones strapped to my head, gazing at the elaborate album covers for hours, reading the lyrics and liner notes over and over (a lost art nowadays because of the microscopic print on CD inserts). I felt an emotional connection. I'd love to sit down with him someday and ask him about his songs and see if he had experienced the same angst I had.

Classic Albums, a popular show on VH-1, analyzes the writing, performing, and production of classic rock albums through the eyes of the producers, engineers, and artists. The show gives us the story behind these popular and influential works. It weaves the story of our teenage years into the story of the artists and their creative processes, two different stories interconnected in a note, a turn of phrase, or guitar solo—a grand drama!

> The truth of the story is not a motto suitable for framing. It is a truth that one way or another, God help us, we live out every day of our lives. It is a truth as complicated and sad as you and I ourselves are complicated and sad, and as joyous and as simple as we are to.[40]
>
> —Frederick Buechner

The human desire to find an overarching story or a metanarrative is hardwired into our brains. It is played out every day in magazines, newspapers, TV, music, and movies. We all convey information in the form of a story whether sipping coffee with a friend at Starbuck's or huddled around a fire in Africa watching a traditional native dance. Each of these stories is but a mere paragraph or chapter in a larger drama.

I am reminded of the award-winning movie *Crash*, which begins with the scene of an automobile accident. We are taken on a journey through the individual stories of each character whose lives momentarily intersected at this horrible event. We quickly see how this simple tragic accident brought together a symphony of narrative in which each character's personal story was melodically intertwined with those of the others.

I encourage you to think about this as you cross paths with your fellow man today. What drama in their lives has just traversed through yours? It's incredible to think that while you read through the lines of your story, you are also a character in someone else's. Maybe if we were more sensitive to the frequently tragic drama played out in the lives of others, we might become more-effective supporting casts in their stories. If we remain unmoved or oblivious to the conflicts in the lives of our fellow man, we are merely engaging in the personal amusement of improvisation rather than the ensemble power of grand theater.

> In the front pews the old ladies turn up their hearing aids, and a young lady slips her six year old a Lifesaver and a Magic Marker. A college sophomore home for vacation, who is there because he was dragged there, slumps forward with his chin in his hand. The vice-president of a bank who twice that week has seriously contemplated suicide places his hymnal in the rack. A pregnant girl feels the stir of life in her. A high-school teacher, who for twenty years has managed to keep his homosexuality a secret or the most part even from himself, creases his order of service down the center with his thumbnail and tucks it under his knee ... the preacher pulls the little cord that turns on the lectern light and deals out his note cards like a riverboat gambler. The stakes have never been higher.[41]
>
> —Frederick Buechner

Masterpiece Theater

Why is there classic literature? Why did my high school English teacher require me to read difficult, old prose written by dead English writers? Why translate the writings of an emotionally unstable Russian into English just to torture a pimple-faced teenager? Most of these books were set in a time and place I couldn't relate to, so why read them? They were required reading because they pointed to timeless truths, and even if I couldn't relate to the book historically, I could still understand the universal struggles, questions, and dilemmas that faced the characters. For a piece of literature to be considered classic, it must transcend its historical and cultural setting and point us to the larger, universal narrative in which we all participate. It sets our minds to wandering, and although we may not be walking the cobblestoned streets of Old London, our minds wrestle with the same questions on the subway in New York.

My dad wrote a book about his life because he was very concerned that he didn't know his parents' stories and didn't want his children to suffer the same fate. His lack of knowledge about his parents' lives made his own story incomplete. He titled his book *My Life to Now*. It was not a collection of facts but of stories. On the cover, he made a statement that I think encapsulates our personal need for larger explanatory stories.

> I have always been upset that the lives of my parents are such a mystery and black hole to me. I decided to make sure that my children at least had something to keep and know about their Dad. Hopefully, while this collects a lot of dust it will be taken down on occasion to read.
>
> —D. E. Strandness, Jr.

Hinduism, which understands God as an impersonal force, treats life as a never-ending series of unresolved ministories or reincarnations during which the problem never gets resolved just recycled or repackaged. The goal is get off the illusory wheel of karmic story. A situation comparable to being locked in a library full of good and bad literature where your task is to keep reading books until you find the "perfect novel" at which point you are allowed to leave and reward your mind with a well-earned eternity of illiterate "zoning out." For the Buddhist, the problem is picking up a book in the first place and then being mesmerized by the story. A story that leads to a lifetime of page-turning suffering. Finally, the atheist blinded by concrete rationality, quickly walks past the classic literature section and makes a beeline for the self-help section and scours the racks for survival manuals.

However, once you introduce a personal God who has stepped into the world, life becomes one big linear story with a beginning and an end, filled in the middle with a universal plot tension that demands resolution. The goal for the Christian then is to dive deeper into the story, understand the narrative tension, and anticipate the climactic final chapter, and in the process become the character he or she was created to be. The Bible gives us the whole script, from beginning to end, and remarkably describes life as we know it. It qualifies as classic literature because it penetrates the heart and points to a unifying truth bigger than us. We cannot just sit in our comfy chair, foolishly trying to extract pithy verses out of context; we must immerse ourselves in the larger metanarrative that's being revealed. If the Bible doesn't inform our lives, the "printer's ink becomes embalming fluid"[42] and leaves us dead to the drama around us. We cannot treat Scripture as Cliff's Notes and miss the beauty of a phrase, metaphor, or poem. The Bible is not only doctrinal truth but also performance knowledge.

> The unified sum and substance of the Bible is theodramatic: it is all about God's word and God's deeds, accomplished by his "two hands" (Son and Spirit) and about what we should say and do in response ... To focus on the propositional content only is to fail to recognize the Bible's divine communicative action, a failure that leads one to dedramatize the Scriptures. The result: a faith that seeks only an abbreviated understanding that falls short of *performance knowledge* ... One can state that "God is good" in a proposition, but it takes a narrative to "taste and see that the Lord is good."[43]
>
> —Kevin Vanhoozer (emphasis added)

Remember, Remember, Remember!

> If the God of the Bible exists, he is not a man in the attic, but the Playwright. That means we won't be able to find Him like we would find a passive object with the powers of empirical investigation, Rather, we must find the clues to his reality that he has written into the universe, including into us.[44]
>
> —Timothy Keller

The Old Testament seamlessly draws us into the larger God story by identifying the Author, setting the scene (creation), introducing the props (plants and animals) and characters (humans), establishing the relationship of the characters (man, woman, and serpent), and laying out the conflict (the fall). God then launches into His salvation storyline, beginning with Abraham. The rest of the Old Testament is essentially a retelling of the age-old conflict and how it is played out in the lives of the people chosen and loved by God. It graphically describes the problem that plagues mankind but graciously offers enticing narrative clues as to how it will be gloriously resolved.

The characters in this story frequently get caught up in the idea that the plot was really about their personal victories when in reality, they were merely the literary devices God used to satisfactorily conclude His story. Throughout the pages of the Old Testament, God constantly called His chosen people to remember His story, remember what He had done, and remember the plotline, all the while warning them of the dangers of trying to write their own narratives.

God's chosen people frequently went off script and foolishly improvised to the suggestions thrown out by their pagan neighbor audience. Why do you think God refers to himself as the God of Abraham, Isaac, and Jacob? Why does He call them to remember the Exodus? God wants His people to remember His story by calling to mind the main characters and plot trajectory because a life of improvisation leads only to ruin.

> And there arose another generation after them who did not know the Lord or the work that he had done for Israel. And the people of Israel did what was evil in the sight of the Lord and served the Baals. And they abandoned the Lord, the God of their fathers, who had brought them out of the land of Egypt. They went after other gods, from among the gods of the peoples who were around them, and bowed down to them. And they provoked the Lord to anger. (Judg. 2:10–12)

God also recognized that the storyline was often so intriguing that the people would get caught up in the drama and forget the Author. The chosen people attempted to avoid this problem by reciting the *shema*, which begins with, "Hear, O Israel: The Lord our God, the Lord is one. You shall love the Lord your God with all your heart and with all your soul and with all your might" (Deut. 6:4–5) and ends with, "I am the Lord your God, who brought you out of the land of Egypt to be your God: I am the Lord your God" (Num. 15:41). This basic liturgical affirmation of Judaism acknowledged God as Author and the Jews' place in God's scripted story.

> Life is the tale of two stories—one finite and frail, the other eternal and enduring. The tiny one—the story of us—is as brief as the blink of an eye. Yet somehow our infatuation with our own little story—and our determination to make is as big as we possibly can—blinds us to the massive God Story that surrounds us on every side … The story already has a star, and the star is not you or me.[45]
>
> —Louie Giglio

A God tied to history is a very scary thing to a culture that wants to live with no strings attached. The word *god* easily rolls from our lips, but the phrases "The God of Abraham, Isaac, and Jacob" or "God, the Father of our Lord Jesus Christ" stick in our throats like bones of accountability. Religion is easy if your God is the great unknown, the eternal, nirvana, or cosmic energy, but it becomes very uncomfortable when He is our Father and we are wayward children, when He is our spouse and we are the adulterer, when He is our God and we are His chosen people.

The Judeo-Christian tradition makes it clear that God stepped into history not to impress us with a Fourth of July fireworks show but to patiently sit with us in the counselor's office as we try to mend the relationship we destroyed with our philandering. The history of mankind is just a series of stories about man trying to exert his independence from God and then God intervening to show man that he is truly dependent on God.

People Plagiarism

According to Genesis, the human race began as monotheists; they knew there was only one Author. It wasn't until after the fall that polytheism developed and man began to create a pantheon of ghostwriters. Despite the fact that God's story was copyrighted long before humans came upon the scene, our ancestral couple engaged in a bold act of divine plagiarism. The Original Sin of mankind was an authoritorial coup. I think if you look at the problems facing the world today, you will see they all stem from man trying to be godlike, characters trying to rest narrative control from the Author and foolishly improvising their lives away.

Once confronted by God, Adam and Eve quickly recognized the absurdity of replacing the word processor of the Author with the color crayons of their personal improvisations. Mankind, banished from the garden, then began to polytheistically spread the blame for its divine ambitions by setting up a pantheon of straw gods that behaved just like them but had divine powers. They paid homage to the undeniable concept of God but ended up playing an elaborate shell game in the spiritual marketplace that allowed them to hide their pretentious desire to be divine under the cover of "god shells" of their own creation.

We know that if we personally claimed to be God, everyone would call our bluff, but if we all winked at each other and created our own little gods, we could absurdly assume divinity without having to prove it.

The King's Speech

How can God as Spirit tell a physical story we can comprehend? Let's begin by asking ourselves how communication occurs in the first place. When human beings communicate with other human beings, they convert immaterial thoughts into physical form, whether spoken or written words. The words are received by others through their eyes or ears and reconverted into an immaterial thought. This interaction makes several assumptions: first, it implies that a thought can be converted into something tangible and real; second, the two people must share a common language; and third, it implies that they share a common ground of experience so the words they send are interpreted through the same intellectual filter.

How does something as nebulous as a thought get converted into something tangible? We see this all the time; consider hydroelectric dams or windmills; they take energy in one form and convert it into another, more-useful form. When we communicate, our immaterial thought information is transduced into another form of word information that cannot be comprehended unless the receiving party understands that physical language. If we don't have a shared physical and emotional structure, we cannot relate to the information being conveyed. Describing a computer to remote aboriginal tribesmen, even if we knew their language, would be incredibly difficult if they had never before experienced one. With these ideas in mind, let's look at God's ability speak our story into existence.

The Bible begins with God creating through speech. God speaks, and something physical comes into existence. God's thought is converted into physical form. Why doesn't the Bible describe God as creating the universe by waving a magic wand or clapping His hands? It makes a big deal about creation being the result of spoken communication. The creation stories of the pagan neighbors, on the other hand, told stories of the world being created because of feuds, jealousy, convenience, and the disemboweling of other gods. In Genesis, God's spoken word is the intermediary between God's creative idea and the physical world such that when we look at the universe, we see the physical representation of God's thought. Just like a dam takes the motion of water or a windmill takes the movement of the wind to create electricity, God's idea is transduced into physical form by His Word. Everything we see around us is therefore the result of God's words. A better characterization of God creating *ex nihilo*, out of nothing, would be creation *ex cogitatio*, out of a thought.

So how is it possible for us to understand God's language? Once again, Genesis gives us the answer. God creates mankind in His image. We have been equipped with enough God infrastructure that we can read and understand the words God spoke. God has outfitted us with the Rosetta Stone of God's Spirit. God's thought is revealed to us through his transduced Word and is understandable to those created in His image! Why do you think humans recognize this Word and animals do not? One simple reason: we were created in God's image and they weren't. God purposely created us so we could read His Word and rethink His thought. A story is a story only if the author's idea can be read or heard by another and reenvisioned in the recipient's mind. God speaks, and the universe is filled with words, man is created, and those words become a story.

> So also no one comprehends the thoughts of God except the Spirit of God. Now we have received not the spirit of the world, but the Spirit who is from God, that we might understand the things freely given us by God. And we impart this in words not taught by human wisdom but taught by the Spirit, interpreting spiritual truths to those who are spiritual ... "For who has understood the mind

of the Lord so as to instruct him?" But we have the mind of Christ. (1 Cor. 2:11–13, 16)

What's even more fascinating is that in the prologue to the gospel of John, Jesus was described as God's creative "Word."

> In the beginning was the Word, and the Word was with God, and the Word was God. He was in the beginning with God. All things were made through him, and without him was not any thing made that was made. (John 1:1–3)

By recognizing Jesus as the Word of God, John clearly revealed how intimately the Old and New Testaments were connected in one, big, God-spoken story. Jesus, the Word, was also described as the perfect image of God. John summarized the plot of God's greater story: people created by the Word fail to recognize the image in which they were created, which leads to all sorts of problems. Please refer to every book in the Bible, every history text, every newspaper, and all the Internet blogs. Sadly, even when the Word was presented to humanity in the human form of Jesus, they still remained blind to the truth.

> He was in the world, and the world was made through him, yet the world did not know him. He came to his own, and his own people did not receive him. But to all who did receive him, who believed in his name, he gave the right to become children of God, who were born, not of blood nor of the will of the flesh nor of the will of man, but of God. (John 1:10–13)

The chosen people tried to write their own ending to God's story. They altered the script and converted the suffering servant into a conquering messiah who would ride into town on His white horse and kick some pagan butt. The bloated majestic militaristic ending to their story, however, was pierced by a cross-shaped spear. Their story revision died on a Roman cross on Golgotha, but in reality, God's story had just reached its unexpected climax.

In a brilliant plot twist, the Author emptied himself and become a character in His own salvation story.

Walter Brueggemann, a respected Old Testament theologian, has an interesting take on God's spoken Word. He describes the sustaining power of God's words as the force that holds back the natural movement of the world to fall apart; he notes that when God stops speaking, the world slips into chaos. For Brueggemann, God's words are not just a one-time event but an ongoing speech that holds the universe together.

School's in Session

God spoke, and school began. The rest of our lives are spent intimately learning his language, connecting the words to the Author, and gaining enough understanding to have a conversation with Him. We cannot settle for just knowing enough God language to ask Him directions to the bathroom; rather, we must expand our vocabulary to the point we can sit down with him and hear His stories. The fact that all people are created in God's image tells us everyone is capable of hearing and reading God's words. Mankind's seemingly unending search for meaning and purpose is merely an attempt to understand the words God spoke into existence long ago. Unfortunately, by removing the Author from this grand drama, we take significance out of the words we hear. We are told they are merely random scrabble letters pulled out of a bag, the literary work of monkeys banging away at typewriters or improvisational comics amusing themselves to death. We need to take out the cultural earplugs of tolerance and relativism and listen to what the world is really saying to us, to hear God's Words, and to immerse ourselves in His story.

Proud Words on a Dusty Shelf

Many people consider religion to be nothing more than dusty, dry doctrine placed on a shelf close enough to give the false assurance of salvation but high enough that they have an excuse for not reading them. The Bible is not just a Christian employees' manual that punches our tickets to heaven; it is an invitation to participate in God's story, a story that is dazzlingly bold and edgy, a story that calls us to a life of danger and excitement. It's a page-turner that can't be put down.

> Christian doctrine becomes dry and dusty only for those who don't believe it with the lively faith that takes action. That God became man in Christ is, on the face of it, an outrageous claim. The resurrection is either the greatest hoax ever foisted on humankind or the unique boundary-bursting, death-defying event that Christians believe it to be. As Dorothy Sayers writes, "It is the dogma that is the drama."[46]
>
> —Chuck Colson and Harold Fickett

Conclusion

I devoted an entire chapter to the concept of story because, as I previously mentioned, our postmodern culture is increasingly telling us that metanarratives are oppressive and intolerant and that freedom is found only when the big picture is abolished and we are free to live in our own isolated little stories created by our own personal truths. Each individual story is allowed to stand on its own, immune from criticism, and must be included in the library of life no matter how bad its grammar or incoherent its story.

Our culture tells us there's no great literature that transcends time, just informational brochures that become obsolete in a lifetime. I would guess that most of you have been guilty at one time or another of thinking or saying, "That may be true for you, but not me." While seemingly innocuous and perhaps even graciously tolerant, it cheapens the word *truth*. Truth has become confused with opinion or preference. Our culture appears to have given up the noble task cultivated throughout history of trying to discover truth. We have thrown our hands in the air and declared it's easier to tolerate the opinions of others than give them the dignity of serious engagement.

I think that a great deal of the emptiness experienced by our culture is because we all feel our stories are incomplete and are disappointed that our frequent attempts at improvisation have done little to fill that void. Our lives are like chapters searching for a book. Deep down, we know we aren't free-standing narratives but part of some great literature, and we want to know the Author. The seemingly unquenchable thirst of humans for purpose, meaning, and spiritual satisfaction is a desire to understand their place in God's world.

> Your eyes saw my unformed substance; in your book were written, every one of them, the days that were formed for me, when as yet there were none of them. (Ps. 139:16)

God has committed Himself to the concept of story; He chooses to work through the medium of narrative. In fact, his plan of salvation involved leaving His seat at the typewriter, emptying Himself of His authoritorial prerogative, and becoming ink on a page, words in His own story, a mere character in His own drama. The narrative idea in His mind was written for all His characters, and He would go to any lengths to make sure that their names were written into His Book of Life.

> Have this mind among yourselves, which is yours in Christ Jesus, who, though he was in the form of God, did not count equality with God a thing to be grasped, but made himself nothing, taking the form of a servant, being born in the likeness of men. And being found in human form, he humbled himself by becoming obedient to the point of death, even death on a cross. (Phil. 2:5–8)

I hope I have made it clear that the concept of story is perhaps the best way of framing the whole worldview discussion. As I mentioned before, all great literature has five essential components:

a setting, props, characters, conflict, and resolution. In the drama in which we find ourselves, the set is the created inanimate universe, the props are the plants and animals, the characters are us humans, the conflict is the problems created when mankind tries to become the Author of a story he didn't write, and the solution is ultimately Jesus Christ.

I hope you will see in the following chapters that the Christian worldview is the only one capable of coherently tying all the aspects of your story together. Your task is to test all your preconceived notions, pieces of the truth, and opinions to see if they make for a coherent story; if they don't, maybe you're just improvising your life. You need to continually ask yourself, do I live in God's world, or does He live in mine?

In the end, I believe a Christian with a story is more powerful than a pagan with an argument. I pray that what I have written will be useful to others on their journeys, but even if it never left my computer, it would still have been worth every minute I spent on it. Like my father, I also hope that one day my children and grandchildren will take it down from the shelf, dust it off, and read it.

> Faith is homesickness. Faith is a lump in the throat. Faith is less a position on than a movement toward, less a sure thing than a hunch. Faith is waiting. Faith is journeying through space and time. So if someone (and this frequently happens) were to come up to me and ask me to talk about my faith, it's exactly that journey through space and time I'd have to talk about.[47]
>
> —Frederick Buechner

Chapter Four

ALL THE WORLD'S A STAGE

Why does the universe go to all the bother of existing?[48]

—Stephen Hawking

THE SIMPLE ANSWER, ALTHOUGH I suspect Stephen Hawking would disagree, is that our grand drama requires a stage on which to be performed. If you believe life is nothing but improvisation, the world becomes just a random backdrop for your selfish performance art. If, however, you see life as a magnificent theatrical production, you recognize the world as a remarkably elaborate stage. The choice is yours—preplanned set or bare improvisational stage. Which is correct? Let's take a look.

> The Heavens declare the glory of God, and the sky above proclaims his handiwork. (Ps. 19:1)

> Biologists must constantly keep in mind that what they see was not designed, but rather evolved.[49]
>
> —Francis Crick

The Happiest Place on Earth

Is the universe a friendly place?[50]

—Albert Einstein

I have always been intrigued by the creative genius of Disney. As a young boy, I tried to construct my own pitiful little Disneyland with masking tape, boxes, and crayons. It was magical to me, but any observer would quickly notice my inability to mimic the incredible detail so characteristic of the Disney enterprise.

I remember one particular Disneyland visit; I was slowly shuffling my way through the line at Thunder Mountain Railroad when my eyes came upon some pigeon droppings on a railroad tie that framed the line to the ride. As I looked at it, I wondered whether it was real bird excrement or some intricate reproduction placed there by the Disney people to make the setting more realistic. Why did I even entertain that thought? I did so because I have always been in awe of the imaginative brilliance of the Disney machine. It would not have surprised me one bit if they had purposely added this seemingly insignificant detail to the décor to add realism to the ride experience. Based on all the detailed evidence around me, I knew there had to be an amazingly creative mind behind it all.

I suspect each one of you has at one time or other encountered something in the natural world that made you wonder if just maybe it had been placed there on purpose. Isn't it strange we can look at the world around us and feel a sense of unity even when we encounter such completely disparate things as clouds, trees, dirt, bugs, octopi, narwhals, or emus? How is it we can sense unity in all this diversity? How can all this apparent chaotic variety give us a sense of peace or calm?

If you just look at it physically, it appears more like a bad MTV music video that repeatedly cuts between seemingly incongruous scenes. None of us, however, would describe the world like that because we somehow see harmony, beauty, and order. The world looks like a great masterpiece. We intuitively sense the work of a skilled Artist and not the random doodles of finger-painting

87

monkeys. We recognize His use of color, light, and texture. We are so enamored with His work that we travel the globe, visiting all His art galleries to acquire an even better appreciation for the scope of His work. The reason we sense the world as a unity is because it was created by one great Artist, and just like the students of any great painter, we know His brushstrokes; the sheep know the voice of the shepherd.

Michael Shermer, an agnostic, conducted a survey in which he asked two questions about the existence of God: Why do you believe in God? Why do you think other people believe in God? The answers were quite illuminating because they highlighted an important intellectual disconnect between the believer and nonbeliever. The number-one reason believers gave for acknowledging the existence of God was the design found in nature, while a sense of comfort or consolation was third. The number-one reason why people felt that others believed in God was comfort/consolation, while design/complexity was in sixth place. The data obtained by Shermer gives us some insight into the frequently heated debates between believer and atheist. It appears that the atheist and believer are not even skirmishing on the same battlefield when it comes to the question of God's existence. Atheists tend to believe that religion is the opiate of the masses, mythically pacifying the ignorant and superstitious as they confront the cruelty of an evolutionary world.

Believers, on the other hand, accept God's existence based on a reasoned evaluation of the order and design they find in the cosmos. It appears that atheists have been beating believers over the head with the wrong stick and now find themselves confronted with the valid scientific challenges of intelligent design theory. Much to the dismay of the atheists, believers aren't primitives huddled in a corner lighting candles and chanting to their God for divine consolation but are intellectuals armed with the God-given tools of science and reason, finding evidence for a creative mind at every level of scientific inquiry. The atheists embarrassingly check their great intellects at the door and waste time trying to defend the world as one highly improbable random mistake, an idea that even ancient man, who identified natural events with the minds of gods, would find quite odd.

They Paved Paradise and Put Up a Parking Lot

Think about this: before there were cities, it was just God and man, side by side working the land, raising families, and creating community. Man was intimately connected to God's creation for survival. However, with the development of the urban concrete jungle, we have progressively distanced ourselves from God's world and become immersed in man's. We don't see God as the source of our water, food, and shelter; rather we see the local Public Utility District, grocery store and mortgage company fulfilling these roles. God's abundance now comes prepackaged and distributed by middle mankind, and we end up losing sight of its source; we surrender the allegiance we formerly had to God and put our trust in the bounty of Costco.

Maybe some of our human unhappiness is based on the fact that we have distanced ourselves from the intimacy we used to experience in God's created order. The cities, the population centers, are more liberal and secular, while the rural Midwest and South, where survival is based on an intimate reliance on the land, forms the Bible belt. The farmer meets God every day in the soil of his wheat fields, while the Wall Street broker may not see, let alone touch, dirt for months. The farmer awakens early to offer prayers to the great provider, while the Wall Street broker awakens early and offers prayers to man's electronic ingenuity.

We live in housing developments that pay homage to the architectural monuments of man's ingenuity and neglect God's concealed but creative order on which they were built. As my friend John Linden pointed out, when we move to the country and are surrounded by nothing but nature, we can't help but reflect on God's power, but when we move to the city and are surrounded by the creative work of man, we can't help but try to place man on the throne. I'm not advocating the overthrow of our social order or the demonization of Wall Street brokers; I'm offering this illustration as a concept to ponder that will help us reprioritize the way we think about this world.

Ask yourself why New York, the financial hub of the United States with all its high rises and concrete, need its Central Park? Why waste strategic land on squirrels and pigeons? Why not make more room for the monuments to man? The reason is simple. In the end, man knows if he is cut off from nature, he is cut off from the last spiritual sanctuary left in his chaotic world. Central Park is like the last vestige of Eden, strategically placed in the center of a city, where people can have a divine encounter with their first love. It represents a chance to refuel their empty "image of God" tanks that have been running on fumes for days and fill them with the high-octane Spirit of the living God.

> But I have this against you, that you have abandoned the love you had at first. (Rev. 2:4)

Nice Weather We're Having

Our grand drama is played out on a particularly habitable planet with a diversity of terrain ranging from the hot, humid jungles of Central America to the frozen tundra of the Arctic, from the dry sand of the desert to the watery depths of the ocean. High-tech celestial dimmer switches illuminate the stage and facilitate its seasonal wardrobe changes. It appears that we humans can't stop talking about the set even with people we don't know. Discussing the weather is not just a convenient way to fill an awkward conversation gap between strangers but a common language everybody can understand and speak. I suggest that when we discuss the weather, we are acknowledging the fact we all share a common stage that impacts the ongoing drama of our lives. Talking about the weather is not a scientific response to meteorological phenomena but a shared critique of a remarkable piece of art.

The Great "I Am" Miller Lite

Picture this scene: Several rugged young men in a boat off the beautiful coast of Maine feverishly trying to complete their long, rigorous day of fishing in anticipation of a good, old-fashioned New England clam bake that awaits them on shore. The next scene finds them on the beach surrounded by family and friends, spreading out a sumptuous meal of fish, lobster, and clams. As the sun begins to set, they raise their glasses of beer, and the wisest (or drunkest) one toasts the group and exclaims, "It doesn't get any better than this."

Some of you may recognize this old beer commercial, but this type of advertising is used to sell a wide array of products. I ask you, in this commercial, what are they really selling, beer or God's beautiful creation? We advertise God and rename Him Miller Lite? In a clever sleight of hand, the advertisers have exchanged the truth for a lie and made God and beer synonymous, as if God's voice would suddenly break in and say, "I'm God, and I approved of this message. Please drink responsibly." Advertisers know God's handiwork moves inventory and have ridden on God's coattails for decades. The next time you watch a TV commercial, look at what is going on around the product and see if you don't catch a glimpse of God's craftsmanship.

The Tonys

The stage sets the scene and establishes the physical environment on which the characters will hit their marks and speak their lines. When the curtain is raised for a Broadway show and the set revealed, what strikes you? Let's take the role of theater critic and ask ourselves what criteria we would utilize to determine whether the set qualifies for the Best Scenic Design Tony Award. First, is it beautiful, evocative, or unique? Second, is it believable, ordered, and coherent? Third, when taken as a whole, does it cause us to lose ourselves in the drama? If after careful deliberation we determine the world around us in fact qualifies for the Best Scenic Design award, we have a final question to answer: whom do we call on stage to accept the award?

Just Say Awe

Several years ago, my family and I took a Caribbean Disney cruise. One of our stops was Key West, an island off Florida's southern coast. After a busy day of touring and shopping, we began our walk back to the ship, and as we approached the dock, we noticed it was becoming quite crowded with tourists and vendors. As we muscled our way through the crowd, we noticed that the aural landscape was punctuated by a tropical blend of many languages that gradually decreased in volume until there was only a smattering of expectant murmurs. It quickly became apparent that we had all gathered on the dock to see the sunset. We quietly watched as the fiery-red sun slowly descended below the horizon, and once it had completely disappeared, the crowd suddenly erupted in applause as if acknowledging a particularly spectacular performance. The only time humans applaud is when they recognize the work, ingenuity, talent, or creativity of a mind. Here we were, a diverse collection of human beings representing many different cultures, climates, and countries, all united by the universal language of natural beauty. It's quite amazing to think this particular twilight show is performed every day of the week to standing ovations and rave reviews.

> The attempt to convey what we see and cannot say is the everlasting theme of mankind's unfinished symphony, a venture in which adequacy is never achieved ... The stillness that crowds the world in spite of our noise ... The search of reason ends on the shore of the known; on the immense expanse beyond it only the sense of the ineffable can glide.[51]
>
> —Abraham Joshua Heschel

Abraham Joshua Heschel, a distinguished Jewish scholar, called this shared awe the ineffable, that which cannot be expressed in words and yet speaks to everybody. Maybe the reason we cannot describe these natural events in words is because we feel so inadequate to repeat what God has just so eloquently spoken. Isn't it amazing that we can grab any human being on earth and meaningfully share a sunset experience without saying a word, without the need for a translator or a Rosetta Stone? In that brief moment on a dock in Key West, we all paid homage to a creative mind, and although most of the people probably didn't even give it a second thought, we had all unwittingly engaged in an act of corporate worship! How many more centuries of corporate worship will it take before we recognize the One we are worshipping? Despite the inability of most people to connect these events with God, it was reassuring to know that at least this diverse group of Caribbean cruisers had the good sense to recognize talent when they saw it.

> The Heavens declare the glory of God, and the sky above proclaims his handiwork. Day to day pours out speech, and night to night reveals knowledge. There is no speech, nor are there words whose voice is not heard. (Ps. 19:1–3)

God spoke the stage into being, and we continue to hear the echo of His words year after year. Sadly, many of us treat them like a soothing wall of white noise, a gurgling fountain in our entryway that temporarily distracts us from the worries of the day. If we listen carefully, however, we can hear Him breathing between His spoken words and feel His heartbeat. Breath and beat, the signs of life, reassure us God didn't just deliver a speech and leave the building but has stayed around long after to answer our questions.

> The imperative of awe is its certificate of evidence, a universal certificate, which we all witness and seal with tremor and spasm, not because we desire to, but because we are stunned and cannot brave it. There is so much more meaning in reality than my soul can take in![52]
>
> —Abraham Joshua Heschel

Order to Go, Please

Why does the set seem so well integrated with our drama? William Paley, the famous religious philosopher, gave the example of a person discovering a watch on the ground during a stroll across the heath.

> In crossing a heath, suppose I pitched my foot against a stone, and were asked how the stone came to be there; I might possibly answer, that, for anything I knew to the contrary, it had lain there forever: nor would it perhaps be very easy to show the absurdity of this answer. But suppose I had found a watch upon the ground, and it should be inquired how the watch happened to be in that place; I should hardly think of the answer I had before given, that for anything I knew, the watch might have always been there ... There must have existed, at some time, and at some place or other, an artificer or artificers, who formed [the watch] for the purpose which we find it actually to answer; who comprehended its construction, and designed its use ... Every indication of contrivance, every manifestation of design, which existed in the watch, exists in the works of nature; with the difference, on the side of nature, of being greater or more, and that in a degree which exceeds all computation.[53]
>
> —William Paley

Even if that person didn't know what a watch was used for, he or she would still recognize it as a complex object and infer it had been created by a mind. Richard Dawkins surprisingly tried to refute this maxim by writing a book cleverly entitled *The Blind Watchmaker*; he implied that evolution was the watchmaker but couldn't see what it was doing. Dawkins, however, committed the evolutionary sin of using the word *watchmaker* in the first place; a word that implies a mind, blind or not, behind the endeavor. When you read the arguments of strict evolutionists, read carefully the terms they use; all too often they smuggle in words that imply a mind, such as *code*, *design*, *master plan*, *language*, and *machine*.

They can't help themselves because the world just looks too darned designed and they are forced to borrow terms not found in their evolutionary lexicons.

A watch is a relatively complex machine, but what if you came upon a heart etched in the sand? Would your first thought be that it had been created by the random forces of waves and wind, or would you think a young couple had stopped there and declared their love for one another? Let's get even simpler; how about a collection of clouds that made the shape of a smiley face? Would you immediately invoke the random movement of condensed water vapor, wind, and light, or would it suggest the work of a sky writer? How about going simpler still, to a vapor trail in the sky? Do you think of a random cloud formation or a pilot flying a jet in a straight line? So what do you see when you look at God's creation, a mind or random chance? It appears it doesn't take much information for us to suspect the work of a mind.

Let's take the other extreme. What about DNA, which is an incredibly complex collection of information? Why would you even for a moment consider random forces as its source when you had just walked on the beach and saw a heart drawn in the sand and inferred a human couple had been there? When you look at the world around you, don't you get the sense you're looking at the work of a set designer?

The God Particle

Physicists appear to have reached an impasse in their understanding of the universe. The old physics took them only so far, and now they have placed their hope in the new physics of quantum theory. Unfortunately, the new physics has created more questions than answers and has highlighted the inability of science to provide a comprehensive explanation for the cosmos. I will spare you all the details, but quantum physics has basically run into problems with the data physicists obtain from subatomic particles because they behave in unexpected ways and are resistant to accurate measurement by classic scientific experimentation. Physics does a remarkable job of describing the world at large but falls short at the subatomic level. This conundrum has generated scientific discussion bordering on the religious and philosophical.

> Physics, which, it was thought, had dispensed with the need of metaphysics, has been transformed by its own proper researches into the most metaphysical of disciplines.[54]
>
> —Carl Becker

Religious people are frequently chastised by members of the scientific community for using a "God of the gaps" argument to prove the existence of God. They compare the beliefs of modern people of faith with ignorant, primitive ancestors who mistakenly ascribed natural occurrences such as thunder and lightning to angry gods. They argue it's just a matter of time before we can explain everything scientifically and eliminate the need for God altogether. In light of the scientifically troubling findings of quantum physics, scientists are actually becoming quite a faith community of their own, building an altar to the unknown god particle.

Scientists working on the Higgs Boson project have recently released new data that may fit the theoretical profile of this particle. While discovering and understanding this particle may give us greater insight into how the universe holds together and functions, it certainly doesn't remove God from the throne.

I think the crazier thing is that science would think the answer to life, the universe, and everything could be reduced to a particle so small that it cannot be directly identified and so elusive that it can be detected only indirectly. I think average people are so totally overwhelmed by the immense, God-shaped hole in their lives that the idea of an infinitesimally minute particle filling it seems absurd.

Why would scientists study something they have not directly seen and yet suspect because of its indirect effects? Oops! Sounds kind of like faith doesn't it? Unfortunately, unbelieving scientists have committed the same religious indiscretion they find so appalling in the believer—faith in something they cannot see but indirectly sense. Maybe they should just accept the fact that they have it half right and drop the "particle" language.

The Bible gives us some insight into this dilemma because it refers to God not only as the Creator of the universe but also as the Sustainer, so maybe this particle is just another wonderful manifestation of God's sustaining power.

> Today, there is a wide measure of agreement, which on the side of physics approaches almost to unanimity, that the stream of knowledge is heading towards a non-mechanical reality; the universe begins to look more like a great thought than like a great machine. Mind no longer appears as an accidental intruder into the realm of matter; we are beginning to suspect that we ought rather to hail it as the creator and governor of the realm of matter.[55]
>
> —Sir James Jeans

Inconceivable! (*The Princess Bride*)

> The most incomprehensible thing about the universe is that it is comprehensible.[56]
>
> —Albert Einstein

Confronted by this intricate, beautiful, and complex set, mankind has been inspired to ask how it got here. Ancient civilizations are full of stories about the creation of the earth. There is even a lot of academic discussion about how these stories may be interrelated or borrowed, but the more interesting question is, why would ancient man ask the question in the first place? I suggest that mankind, even subconsciously, has perceived nature as an intricate set for a story, whether it was the loving creation of the one true God or the battlefield of the impetuous, spoiled gods of the Greek and Roman pantheons.

Critics of religion point to primitive man's fear of the unknown as the stimulus for creating mythical deities and angry gods thunderously yelling and throwing lightning bolts, but I find it even more interesting that primitive people recognized that what they saw had the qualities of a mind. Why else would they try to explain unknown things in terms of intelligent beings, even if those beings happened to behave like spoiled children? They didn't invoke random chance because they knew what they saw looked more like a thought or intention that could come from only one place, a mind. Even the pagan attributing the seasons to the visitation rights of Persephone's separated parents knew there was a reason for the order they saw in nature. It appears that intelligent design theory, not random chance, has always been mankind's default understanding of the origin of the world.

Despite the shared reference to a mind or minds in all the creation stories, there are striking differences between the biblical creation narrative and the ancient creation myths. The Genesis account sounds more like a textbook than a myth. It describes an ordered, sequential creation from the large cosmic to the small earthly, from land and sea to bird and bee. God is described as intentionally creating the universe good and making mankind the pinnacle of His work. The ancient Near Eastern creation myths depict a chaotic situation in which the world is accidentally created because of the gods' inability to play nice with one another. Mankind was created to do all the work so the gods would have more free time to behave like unsupervised teenagers, partying all night and sleeping until noon. Genesis describes the world as very good only after man was created, which I argue is when the story begins. The set and props that are good become very good only when actors enter the stage.

> Maybe the cosmic rumblings of light and energy produced by the Big Bang that we detect with our technologically advanced divining gadgets may actually be the echoes of God's voice declaring, "It is good, it is good, it is good."
>
> —Author

Well, says the atheist, mankind is a pattern-creating animal, and all this talk of order is just mankind's admirable efforts to put an ordered façade on random reality. I have to disagree with my atheist friends. We humans have too short of an MTV attention span to try to create order if there isn't any. Randomness, as it turns out, is exceedingly boring, and humans don't want to waste their precious time with it. Do you think scientists would perform research if they concluded it was all due to random forces? Isn't it ironic that the evolutionist is exceedingly good at ordering words on a page, ordering pages into books, laying out an orderly discussion about the ordered complexity of life, and then come up with the astonishing conclusion that it all arose randomly? Doesn't that strike you as odd?

Preferred Seating

In their book *The Privileged Planet,* Jay Richards and Guillermo Gonzalez make the case that not only does this world appear designed but also that our planet is situated in the solar system in such a way that it gives us an unprecedented viewpoint from which to make detailed scientific observations.

> Even more mysterious than the fact that our location is so congenial to diverse measurement and discovery is that these same conditions appear to correlate with habitability. This is strange, because there is no obvious reason to assume that the very same rare properties that allow for our existence would also provide the best overall setting to make discoveries about the world around us ... It cries out for another explanation, an explanation that suggest there's more to the cosmos than we have been willing to entertain or even imagine.[57]
>
> —Jay Richards and Guillermo Gonzalez

If we were living anywhere else in the galaxy, we would not have the proper atmospheric conditions to make any predictions about how the universe works. An atheist could argue that the idea of a finely tuned universe perfectly suited to life is just another way of saying the conditions are perfect because they are the only possible conditions that could have produced us. The more interesting point is that the universe has somehow provided the perfect setting to be investigated. In other words, it has introduced transcendence; it has made it possible for man to step outside of himself and ask scientific questions about the origins of the universe. It appears that God has opened up His Theater, handed us bags of popcorn, and escorted us to the best seats in the house.

> It's all a matter of keeping my eyes open, Beauty and grace are performed whether or not we will sense them. The least we can do is try and be there ... so that creation need not play to an empty house.[58]
>
> —Annie Dillard

Let's Get Away from It All

So far, we have seen that the set is awe inspiring and ordered, but does it draw us into the story? In the immortal words of Ty Webb in the movie *Caddyshack*, we need to "be the ball"; we need to "be the drama" and enter into it to see if it all makes sense. We are observer as well as participant, audience as well as actor. We participate in our own drama and yet are very aware of the subplots swirling about us. We need to ask ourselves if this world draws us into the action.

> They say there's no place quite like home
> A charming thought and pure
> But until the world we roam
> How can we be sure?[59]
>
> —Dennis and Adair

We are strangely attracted to our set's beauty and its ability to bring peace to our embattled souls. Every summer in Spokane,

a great number of my friends, acquaintances, neighbors, and coworkers disappear to their lake places to recharge their batteries and get away from it all. Why do we humans feel the need to build cabins in the mountains or homes on the shore of a lake or ocean? Why do we get a little peeved at rich people when they buy the choicest land with the best views and then place "No Trespassing" signs in the sand of their beachfront property? Truth be told, if we had the money, we would probably do the same thing, but why? When you get down to it, nature is dirty, windy, wet, and full of ants and mosquitoes. Trees fall on our cabins in the mountains, flooding ruins our riverfront homes, and the siding of our beach bungalows gets weather-beaten by storms. We even try to make nature more convenient by bringing it into our homes. We have pets and plants, waterfalls in our backyards, and trickling water features in our foyers. We seem to get a peace from these that only nature can provide, a peace that demands an explanation.

> This thing that bewilders the intellect utterly quiets the heart.[60]
>
> —G. K. Chesterton

We try to buy up all the great views, and we travel to exotic, beautiful locations for vacations. What is it about tropical beaches, rainforests, or rugged coastlines that attract us? Why do retreats take place in beautiful locations and not in the inner city? Why do we go camping in the mountains, visit national parks, take Alaskan cruises, or fly to Hawaii? Somehow, nature restores a balance to our lives that we lose in the daily grind.

I remember a particular vacation in Honolulu; we stayed in a hotel just across the street from Waikiki beach. We had a beautiful ocean view, but unfortunately, we also had a view of the street, where life hectically and continuously churned. My idyllic dreams of sitting on the hotel deck, sipping coffee and reading a good book while admiring the beautiful blue ocean and feeling the warm tropical breeze on my face, was interrupted by the exhaust of the cars below and the carnivorous sounds of a garbage truck

devouring human refuse. I quickly found out that civilization in proximity to nature's beauty is unfortunately still civilization.

Tropical Treasures

Why do we go to uncomfortable extremes to encounter the beauty of nature? On the island of Maui, one of the touristy things to do is to drive to the top of the dormant volcano Haleakala to see the sunrise. You get up in the ungodly early hours of the morning, drive several hours in the dark until you reach the top, step out of your rental car dressed in only tropical floral attire, and meet with an unexpected frigid wind. You huddle together, wrapped only in the inadequate small towels you brought from the hotel, and wait for the sun to rise. Undeterred, you stand elbow to elbow, shivering with your fellow man just to experience the beauty of a sunrise. What a silly, inconvenient thing to do if there wasn't something beyond the mere physics of light, color, planetary movement, and sun's rays that you expected to encounter. Couldn't you have just bought a postcard?

As the sun begins to rise, what do you think you hear? Nothing but contemplative silence. Whether you are an atheist, agnostic, or person of faith, you have just once again engaged in act of corporate worship!

> Reverence is one of man's answers to the presence of mystery ... When we stand in awe, our lips do not demand speech, knowing that if we spoke, we would deprave ourselves. In such moments talk is an abomination.[61]
>
> —Abraham Joshua Heschel

Another touristy thing to do on Maui is to make the long, nauseatingly winding drive to the town of Hana to see the seven sacred pools. Unfortunately, my family attempted this pilgrimage on an exceedingly rainy day, and the seven sacred pools were one torrential pagan river. Though some days offer a better view than others, tourists make the trek day after day. The natives recognized

these sites were sacred manifestations of the minds of a god or gods. It was only later that fallen mankind exploited them for monetary advantage. Why would we inconvenience ourselves with sleep deprivation and long, winding car rides to see a sun rise over a volcanic horizon or a unique collection of mud puddles?

> The repetition in nature may not be mere reoccurrence, it may be a theatrical encore.[62]
>
> —G. K. Chesterton

And the Award Goes to ...

I think you can see that the set which God created fulfills all the Best Scenic Design Award criteria I've set forth; it's beautiful, ordered, and able to hypnotically draw us into the larger drama. If you accept this premise, it raises an interesting question: who do we hand the award to? All these criteria reveal the work of a mind—the creative work of an artist, the technical expertise of an engineer, and the spellbinding narrative of a storyteller. How could we ever attribute these qualities to merely random forces? I'm sorry, but we humans are far too sophisticated to be entertained or amused by haphazard events. If I handed people sheets of random letters, the first thing they would do would be to search for some sort of order, some message or word, and if that proved unsuccessful, they would quickly put it down and move onto something more interesting. I suggest that God spoke in the beginning, and we haven't been able put His script down since.

Luke, I'm Your Father

Those of you who are parents are quite familiar with the repeated challenges to your authority offered up by your children. They meet seemingly simple requests such as picking up socks and putting away dishes with defiant requests for metaphysical explanations for the necessity of such menial tasks. Our default response to their universal childish whys is our adult, erudite, "Because I'm your parent!"

While it seems to lack suitable argumentative substance to meet the discerning tastes of our rebellious teenagers, it implies something they seem to be persistently oblivious to, the fact that we as parents have knowledge they are incapable of fathoming. We are forced to point out to them that until they can provide their own food, clothing, and a roof over their heads, they had best not question our wisdom. They are oblivious to all the things we have done behind the scenes to make their existence palatable. We have cleaned up their vomit when they were sick and have made their beds when they forgot. We have created the conditions that protect them, feed them, and allow them to live and play Halo another day.

In His role as parent, God faces a remarkably similar situation when confronted by the unreasonable demands of His rebellious children. He also has to make it abundantly clear to His kids that before they get too bent out of shape because they lost their jobs or their cats died, they need to remember He created the air, food, and water that gives them the strength to complain in the first place.

One of the most fascinating stories in the Bible is that of Job. He had his life of luxury toppled and ended up suffering financial, familial, and physical loss. He was perplexed as to why this had happened to him. He received unhelpful explanations from his wife and friends and ultimately recognized he needed an answer from God. God responded by making it clear to Job that only when he was capable of creating and maintaining a universe would he be able to understand the answer to his question. God reminded Job that He was the Author, Set Designer, and Director of an immense theatrical production and that Job was merely a character in a smaller subplot—a unique and cherished character, but a character nonetheless.

> Then the Lord answered Job out of the whirlwind and said: "Who is this that darkens counsel [my story] by words without knowledge? Dress for action like a man [character]; I will question you, and you make it known to me. "Where were you when I laid the foundation of the

earth [built the set]? Tell me, if you have understanding. Who determined its measurements—surely you know! Or who stretched the line upon it? On what were its bases sunk, or who laid its cornerstone, when the morning stars sang together and all the sons of God shouted for joy [established the storyline]? (Job 38:1–7, my additions)

In essence, God answered Job's juvenile questions with, "Because I am your Father." The Author of our grand drama points the characters' attention to the stage on which their story is allowed to be played out and says, "I am the Author, and you are the characters. Until you are capable of creating your own stage, stop your whining!"

We do, however, need to be careful how we understand the language of parenthood when applied to the world. Nature is frequently referred to as Mother Nature, but she is not our mother; she didn't give birth to us; we exist alongside her, but she teaches us nothing about the meaning of life. She only points us to the source of all good things.

The main point of Christianity was this: that Nature is not our mother: Nature is our sister. We can be proud of her beauty, since we have the same Father; but she has no authority over us; we have to admire but not to imitate.[63]

—G. K. Chesterton

Taggers

Since the fall of Adam and Eve in the garden, a tension has existed on the set. We have ridden a fine line between working God's creation and exploiting it. We have paid homage to nature in song, paint, and the written word but have desecrated it by tagging it with the graffiti of modernity. We have progressively distanced ourselves from its calming presence by encasing ourselves in concrete cocoons, unable to see the mountains for the smog; we've paved over paradise with a parking lot.

Unfortunately, environmentalism has become a divisive issue because it has become so intertwined with politics. Evangelical Christians are frequently seen as the prime instigators of the rape of the planet because of the misunderstood command of God to "have dominion" over the earth. God-ordained dominion over the planet is thoughtful environmentalism, but sinful dominion is exploitation and pollution. Of all people, Christians should be the most passionate about the environment because they know the drama completely breaks down when the set becomes uninhabitable.

Since we recognize the world as a great masterpiece, we dishonor the Painter when we spray paint His canvas with graffiti. God made it clear that what He had created was "good." The Bible's favorite point of reference for God's sovereign power and majesty is the creative work of His hands, and when His authority is questioned, He puts forth the magnificence of nature as evidence of His glory. Why would God, who puts so much stock in His creation, allow irresponsible humans to abuse it? If nature is the signet ring of God's sovereignty, we must approach it with kid gloves. Desecration of the planet is an abomination. Our future is intimately interwoven with the fate of nature, and so we Christians, who have been given the responsibility of being stewards of this planet, need to be the most zealous environmental advocates of all. We can argue over theories of global warming, but we all agree that sitting in a closed garage with a running car is lethal. Why do we hold pollution hostage to quarrels over the science of global warming or the big business of energy?

God calls us to be stewards of this planet; anything short of that is rebellion. How dare we hold nature hostage to our own sinful nature! We do, however, need to proceed with caution because even this noble venture can be derailed by our sinful nature, and preserving the planet can become a thinly veiled excuse for selfish financial gain.

I suspect that most people would accept some blame for polluting our planet; they would feel some guilt for not recycling, driving their cars too much, or using gas-driven weed whackers. We are repelled by the sight of garbage on the shore of a pristine beach and disgusted when we explore the rocky shoreline only to see Mr. Pibb looking up at us from the bottom of a crystal-clear tide pool.

We feel guilt for what we have done to the planet because as beings created in God's image, we understand what it means for God to declare something "good." If Michael Shermer is correct in his polling, Americans believe in a God because of the beauty, order, and complexity they see in the world. Do you really believe that a god that made everything and declared it all very good would be okay with the pollution and exploitation of His creation? Do you think an artist would be okay with someone taking his masterpiece and using it as a doormat to wipe sinful refuse off his shoes? Our passion for the environment is God's passion.

> The world that we have long held in trust has exploded in our hands, and the stream of guilt and misery has been unloosed which leaves no man's integrity unmaimed.[64]
>
> —Abraham Joshua Heschel

Surprisingly, many environmentalists have no religious affiliation at all, or if they do, they adopt a Mother Earth–type of spirituality that they uncomfortably link to a purely material evolutionary explanation for the world. It is uncomfortable because it lacks any basis for an environmental mandate. We are reduced to the most highly evolved animals merely acting appropriate to our evolutionary level; we therefore cannot be blamed for the desecration of the planet. How is it that I, the most highly evolved creature, can be held responsible for the evolutionary inferior life forms I may need to trample on as I forage and mate my way through life?

You could argue that unpolluted water will help us live long enough to procreate and pass on what Richard Dawkins calls our "selfish genes," but it doesn't demand that we save spotted owls. The only way mankind can be held accountable is if he transcends the world around him and has been given an environmental mandate. Mother Earth spirituality unfortunately is a worldview without a mandate because it views humans as no different from rocks, dolphins, or mosquitoes and lacks the credibility to single out mankind as either planetary villain or savior. Evolutionary environmentalism has a nice ring to it, but it's just toothless sentiment, because there's no obligation to make things better, while Christianity holds up care of the planet as an obligation imposed by God Himself. When mankind fell, he dragged nature down with him, and it is therefore only when mankind is redeemed that it will all be set right. The Original Sin of mankind fractured a perfect world, and the planet groans as it patiently awaits repair, a repair that will occur only when we humans are adopted as children of God. We are responsible for His creation, and the restoration of the entire planet is intimately tied to our salvation. That sounds like a pretty strong environmental mandate to me.

> For the creation waits with eager longing for the revealing of the sons of God. For the creation was subjected to futility, not willingly, but because of him who subjected it, in hope that the creation itself will be set free from its bondage to decay and obtain the freedom of the glory of the children of God. For we know that the whole creation has been groaning together in the pains of childbirth until now. And not only the creation, but we ourselves, who have the first fruits of the Spirit, groan inwardly as we wait eagerly for adoption as sons, the redemption of our bodies. (Rom. 8:19–23)

Trouble in Paradise

While nature is universally seen as a soothing balm for our embattled souls, it is also capable of instilling fear and causing suffering. It periodically erupts in dramatic and terrifying displays of power such as hurricanes, tornadoes, earthquakes, forest fires, droughts, and floods. While these are frequently disastrous to the props and characters in our drama, science is beginning to recognize these cataclysmic disruptions may be important for the health of the planet's ecosystem.

Critics of Christianity may acknowledge the fine-tuning of the set but will quickly point to the cruelty of it all, the Indonesian tsunami, Hurricane Katrina, and the Haitian earthquake to name but a few. However, most people would not call these natural phenomena evil in themselves. Despite the devastation, we are fascinated by the power of nature. We have television shows about storm chasers who risk their lives to film tornadoes, surfers waiting on the beach for the big tsunami waves, and the seemingly endless news coverage of hurricanes bearing down on big cities. Isn't it interesting that mankind is the only creature capable of predicting, warning about, preparing for, and mopping up the consequences of these natural disasters?

The stage is just behaving like a stage, setting the scene, but it is the response of us characters that creates the drama. How do we understand this tension between the awesome, strangely appealing power of the hurricane and the deaths of those in its path?

> The sea is not less beautiful in our eyes because we know that some times ships are wrecked by it. On the contrary, this adds to its beauty. If it altered the movement of its waves to spare a boat, it would be a creature gifted with discernment and choice and not this fluid, perfectly obedient to every external pressure. It is this perfect obedience that constitutes the sea's beauty.[65]
>
> —Simone Weil

We don't blame the tornado for acting like a tornado, so whom do we blame? Atheists say it's just bad luck, but the man on the street finds this explanation unacceptable and feels somebody must pay. The anger usually turns either toward God for allowing it to happen or to mankind for failing to adequately prepare for it. Those who don't believe in God have no choice but to absurdly make mankind at least an accomplice in the tragedy. Listen to the news reports after a disaster and you'll hear how quickly it turns into a mankind blamefest: failed disaster preparation, slow response of emergency services, and lack of FEMA funding. If, however, you believe in God, you are faced with a problem: how does this naturally occurring "evil" suggest a benevolent and loving Creator? As a Christian, you have been given some interesting insight. God created everything; it was "good," and He created mankind to care of it, and it was "very good."

> The Lord God took the man and put him in the Garden of Eden to work it and keep it. (Gen. 2:15)

Then a terrible thing happened on the way to the perfectly balanced planet; Adam and Eve tripped over the root of pride and fell headlong into a state of sin, but as they tried to right themselves, they grabbed the curtains of creation and pulled them down with them. Three relationships were simultaneously broken: God and man, man and woman, and man and nature. The ground became cursed and would bring us pain and hardship.

> *Cursed is the ground* because of you; in *pain* you shall eat of it all the days of your life; *thorns and thistles* it shall bring forth for you; and you shall eat the plants of the field. By the *sweat* of your face you shall eat bread, till you return to the ground, for out of it you were taken; for you are dust, and to dust you shall return. (Gen. 3:17–19, emphasis added)

The Genesis account gives the most satisfactory explanation for the discrepancy between the magnificent power of a hurricane and the deaths left in its wake, the ecologically restorative power of a raging wildfire and the homes burned in its path; these are echoes of God's once "very good" creation muted by the cacophony of Original Sin.

Total Perspective Vortex

Critics of Christianity have a very difficult time denying the beauty, order, and awe evoked by the world around them, so they are forced to try another tactic—crush us under the sheer weight of

God's creative output. They assert that we are so microscopically small when compared with the immensity of the universe that we just have to be insignificant. We are but an evolutionary tear in a vast, purposeless ocean.

> Space is big. Really big. You just won't believe how vastly, hugely mind-bogglingly big it is. I mean you may think it's a long way down the road to the chemist, but that's just peanuts to space.[66]
>
> —Douglas Adams

Douglas Adams once again gives us some insight in his book *The Restaurant at the End of the Universe*. In one particular scene, Zaphod Beeblbrox, the arrogant president of the universe, is forced to enter the Total Perspective Vortex, a machine that allows those who enter it to see their puny existence next to the vastness of the universe. People who had previously entered the machine had their brains annihilated by the awareness of their complete insignificance in the cosmos.

> You can kill a man, destroy his body, break his spirit, but only the Total Perspective Vortex can annihilate a man's soul! The treatment lasts seconds, but the effects last the rest of your life![67]

Zaphod is placed inside the vortex, and to everyone's surprise, he comes out alive and well. When asked what he had experienced when confronted with the miniscule reality of his little life, he replied, "It just told me what I knew all the time. I'm a really terrific and great guy."[68] Only Christians can enter the vortex and come out assured of their significance, because the Creator of the universe declared it was man who made it all special. In Genesis, God didn't declare His creation to be "very good" until He had created mankind. The universe, rather than annihilating mankind, actually makes him even more extraordinary.

Walks Like a Duck, Quacks Like a Duck, but It Only Looks Like a Duck

> One of the greatest challenges to the human intellect, over the centuries, has been to explain how the complex, improbable appearance of design in the universe arises. The natural temptation is to attribute the appearance of design to actual design itself. In the case of a man-made artifact such as a watch, the designer really was an intelligent engineer. It is tempting to apply the same logic to an eye or a wing, a spider, or a person.[69]
>
> —Richard Dawkins

Our critics are frequently forced to admit that the set does look designed, but then they are placed in the uncomfortable position of having to deny their keen scientific intuition and light candles and mindlessly chant, "I do believe in evolution, I do believe in evolution, I do believe in evolution." Confronted by the design and information that saturates our world, they are forced to retreat into their scientific catacombs and scratch pictures on the walls of advanced aliens that seeded our planet with life. I am fine if they want to accuse us Christians of clinging to myth and fantasy, but they need to apply the same criterion to their own fanciful speculation.

Parlay

Many of us were introduced to the concept of *parlay* by watching the entertaining movie *Pirates of the Caribbean*. A pirate captured by an enemy has the right to declare parlay, or temporary protection, until he has an audience with the enemy captain. As we navigate the treacherous waters of life, we frequently find ourselves captured by the pirates of either religion or science, and instead of trying to jump overboard and escape, we need to declare "Parlay!" and seek a meeting with our captors to work out our differences and achieve an accord.

We religious folks and scientists are not foes; we are allies, but we have become so comfortable in our private ports of call that we don't even bother to drop anchor in the others waters for a meet and greet. The problem with science is that it tries to tell us things about the big world outside while cloistered in its sealed, sterile laboratory playing with atomic accelerators and protein electrophoresis gels. Scientists forget to walk the stage, look at the sunrise and sunset, feel the wind, and take in the fragrance of the flowers. On the other hand, the religious among us need to interrupt our walk through the rose garden, stop and peer through the laboratory window, and marvel at the gift of intellect, curiosity, and technology at work in the brilliant minds of the scientists created in God's image. We are incomplete without each other.

Science deviated from the vision of its founding fathers, who viewed it as another way of seeking the mind of God. Science stormed the gates of heaven, pillaged the pantheon, and returned with nothing but the material elements of earth air, fire, and water. Unfortunately, when it arrived back on earth, the people were not as grateful as it had hoped. Since then, the people have frantically tried to rub sticks together and rekindle the spiritual fire of God the scientists had tried to douse with the incomplete water of human reason. Unfortunately, we Christians have also spoken ill of science as we sit in our air-conditioned churches, watching computer-generated PowerPoint sermons projected onto giant, technologically advanced, motorized screens.

> What is the difference between a cathedral and a physics lab? Are they not both saying: Hello?[70]
>
> —Annie Dillard

Conclusion

God has spent an eternity, planning, organizing, and building a set for His grand drama. He stands back and admires the stage and declares it very good. Not content to just look at it, He strolls through it to enjoy what He has done. But as He walks along the garden path, He hears the derisive muttering of the crowds: "The water's too cold! The sun's too hot! The people are too selfish! There's too much maintenance required!" They grab Him from behind, bind Him, mock Him, spit on Him, convict Him of scientific high treason, and sentence Him to death. A cosmic coup has occurred; the Creator has been overthrown by the created. God is dead! Or is He? Wait! We are reminded of the words of Mark Twain: "The rumors of my death have been greatly exaggerated." "I live!"

All evolutionary theory really did was carpet over the evidence of a Creator, but the carpet is beginning to smell and fray, and the people have realized it's time to replace it. They pull back the carpet and discover a beautiful, solid, hardwood floor underneath. They are confronted with a dilemma: cover the floor with new carpeting that will soon wear down and smell, or leave a natural, beautiful, hardwood floor for all to see.

You are presented with the same choice—carpet or wood floor, the pink shag of evolution or the hardwood floor of intelligent set design, the smoke-filled improvisation club or the Sydney Opera House. The choice is yours, but I implore you to critically think through your decision. I hope I have offered enough evidence to help you recognize that your personal drama is played out on an award-winning set. It is evocative and well-constructed, and it hypnotically draws us all into the drama swirling all about us.

But wait, there's more! The set is full of all sorts of props that demand our attention, objects that are incapable of creating a story by themselves but are intimately associated with the story in progress. Like James Bond touring Q's high-tech laboratory to see the latest spy gadgets, we have the opportunity to stroll God's creation and be amazed at all His intricate prop inventions.

Chapter Five

PROPPED UP

W HAT'S THE FIRST THING YOU think of when you hear the word *prop*? Do you envision the phantom's mask in *Phantom of the Opera* or the revolving barricade in *Les Misérables*? How about Sandy, the dog in *Annie*? An elaborate Broadway set is incomplete without props. Wikipedia defines a theatrical prop as "an object used on stage by actors to further the plot or story line of a theatrical production … the difference between a set decoration and a prop is use."

Alone, a prop is incapable of creating a plot or storyline, but in the hands of a character, it can magically accentuate the action on stage. I suggest that in the grand drama of our lives, the animal and plant kingdom represents the props. I want to make it clear that I don't use the word *prop* derogatorily, only descriptively, because props are absolutely essential to the story and without them the stage would feel quite empty and incomplete.

Our infatuation with props starts the moment the morning sun's rays jump-start the slumbering metabolism of our cats. Stomachs grumbling, they pat us on the face, hoping to awaken us to our covenantal feeding duty. We stumble into the kitchen, water the plants, put a leash on the dog, and go for a walk. The details may differ, but I suspect that if we took a close look at our lives, we'd be amazed at just how much the props contribute to our life stories.

My daily performance is enhanced by four cats, three horses, a small orchard of fruit trees, and a vegetable garden. My coheadliner wife, perhaps one of the best "prop" stewards I have ever met, also knows a good prop when she sees one and has become very active in fostering wayward pregnant cats for the Humane Society.

When you attend a Broadway show and the curtain goes up, you may be temporarily amused by the intricate stage and props but will be restless until the action begins. You may be magically transported to the phantom's opera house or to a French battlefield, but if the story doesn't begin soon, you'll hop out of our seat and indignantly march to the box office for a refund. Viewing a set decorated with props but without any actors is about as exciting as watching grass grow. What do the props contribute to any theatrical production? If the props are incapable of creating a story, what do they bring to the drama performed on stage? What makes them distinct but limited?

> But ask the beasts, and they will teach you; the birds of the heavens, and they will tell you; or the bushes of the earth, and they will teach you; and the fish of the sea will declare to you. Who among all these does not know that the hand of the Lord has done this? In his hand is the life of every living thing and the breath of all mankind. (Job 12:7–10)

Propaganda

The animal and plant props in God's story are unique; unlike the set, they are living organisms that require nourishment; they procreate and ultimately die. They are similar to the human characters because they are carbon-based life forms whose physical beings are coded by DNA. I think it is pretty obvious to most people just how different the props are from the set, but the distinction may be fuzzier when they are compared with the characters. One of the major implications of evolutionary theory is the proposition that man is nothing more than a fancy prop. Is that true?

Despite media illusions to the contrary, props are incapable of creating a story themselves. Documentaries, movies, and cartoons frequently depict animals as characters in interesting dramas; bucks involved in leadership power plays, guerrilla warfare between cats and mice, and the psychological struggles of bees and ants trying to exert their individuality in the rigid hive or anthill hierarchy.

Each of those scenarios, however, is dramatic only when man gets his hands on them and laces them with words that imply human struggle. We lend nature the tools of our dramatic trade to help it tell a story even though it seems uninterested in hearing it. I don't think lions would be offended if we used Pee Wee Herman's voice instead of James Earl Jones's voice for Mufasa in *The Lion King*. Man's delight in anthropomorphizing nature has a long and celebrated history, from painting on cave walls, to fashioning golden calves, to making the movie *Ice Age*.

As children, we delighted in many of Aesop's fables such as *The Tortoise and the Hare* and *The Wolf in Sheep's Clothing*. In each of these stories, however, the animals were transformed into characters to portray uniquely human problems. All a recently hatched baby turtle knows is that it is somehow supposed to go to the sea—no planning or strategy needed, no regaling its buddies with stories of how close it came to death. The drama we superimpose on the animal world is just another way for humans to express their seemingly unquenchable desire to tell stories.

A Bug's Life

I suspect most of you have seen the movie *A Bug's Life*. The title is misleading because it doesn't really portray the life of a bug, which in actuality is quite boring, but the life of a human in ant's clothing, which is quite interesting. It's a story of human struggles magically transported into an anthill setting. The proppy ant becomes thought-provoking only when we make it into a character.

Isn't it interesting that we love to depict animals with human characteristics, but when the tables are turned, when man is transformed into an animal, it's usually frightening or demeaning? These include stories about vampires and werewolves forever cursed to live as feral animals and frog princes and beasts rescued by romantic kisses that transform them back into humans.

The Eastern religious traditions understand this concept by recognizing that reincarnation as a slug is a karmic step backward. Our culture seems to forget its evolutionary roots and continues to entertain itself by indirectly acknowledging just how unique human beings truly are.

Beached Whales

Why do we hold humans to a higher standard than animals? Why are we frequently called to task for polluting the environment, clearing rain forests, and expanding our carbon footprint and yet don't get after bears for pooping in rivers and making the water undrinkable? If we accept the fact that there will be animal casualties in the evolutionary battle, that a species may become extinct, why do we relocate overpopulated wolves or breed rare white tigers? How is it possible for us to cry transcendental tears for an extinct species if they were just an evolutionary misstep we had to climb over on our way to the top of the survival pyramid? Why do we feel responsible for mopping up the mess evolution leaves in its wake? Why would our selfish human genes have any interest in the genes of the spotted owl or the white tiger? We run to the aid of beached whales, keeping them moist, while we try to get them into the water and direct them back out to sea. We issue fishing licenses, regulate hunting seasons, and boycott tuna caught with nets that kill dolphins. Why do we care about a species going extinct? Why do we waste evolutionary resources estimating the diminishing number of a rare species and instituting breeding programs to repopulate it? Why do humans care about the threatened mountain gorilla when the mountain gorilla doesn't care for starving African children? Why do we feel the need to protect animals from the very evolutionary forces that "created" them?

We do all this because we know a life without unique props is unacceptable. As actors and actresses in God's story, we have an affinity for the props and feel, quite rightly, that a stage production without them is stifling, unoriginal, and bland. Anything that threatens their existence, whether extinction, pollution, or scarcity of resources, is unacceptable.

God declared that the set and props were good, a fact that prior to the creation of man was evident only to God. The set and props couldn't recognize this goodness because they were incapable of stepping outside themselves and pondering their situations.

Interestingly, when God created mankind, everything was transformed from "good" to "very good." What had man brought to the table that accentuated God's already "good" creation? Ask yourself, is art in fact art if there's no one to appreciate it? Would an art gallery be an art gallery if there weren't people to peruse its displays? God needed to create patrons of the arts to obtain third-party verification for His creative genius. He needed beings capable of stepping outside God's painting and admiring His use of texture, color, and lighting. This third party, however, had to be able to appreciate art in the first place, which is possible only if the third party has an artist's heart, and so, He created mankind in His own artistic image.

> I cannot conceive the necessity for God to love me, when I feel so clearly that even with human beings affection for me can only be a mistake. But I can easily imagine that he loves that perspective of creation which can only be seen from the point where I am.[71]
>
> —Simone Weil

It appears that only the monotheistic traditions can claim a unique relationship with the props. Atheism has the weakest environmental claim of all because it endows mankind with only one responsibility, survival, and it doesn't matter what mankind tramples on to get there. We cannot evolve responsibility for other species if it in any way inhibits our ability to survive. Our evolutionary prowess can cause us to overhunt the buffalo but doesn't require us to establish repopulation programs.

Pantheistic religions, those that claim God is everything and humans are just one of many equal parts of "God's" divine nature, have a very strong environmental focus, but pantheists' beliefs don't support their activism. They cannot theologically separate man from nature and make man a villain or a savior because that would be theological arrogance. Man may feel sorrow for some of his technological travesties, but he's not obliged to make things better. Only when mankind has been given a transcendent mandate to care for the planet can he be held accountable.

Buddhism, while it admirably promotes environmentalism and discourages the killing of even mosquitoes, also doesn't have philosophical support for its beliefs. Nirvana, the extinction of the illusory self and the illusory world, seems to create only an illusory responsibility to the illusory environment.

Similarly, the basic Hindu understanding of the world is that we are stuck on the wheel of karma and need to get off to be reunited with the impersonal oneness of Brahman. The ultimate spiritual goal is to jump the physical ship. While Hindus have prohibitions against cruelty to animals, it's primarily because they don't want to be responsible for stepping on a karma-challenged relative. Reincarnation as an animal is a step backward and relegates animals to small cogs in their salvation machine. Once again, they don't have the doctrinal worldview support for their environmental stance.

Christianity, however, calls man to the carpet for messing up the world and intimately links his fate with that of the rest of the planet. We are responsible for the dilemma, we groan together with nature, and it is only our redemption and God's coming kingdom that will set it right. Now that really sounds like environmentalism!

Suitable Helper

Since it appears Christianity is the only faith tradition that can claim an environmental mandate, let's take a look at the scriptural evidence. As I previously discussed, the primary factor distinguishing us from plants and animals is that we were created in God's image.

The only time in the creative process that God referred to something as being "not good" was when He acknowledged it was not good for man to be alone. In the first-ever recorded petting zoo, God gave Adam the opportunity to test the limits of the animal-man relationship by parading the animals before him to find a suitable helper. The Hebrew word for helper is *ezer*, one who is capable of doing something for someone that they are incapable of doing for themselves. God allowed this animal-as-helper experiment to be conducted so Adam would clearly understand the unbridgeable gulf between animals and man.

If man had just evolved, you would think he might have been able to party with his ape relatives. Adam, however, quickly realized the animals were incapable of the one interaction he most desired, the ability to share stories. Even though the animals were not found to be suitable helpers, we need to remember God gave animals the dignity of at least being considered potential companions.

> Then the Lord God said, "It is not good that the man should be alone; I will make him a helper fit for him." So out of the ground the Lord God formed every beast of the field and every bird of the heavens and brought them to the man to see what he would call them. And whatever the man called every living creature, that was its name. The man gave names to all livestock and to the birds of the heavens and to every beast of the field. But for Adam there was not found a helper fit for him. (Gen. 2:18–20)

The Name Game

Despite the fact that animals couldn't be suitable helpers, Adam marveled at their uniqueness, and with God's blessing, he named each one. Adam, it appears, engaged in the first biological research by classifying every animal by name. Naming someone or something had a great deal of significance in the Hebrew culture. A name was conferred by one in authority and denoted a purpose or told a story. Adam's act of naming therefore placed him in a position of authority over the animals, dominion if you will, but a dominion that implied responsibility and not exploitation.

> God is perfectly capable of naming every animal and giving Adam a dictionary—but he does not. He makes room for Adam's creativity—not just waiting for Adam to give a preexisting right answer to a quiz but genuinely allowing Adam to be the one who speaks something out of nothing, a name where there had been none, and allowing that name to have its own being.[72]
>
> —Andy Crouch

The Old Testament is full of vignettes about names that told stories, such as Abraham and Sarah finding humor in the absurdity of having a son at an advanced maternal age and naming him Isaac, which means *laughter.* Jacob, after he wrestled with God, had his name changed to Israel, which means *one who struggled with God.* God used names to put His stamp of authorship on every page of His story. We carry on this same tradition by naming our pets. We generally don't name our plants, but we would feel oddly remiss if we didn't name our dog or cat. Why? By giving them a name, we imply ownership and significance and connect them with stories. My youngest daughter named our dog Sunshine Nicholas because good old Saint Nick delivered him to our doorstep on a particularly sunny but chilly December day. A pet without a name seems so wrong to us, but is useless baggage to our cats, unless of course, food is on the line. Names are important, and even in the 1970s, we seemed to think that it was necessary to name our pet rocks.

Apples, Mathematics, and Responsibility

While I lump plants and animals into the category of props, we all recognize they are different entities. The mere existence of vegetarians underscores this point; they clearly know the difference between eating a chicken and an apple despite the fact they share a common form of biological information. The biblical account of creation once again gives us insight into these differences.

> And God said, "Let the earth sprout vegetation, plants yielding seed, and fruit trees bearing fruit in which is their seed, each according to its kind, on the earth." And it was so. The earth brought forth vegetation, plants yielding seed according to their own kinds, and trees bearing fruit in which is their seed, each according to its kind. And God saw that it was good. (Gen. 1:11–12)

> And God said, "Let the waters swarm with swarms of living creatures, and let birds fly above the earth across the expanse of the heavens." So God created the great sea creatures and every living creature that moves, with which the waters swarm, according to their kinds, and every winged bird according to its kind. And God saw that it was good. And God blessed them, saying, "*Be fruitful and multiply* and fill the waters in the seas, and let birds multiply on the earth." (Gen. 1:20–22, emphasis added)

The difference between the creation account of plants and animals is found in the phrase "be fruitful and multiply," which God applied to animals but not plants. Plants passively reproduce, while animals actively reproduce. Since animals actively seek mates to procreate, they needed a more in-depth set of rules to govern their behavior to ensure successful reproduction. Animals were given instincts, which guaranteed they mated during favorable reproductive seasons and utilized preprogrammed caring mechanisms such as pouches, nests, and burrows to ensure the survival of their young. These behaviors are intimately linked to the changing scenes on the stage, and the animals take their cues from each new scripted setting.

In the creation of mankind, God took it to a different level. God had generically instructed the animals to be fruitful and multiply but then personally spoke the same commission to the man and woman. The animals were given a corporate, instinctual mandate they had to obey, while man was given a commandment to ponder. When was the last time you saw a bad animal parent? Why don't we ever see a father quail neglecting his babies as they cross the road just because he's too busy grooming his plumage and yet frequently see human parents abusing, neglecting, and exploiting their children?

Animals know only good, but mankind unwisely chose to also know evil, and our children have suffered the consequences of this knowledge ever since. We share the ability to be fruitful and multiply with animals, but we have, for better or worse, also been given the capability of contemplating those reproductive decisions.

Stewards

God also gave man responsibility for the rest of His creation. While it is described as having dominion and subduing, it was never meant to give us license to do whatever we wanted to the environment. What He really did was give us a higher calling. He asked us to be curators of his museum, responsible for creating displays and cataloguing His great works.

> And God blessed them. And God said to them, "Be fruitful and multiply and fill the earth and subdue it and have dominion over the fish of the sea and over the birds of the heavens and over every living thing that moves on the earth." (Gen. 1:28)

As beings created in God's image, we understand what God means when He calls something good, but we also understand that our knowledge is incomplete. Our imperfect understanding is what drives the scientific enterprise. We want to comprehend the mind of the Maker by studying what He has created, but we also want that knowledge to make us more skilled caretakers. We study the props, catalog them, learn about their eating and mating habits, and follow their migratory patterns to help us do a better job of taking care of all His creation.

Pet Etiquette

If, as the evolutionist declares, I share my personality traits with the animal kingdom and the differences we see are just matters of degree, why doesn't my cat periodically leave me a thank-you note for feeding it and cleaning its litter box? What's up with that? I could justifiably be disappointed if I didn't get a thank-you note from another human being, but why does my evolutionary brother get a free pass in the politeness category? The only way for the evolutionist to deny this vast chasm between man and animals is to make man look stupider or make animals look smarter. Despite the astounding displays of human stupidity celebrated by the Darwin Awards and the trend of outfitting poodles with fashionable sweaters, the gulf between animals and man remains.

To provide evidence for our connection with the animal kingdom, scientists try to teach our evolutionarily inferior ape brothers to communicate. We arrogantly seem to think acquiring human communication skills is a good idea, but what if we teach an ape to read and it gets hold of a copy of Nietzsche and decides it's better to commit suicide than live a life meaninglessly pursuing bananas?

Maybe it's better to accept the fact that our humanness is revolutionary and not evolutionary. Maybe we should be content to let our ape friends throw poop at one another rather than force them to suffer from an existential crisis they're woefully incapable of handling. When we train animals to do human-like things, we are not appealing to their sense of intelligence but rather to their desire for food. Why will a dolphin jump through a hoop for a fish but not a diploma?

We have philosophers, for heaven's sake, people who seek knowledge for the sake of knowledge when it would make far more sense for them to get in line and buy a ticket for the natural selection lottery. In our grand drama, the characters don't want to be props, but they somehow feel that the props should want to be characters. Isn't that odd?

Sadness on the Savannah

I came across one particularly poignant example of this vast difference between animals and man in a documentary televised on the Animal Planet channel. It was a story about some abandoned lion cubs that had been rescued by a man; he took them in and raised them with the intention of releasing them back into the wild once they reached young adulthood.

The day finally arrived to set them free, and like any good parent, this man was conflicted. He was very sad to release them back into the savannah but very proud they had grown so strong and independent.

He monitored them carefully from a distance to make sure they were adequately prepared for life in the wild. One particular day, he observed one of the lions stalk, kill, and eat a young antelope. Once again, the man was very conflicted. He was proud the lion had demonstrated natural survival skills but horrified that it had been at the expense of an innocent antelope. He was happy the lion was acting like a lion but sad it wasn't acting like a human.

If we really are just highly evolved animals, we cannot justify our horror at the death of a seemingly helpless antelope. There is something deep inside us that recoils at the apparent cruelty of the "circle of life" no matter how well animated or beautifully scored. We feel comfort when our cat curls up in our lap but disgust when it brings us a dead mouse. If we are nothing more than evolved animals, we cannot be appalled by any animal behavior. Predatory hunting, rape, abandoning a weaker member, or extinction should then be nothing but the consequences of survival of the fittest. It may sound harsh, but there's "no crying in evolution."

> The more we really look at man as an animal, the less he looks like one.[73]
>
> —G. K. Chesterton

My home is on the outskirts of Spokane, where farmland still exists and nature continues to function largely undisturbed. Every day I see deer, hawks, quail, and even an occasional moose. Despite the regularity of such encounters, I continue to call family members to the window and pull out the binoculars and cameras so we can share and record these encounters. Why are we enthralled with these creatures even when these sightings have become routine and all we see them do is eat and walk? What is the fascination? Is it perhaps the image of a creator in me marveling at the work of the ultimate Creator?

Duck Envy

If you could be any kind of animal, what would it be? My response has always been a duck, because ducks just leisurely float around on the surface of a pond, paddling through life without a worry or care patiently waiting for humans to come by and toss them a breadcrumb now and then. Other people would choose a gazelle because of its grace or a lion for its bravery. If you think about it, aren't we just placing our human ideals on animal bodies? In reality, animals live as either predators or prey, and their apparent freedom, grace, or courage is appreciated only as a human illusion; for them, it's just about survival.

If you look at the animal world objectively, you see conformity and predictability, but when you look at man, you see individuality and unpredictability. The instinctual constraints imposed on animals ensure things generally go well; they know where to find food, shelter, and mates and how to rear their young. They don't need laws or police to enforce the animal order because they are bound instinctually to the script. Human characters, on the other hand, have been given artistic freedom and are encouraged by the Director to ad lib within the fairly loose constraints of the storyline. While a lion roaming the savannah is often held up as the image of truly being "born free," that freedom is an illusion because the lion is just a prisoner in a cage of instinct. Humans have true freedom because they can decide to assume their roles or not, perform or improvise, and even choose to exit the production without the Director's approval.

Gimme Shelter

Despite the significant differences between the props and characters, we, the characters, know that a drama without props is unacceptable. We feel we need to look out for them just as an older brother or sister would look out for a younger sibling. The evidence for our concern is found everywhere. We integrate them into the story by forming organizations such as the Humane Society, Greenpeace, PETA, and the EPA. We set up relief funds for animals on the verge of extinction, we have shelters for stray cats and dogs, we reserve forests for spotted owls, and we rescue beached or misguided whales. If we allowed the natural selection wheels to turn, many a beautiful and unique animal would be crushed under evolution's oppressive weight, merely collateral damage in the battle for the survival of the fittest.

If you believe we are merely evolutionary accidents, you don't have the worldview credibility to criticize someone for wearing an exotic fur. If you happen to be an evolved caveman freezing to death, a fur coat would seem a pretty good idea, and if at the same time it makes you "look marvelous," all the better, as you sit atop the evolutionary pyramid.

Conclusion

I hope I have convinced you that plants and animals function as props in our grand drama. They can certainly enhance a story but are incapable of creating one. It is only when man appears on the scene that grazing sheep can become the story of a shepherd and a lost sheep or a mustard seed can become the kingdom of God.

It's interesting that Jesus frequently used fig trees, camels, and wolves as props to make His points; He seemed to find them more effective than direct references. If the Author of our faith holds them in such high esteem, it may behoove us characters to do the same. Jesus brought His message to the people but never hesitated to use a good prop to illustrate His point. He was not deaf to the groans of the props but knew their liberation was possible only through the redemption of mankind.

> Consider the ravens: they neither sow nor reap, they have neither storehouse nor barn, and yet God feeds them. Of how much more value are you than the birds! (Luke 12:24)

We need to be mindful of the clear differences between the props and characters; when we confuse them, we end up engaging in all sorts of delusional worldview contortions. Plants and animals are key ingredients in God's narrative vision; they allow the characters to enhance their performances, and without them, the stage would feel quite empty. Why then did Jesus say that the human characters were more valuable than the "bird" props? Let's meet the cast of this amazing drama and find out why.

Chapter Six

MEET THE CAST

Men go to gape at mountain peaks, at the boundless tides of the sea, the broad sweep of rivers, the encircling ocean and the motion of the stars, *and yet they leave themselves unnoticed; they do not marvel at themselves.*[74]

—Augustine (emphasis added)

A PLANET WITHOUT CHARACTERS MAY spin along effortlessly. The weather will cycle through its seasons, volcanoes will erupt, and animals will mate, but it will remain nothing more than a picture postcard of a vacation never taken unless you see characters with floral shirts and plaid shorts in the foreground. Is a sunrise over Haleakala beautiful if there aren't any shivering tourists to see it? Do fish actually try to find Nemo without Disney/Pixar? Do my cat and I actually get group therapy without Jackson Galaxy?

We all know that sets and props are incapable of generating a story and that only when human characters appear on the scene does the action begin. What is it about these human characters that makes them uniquely qualified to add drama to this world? We have already explored some of these differences in our discussion about the props, but let's dig deeper because, as I mentioned in the opening chapters, one of the biggest barriers to understanding the fact that we live in God's world and are special characters in His story is the mistaken notion that mankind is not unique.

Unfortunately, this has become a major stumbling block to any reasonable cultural dialogue because for Christians, man is the pinnacle of God's creative work, a being formed in His image, while for the atheist, man is just a remarkably lucky mistake of genetic replication who represents nothing more than a point on the animal continuum. The way we understand mankind is not some theoretic curiosity; it has profound implications for the way we live together on this planet. We earlier addressed the concern over the death of story, but let us turn our attention to the other major concern, the death of man.

The Human Zoo

> And if we deny the things that make us truly human, then we will create a culture that is, by definition, inhuman.[75]
>
> —Chuck Colson

How often were you disappointed after you visited a zoo because the lions, tigers, and bears (Oh my!) were all sleeping? You probably considered it a good visit if you saw the animals walk or eat. Why do we get into big lines to feed giraffes food pellets? The biggest thrill at my most recent zoo visit was seeing a gorilla throw his poop. Discontent, we humans then go home and plop *Finding Nemo* into the DVD player and watch interesting fish engaging in an exclusively human drama. Why do we let animals off the hook and not demand more for our hard-earned zoo admission dollars?

Did you ever wonder why reality TV has become so popular? If you think about it, it's nothing more than a high-tech human zoo, mankind placing his fellow man in carefully monitored cages, manipulating the environment, and recording their responses.

One of the most popular reality shows, *Survivor*, takes people from diverse backgrounds, places them in harsh environments, and films their triumphs and failures. It's fascinating to see how people adapt to demanding, new environs while trying to get along with other socially challenged human beings.

If we placed gorillas in the Arctic and recorded their exploits, I suspect it would be boring and exceedingly cruel. The evolutionist may say mankind has evolved the capacity to creatively adapt, but why is there such an incredibly large behavioral gap between the smartest animal and the dumbest human? Where are the behavioral intermediaries that give us clues about the evolutionary source of my creative adaptability? Please don't tell me monkeys using sticks to dig ants out of a log or to hit each other over the head qualifies as early evidence of human intelligence. Even if you give those Arctic gorillas nails, wood, fishing poles, and matches, they would still die of hypothermia and starvation.

Isn't it interesting that the props in God's story are physically well suited to their particular environments while the characters are not, but the characters are able to inhabit any environment they choose? Eskimos inhabit the frozen north while nomadic peoples populate the scorching desert. If you took a white artic fox and placed him in the tropics, it would be immediately eaten. If you placed an iguana in the artic, it would freeze to death. Why can you take a man born without a thick coat of fur and place him in the artic, watch him hunt down a polar bear, make a coat of fur, build a house out of ice blocks, and learn to find the breathing holes of seals to capture them for food?

> That an ape has hands is far less interesting to the philosopher than the fact that having hands he does next to nothing with them.[76]
>
> —G. K. Chesterton

I'm Not an Animal!

Many of you may remember the story of John Merrick, the Englishman afflicted with the severely disfiguring disease neurofibromatosis. His life was popularized in the stage play and movie *The Elephant Man*. You will recall that because of his grotesque appearance, he was exploited and mistreated. In his grief, he cried out the memorable line, "I am not an animal! I am a human being! I am ... a man!"[77] It seems that when the rubber meets the road, we humans don't like being treated like circus animals. Unfortunately, that is exactly the verdict the evolutionary jury has come to.

If you accept a materialistic evolutionary view of mankind, you have no choice but to admit you are an animal, maybe more clever than other animals, but an animal nonetheless. The good news is that if you look at the way our society thinks and behaves, you will see it treats mankind as if he is truly unique and invokes his animal ancestry only when he needs to justify his bad behavior.

Our current postmodern culture has made it abundantly clear that denying a spiritual component to human nature is absurd, but ironically, it still accepts a purely naturalistic explanation for the origin of life. Why do we live like spiritual beings but cling to an evolutionary theory that declares we're just animals? I suspect it allows us to be a member of the spiritual pantheon with an asterisk by our names, markers in our particular stories that give us a ready excuse for not acting like gods. If we ever get hauled into little god court for bad behavior, we can always claim the animal-instinct defense. It's much easier to cover up our bad behavior by claiming we are merely cats that don't always use the kitty litter box.

> Man is not merely an evolution but rather a revolution.[78]
>
> —G. K. Chesterton

What exactly do we mean by *unique*? The Encarta world dictionary defines unique as "being the only one of its kind, very unusual, aberrant, atypical, abnormal, exceptional, extraordinary, freaky, odd, peculiar, phenomenal, rare, singular." Don't you think that some or all of these descriptors apply to you or perhaps more accurately to your neighbor lady with the twenty cats? Atheists want to level the animal kingdom playing field by spending all their time pondering the physical similarities between animals and man while conveniently neglecting to explain the vast differences between the minds of animals and man. Isn't it interesting that scientists gathering data from the Large Hadron Collider can think they are just a couple million years removed from monkeys using sticks to dig termites out of a log? Unfortunately, only a handful of evolutionists have the guts to talk about the disturbing consequences of their deeply held theory that declares man is not special!

> Animal liberationists do not separate out the human animal, so there is no rational basis for saying that a human being has special rights. A rat is a pig is a dog is a boy. They are all mammals.[79]
>
> —Ingrid Newkirk

If you assert that man is just a more highly evolved animal, you are left with only instinct to explain his actions. You can appeal only to the built-in mechanisms of behavior seen in the animal kingdom to explain the behavior of man. The best reason you can give for people traveling from Spokane to Palm Springs every December is the need to fly south for the winter. Canning fruits and vegetables is nothing but hiding nuts in the ground to make sure you have food available when the snow sets in.

Instinct doesn't grant the ability to anticipate or plan for future wants and desires. Instinct doesn't prompt us to save money for our kids' college funds or plan for family vacations. Instinct doesn't plan; it reacts. The beauty of appealing to instinct, however, is that it allows us to live in the selfish introspection of the here and now rather than in the altruistic anticipation of the future. If we lived by instinct, global warming would represent just a particularly pleasant fall, and bankrupting the Social Security promise we made to our children would be more like a squirrel finding an extra nut to snack on during the winter. Survival of the planet is irrelevant as long as you have a warm cave in which to hibernate.

What is even stranger is that we talk about instinct at all. Instinct is instinct, and once you contemplate it, you no longer embody it. By definition, "instinct is an inborn pattern of behavior characteristic of a species" (Encarta), so to discuss instinct is to step outside our animal nature, which would seem to disqualify us from being mere animals.

Controlling instinctual behavior is an oxymoron when it comes to considering animals but a transcendent feature of mankind. To speak of instinct in the abstract violates the rules of the animal instinct game. Controlling instinct implies that there is a standard above instinct by which we can contemplate instinctual behavior. Where did it come from? Instinct is often blamed for some of our atrocious behavior, but once instinct becomes abstract, it falls into the category of sin.

I Think, Therefore I Am (Different)

In nature, we see gradations of animal intelligence, which fits in nicely with evolutionary theory, but once we encounter mankind, we recognize a huge gap between the smartest animal and the dumbest human. Despite the amusing videos of the world's dumbest criminals and of apes that have learned a few words of sign language, the gulf remains. It seems to me that if we evolved from animals, we should expect to see more evidence of a verifiable intelligence continuum.

> There may be a broken trail of stones and bones faintly suggesting the development of the human body. There is nothing even faintly suggesting such a development of the human mind.[80]
>
> —G. K. Chesterton

If you think about it, when you remove man from the world, the characters from the play, you are not just eliminating an evolutionary chink in the animal chain but are also removing a transcendent mind from the world. You can see this in the frustration of scientists unable to find comparable minds in animals who then are forced to turn to the rather questionable search for extraterrestrial intelligence.

Why are documentaries about alien life so popular? When I was growing up, the mere mention of space aliens was met with jeers and snickers from the scientific community, but now it has become almost mainstream. The dogmatic denial of a creating intelligent mind fostered by many in the scientific community has embarrassingly forced them to adopt their own creation mythology featuring highly intelligent aliens seeding meteors and propelling them our way. They see a mind behind it all but refuse to let a consequential God into the picture. Their brains know there must be intelligence, so they import it from a less-demanding source, space aliens. Why would we assume our exceedingly unlikely evolutionary appearance was somehow replicated elsewhere in the universe and had created beings of equal or greater intelligence? Why would we assume they would have evolved language, mathematics, and science? The reason is that we subliminally see the work of a mind all around us but have somehow confused Him with little green men who say, "meep, meep."

A Monkey's Uncle

Why does our closest ancestor, the ape, make for a worse companion than man's best friend, the dog? Doesn't that seem odd? It would seem to me that our best friend would be our most recent evolutionary relative. We should be able to sit down for tea and ponder all the great evolutionary changes we have experienced. Maybe we could even take a walk and reminisce about those we lost along the way, like the stroll the finalists in *Survivor* take in the last episode, stopping at the torches of each contestant voted out because of his or her inadequate social and physical-survival skills.

How did we come to the conclusion we humans are the most highly evolved animals anyway? Isn't that a bit presumptuous? How has the development of angst, suicide, spirituality, relentless pursuit of purpose, caring for the poor and disabled, and the Special Olympics given us any kind of evolutionary advantage? Maybe we are the evolutionary dead ends and animals have evolved beyond us instead of the other way round. Maybe one day, all our books, computers, and digital watches will be just archeological artifacts of a failed intermediate species.

In his book *The Denial of Death,* Ernest Becker considers all our unique human qualities to be just symbols we create to deflect and pacify our fear of death. The inner guilt and angst we experience is due to the knowledge that we are living a lie and that we are actually just deluded animals covered with the colorful wrapping paper of human symbolism. I find it interesting that he goes to great intellectual lengths with his uniquely human gifts of reflection, contemplation, and intelligence to declare we are not special at all. Why do we need such complex theories to make us aware of our own insignificance? What we really need is a book to explain why we need to write a book about how insignificant we are.

Isn't it surprising that after thousands of years of becoming increasingly smarter and more resourceful, our biggest accomplishment is discovering just how inconsequential we are? Congratulations, mankind! You have become so advanced that you can now prove your insignificance!

> Christian thought elevated man to something with divine potential while scientism, naturalism tries to make him return to swinging in the trees.[81]
>
> —David Bentley Hart

> The modern objective consciousness will go to any length to prove that it is not unique in the Cosmos, and by this very effort establishes its own uniqueness. Name another entity in the Cosmos, which tries to prove it is not unique.[82]
>
> —Walker Percy

Transcendental Mediation

The odd thing about the efforts of many atheists to demote mankind to the lowly status of mere links in the evolutionary chain is that they have to dabble in the "dark arts" of transcendence to prove their point. They have to step outside of evolutionary theory to gain enough perspective to declare we don't transcend anything. I argue that the very act of declaring that a human being is insignificant is quite significant.

Despite the fact that the props and characters share a life-giving code, the characters are strangely the only ones able to transcend it. Richard Dawkins, however, suggests that we don't transcend our DNA but are actually under its rigid control. He describes our DNA as "selfish genes" whose only goal is to make sure that their information is propagated and that we humans are merely convenient biological conduits for their replication.

> DNA neither knows or cares. DNA just is. And we dance
> to its music.[83]
>
> —Richard Dawkins

If he is right, why am I capable of committing suicide or wiping out the planet with an atomic device? It appears he has it backward; humans are the ones pointing the gun at the feet of its DNA and demanding that it dance to their tune. Don't you find it odd that the poster boys and girls of natural selection have evolved the ability to destroy themselves?

The selfish gene has become a slave to its own creation. In addition to man's ability to destroy the gene pool, he has also "evolved" the remarkable ability to look under the genetic hood and tinker with its parts. He can clone sheep, selectively breed plants and animals, prolong life, and even commit the treasonous act of allowing "inferior" genes to replicate. He is even developing gene therapy to repair harmful mutations. It appears that the deluded "selfish gene" has developed a bit of a God complex and is in need of therapy. The seemingly inviolable law of natural selection has been thrown out of court and is now being legislated from the human bench.

I'm Not a Number

> Endless invention, endless experiment,
> Brings knowledge of motion, but not of stillness;
> Knowledge of speech, but not of silence …
> Where is the life we have lost in living?

Where is the wisdom we have lost in knowledge?
Where is the knowledge we have lost in information?[84]

—T. S. Eliot

Sadly, our world has gravitated toward a scientific explanation for everything and in the process has reduced people to mere data. Meaning is confused with facts and figures. We begin generating data from the moment of our birth by assigning an Apgar score at the first and fifth minute of life, a numerical assessment of the physiological transition to life outside the womb.

The data generation doesn't stop there; we record the babies' weights, lengths, and head circumferences and plot them on graphs to see if they fit within normal parameters. I remember being urgently called to the emergency room to attend the delivery of a baby whose mother had been unable to make it to the labor and delivery floor in time. After completing our work, the ER nurse demanded an Apgar score so she could complete her paperwork. The birth she had just witnessed and assisted in was insufficient to document the baby's existence; she needed some numeric data. The amazing birth experience is frequently dwarfed by the amount of required paperwork and documentation. The almost magical birth of a baby is reduced to the level of a ticker tape display effortlessly gliding along the bottom of our TV screens informing us of the numeric worth of our human stock investments. Thankfully, parents bring some sanity to the birth process and compare the baby's toes, eyes, and ears to Mom's or Dad's. They want to stop all the measuring and hold their child.

It appears that the rest of the world is already writing a boring, fact-laden documentary of our lives when we have just begun to write our own literary masterpiece. If you thought *War and Peace* was daunting, you should see the monumental works of data generated by the elderly with every new hospital admission.

I have to admit that as a neonatal physician, I was extremely good at reducing babies to bits of data. Once a baby was admitted to the neonatal unit, we would immediately attach devices to their delicate bodies to monitor their heart rates, respirations, oxygen levels, and blood pressures. We had effectively downgraded these little humans to information generators. We reduced their valiant struggle to breathe to respiratory rates and their anxieties and discomforts to numeric pain scores. We placed them in incubators or on hot beds and instructed the parents to minimize touching and talking because of the fragility of their babies.

While these measures were essential for proper medical care, we frequently encountered resistance from parents who just wanted to hold their babies even if that might jeopardize their treatment. Why were these parents so insistent on touching and holding their babies? They knew medical care was incomplete without the human touch. Parents understand that humans must be welcomed into this life with an embrace or hug and not by measuring tapes, needles, and blood pressure cuffs.

I have also noted a very curious thing during my years of neonatal medicine; even when I attended the birth of a baby from the most dysfunctional of families that already knew that their baby would be placed in foster care—the birth was almost always a magical moment. All the hostility and anger briefly melted away. The family members who had been beaten down and abused their whole lives and had suffered from extremely bad lifestyle choices were confronted with a pure, innocent, human life, and they seemed to be captivated by thoughts of what could have been in their own lives and renewed hopes for this new life. These babies were frequently given names such as Hope, Destiny, Heaven, and Joy as if such names were amulets that would ward off the Devil the parents had already danced with.

Portfolios or Poetry

The problem with the enormous amounts of life data we accumulate is that it's meaningless when we die. When we attend a funeral, we don't care about the physical data of the deceased but rather how the deceased had transcended it. A eulogy would be quite sad if all we heard was, "Here lies Bill, born 6/10/1954,

140

birth weight 7lb 6oz, Apgar score 6 and 9, AGA (appropriate for gestational age). Educated up through a master's degree in economics. Worked fifty years, spawned three children who spawned three grandchildren, and died of cardiac failure 12/5/2008, amen." We want to know about Bill's passions and hobbies and how he had touched the lives of others. We hope to hear a story full of poetic nuance, plot twists, and conflict resolution. We are quite uncomfortable attending the funerals of those who never transcended their facts and figures and who left nothing behind but a stock portfolio as the only evidence they had walked the earth. If we are just animals that forage, fornicate, and die, why do we feel compelled to conduct funerals and offer eulogies?

> Just as character can only be truly rendered in narrative form, so the answer to the question "Who am I?" can only be given if we ask "What is my story?" and that can only be answered if there is an answer to the further question, "What is the whole story of which my story is a part?" To indwell the Bible is to live with an answer to those questions, to know who I am and who is the One to whom I am finally accountable.[85]
>
> —Leslie Newbigin

Companies carefully review the educational and employment histories of prospective employees to get a sense of their ability to perform the work. The most crucial aspect of the hiring process comes down to the interview. Employers need to see prospective employees face-to-face to see how they transcend their data; that's ultimately the measure by which the employer will determine which applicants will fit in. You would never base a friendship or romantic relationship on data. Even in this age of online dating services and personal profiles, there must be a first date before wedding arrangements are made.

Genuine People Personalities

Even though we see that each character in our story is unique, we still recognize several basic personality types such as pessimists, optimists, pragmatists, realists, and idealists. Why would a particular set of natural selection forces brought to bear in the same region evolve one creature that wants to read poetry next door to someone who wants to blow things up? It almost appears as if there's a specific societal role for each personality type. This fact would seem odd if the appearance of man was based just on survival of the fittest but makes perfect sense if we were characters in a story. Don't you think it would be a survival distraction if I needed to build a shelter and my environmentalist tribe mate stopped me because cutting down a tree would displace his treasured spotted owl? What if a tribe needed to take up swords to defend against a warring enemy but the tribal painter wanted to take up his paintbrush and compose a watercolor of the sunrise?

Unfortunately, many a worldview is constructed from the perspective of only one particular personality type, failing to take into account the fact that a worldview is valid only if it works for everybody. The Bible has a portal of entry for each of these distinct personalities. The realist is pleased with the historical detail of the narrative books of the Bible, the idealist finds God in the poetry and songs of the psalms, the pragmatist finds God in the logical axioms of the proverbs, the pessimist finds God in the honesty of Ecclesiastes, and the philosopher finds God in the letters of Paul. I think our postmodern friends would be quite pleased to see just how much God encourages and embraces diversity. The Bible speaks of each person as a unique creation whose every hair is counted and known by God. God created a beautiful landscape, but we must not forget He also painted intriguing people in the foreground, each with his or her own fascinating story.

Ghost in the Machine

Atheists are haunted by the clanging chains of the spiritual ghost wandering their fine-tuned physical factory and cannot escape the fact that humans are composite physical and spiritual beings. Most people acknowledge we share some physical similarities with animals but also recognize there are spiritual qualities that make us unique. Humans are in the difficult position of having one foot in the spiritual world and one foot in the physical world. We are puzzled by the fact that our minds can turn to the heavens and contemplate the universe but then quickly crash to earth as we feel the demands of our progressively distending bladder. We are perplexed when the untimely passing of gas ruins the quiet contemplation of a room of mystics as they contemplate the God within; we are bewildered when our biology fouls the air of our spiritual aspirations.

The materialist tries to pull the physical world away from the spiritual while the religious tries to pull the spiritual away from the physical, and we end up either pulling a muscle or ripping the seat of our pants in our attempt to perform the cosmic splits. Unfortunately, both sides have pulled so hard that the previously united physical and spiritual wishbone has been broken, and both sides are claiming the bigger piece. As physical and spiritual creatures, we are the only ones capable of uniting the two worlds, and we should resist every attempt to separate the two. In the beginning, God married the spiritual and physical by creating us in His image, but unfortunately, our culture has filed for divorce due to irreconcilable differences. The question becomes, are these differences really irreconcilable?

> We are not human beings having a spiritual experience,
> we are spiritual beings having a human experience.[86]
>
> —Teilhard de Chardin

One of the problems we encounter when returning from spiritual forays into the heavens is reentering our physical airspace. We cannot remain in the transcendent realm very long without having to go to the bathroom, eat a meal, or get some sleep. This difficult transition between the two is a constant source of human angst.

> The spectacular miseries of reentry—especially when the transcendence is so exalted as to be not merely Adam-like but godlike. It is difficult for gods to walk the earth without taking the form of beasts.[87]
>
> —Walker Percy

Walker Percy describes the attainment of transcendence as the "partial recovery of Eden." I argue that it is more like a brief peek through the gate into Eden, a glorious glimpse into a garden we previously walked but can no longer enter for fear of being slashed by a fire-sword–wielding angel.

We often experience these brief moments of spiritual transcendence when reading Shakespeare, viewing a Rembrandt, or listening to Mozart but blink our eyes and find ourselves once again selling paper in Scranton. Reentry is a difficult transition. How can I bring Eden to Scranton or take Scranton to Eden? Jesus made it possible by tearing the curtain and establishing a temple for God in our own bodies. The once-portable tabernacle that had become fixed in Jerusalem was once again free to travel.

We all contain a dwelling place for the transcendent Holy Spirit to reside, but instead of acknowledging we are vessels for holiness, we make ourselves into divine forgeries. We intellectually understand we are made in God's image but go to extreme lengths to make ourselves unrecognizable to God. Our spirits groan. We take our image of God to the beauty salon, get its hair and nails done, apply heavy layers of makeup and eyeliner, and end up looking like sad clowns. We are supposed to be temples in which the bride and Groom exchange vows, but instead, we end up looking more like a Las Vegas marriage chapel.

Walker Percy compares the dilemma of physical immanence and spiritual transcendence with a spacecraft reentering earth's atmosphere after a space mission. Most human beings want to periodically enter divine airspace but soon run out of oxygen. As they scramble to return, they have to face the uncomfortable heat of imminent reentry.

Interestingly, all other faith traditions place the power of transcendence in the hands of the religious elite, such as the New Age guru, the shaman, or the monk. Jesus, on the other hand, had the audacity to say that it would be the poor, the weak, the suffering, and the outcast who would see the kingdom of God. The rest of the world looks at them and pities their immanence, but Jesus tells them they are the only ones capable of entering the transcendent kingdom. Why would that be? The people Jesus described in the Sermon on the Mount were more acutely aware of their need for a Jesus spacesuit and once outfitted could enter the heavenly realm without having to gasp for breath in the vacuum of holy space.

Mankind is unique because he exhibits qualities that come from the heavens above and the earth below, and he spends most of his life trying to reconcile the two. I think a great deal of our human unhappiness finds its source in our inability to successfully meld them. Which worldview can best harmonize these two seemingly incompatible realms? Atheists and evolutionists solve the problem by demoting spiritual longing to chemicals and neural pathways in our brains. Pantheists bring the transcendent down to earth and have it inhabit every material thing. Hindus claim our spirituality is a divine spark buried deep in our physical bodies seeking to be released from its biological prison to unite with the ultimate divine. Buddhists tell us that spirituality is achieved by completely extinguishing the physical illusion of the self. These alternative religious solutions basically suggest that ultimate spirituality is a corporate blandness in which our personal distinctiveness is lost in a larger, nameless, faceless spiritual essence. If this is true, why do we spend our lives trying to establish our unique individualities on this planet instead of hoping to be homogenized in some divine cosmic blender? I find it quite interesting that our progressively postmodern culture, which cherishes individual expression and personal truth, unquestioningly accepts religious beliefs that turn us into just spiritual bricks in the wall.

Christianity, on the other hand, not only recognizes but also encourages our individuality. God made us all unique. He knew us before we were created. Our quest, therefore, is to discover the unique spiritual and physical beings God created us to be. As physical beings created in the image of a spiritual God, we sense the importance of both realms in our lives. The fall, however, obscured this connection, and we see our true nature only dimly.

The good news is that we are not alone in this incredibly important task. He has equipped us with our own personal GPS, God Personality Sensing unit. Since we are created in His image, we have access to this remarkable God app, but sadly, most of us behave like proud males lost in the city, carelessly turning down every wrong street and defiantly refusing to pull over and ask for directions. For those of us who are technologically challenged, there is another time-tested option, the Bible, a several-thousand-year-old road atlas that tells us exactly how to get there and describes all the sights along the way.

We Christians, however, should be most comfortable moving between realms because we know we're on a journey accompanied by a tabernacling God. We know Jesus tore the curtain and made it possible for the Holy Spirit to dwell in us, sparing us from the dangers of spiritual space-shuttling. We know that when creation is restored, God will dwell with His people as He did in the garden without the need of temple walls. We will experience the complete, seamless restoration of the physical and spiritual realms that were originally intended in the garden before the fall.

First Responder

> What are human beings that you are mindful of them?
> (Ps. 8:4)

How do we account for man's uniqueness? Evolutionary theory says we are no different from animals. Buddhism considers humans to be temporary collections of impersonal aggregates whose special status is an illusion. Hinduism considers everything in the world to be pieces of diluted divinity housed in illusory bodies that accidentally spilled out of the impersonal Brahman. Mother Earth spirituality considers humans to be just different manifestations of the same universal spirit. In each case, there is nothing special about mankind, but why do people behave as if they are so darned special?

> The Bible is primarily not man's vision of God but God's vision of man. The Bible is not man's theology but God's anthropology.[88]
>
> —Abraham Joshua Heschel

The Genesis account of the creation of mankind explains why we feel so different from the rest of nature. Mankind is described as being planned, desired, loved, and made as a unique physical and spiritual unity. Man has a distinctive role as a bridge between the physical world and a spiritual God, a sort of middleman between the Creator and the created.

If we are a bridge, what type of traffic moves across it? Man transports God's spiritual wishes to a physical planet by being a steward of God's handiwork, but he also ships the planets' physical praise back to God by being the mouthpiece of gratitude for the universe. We are the only creatures capable of pondering God's amazing craftsmanship, and without man, the universe would be guilty of cosmic disinterest. Mankind is, in essence, God's first responder, the only being capable of meaningfully responding to what God has done.

Valiant first responders are characterized by their ability to quickly assess a situation, understand the seriousness, and bravely enter into the fray. As Christians, we are called to be just as courageous. We have been trained to recognize God's creative work, we understand the seriousness of failing to acknowledge it, and we are willing to put our lives on the line for others to prevent them from being consumed by the fire.

Image of God

The biblical account of man being created in God's image provides the best explanation for our uniqueness. Genesis emphasizes the significance of this event in two crucial ways. First, God didn't take man's creation lightly; it required a high-level discussion between God and His heavenly host, variously interpreted as early allusions to the Trinity or His council of angels.

> Then God said, "Let us make man in our image, after our likeness." (Gen. 1:26)

Second, it was only when mankind appeared on the scene that God could call rocks, plants, and animals "very good" instead of just "good." Mankind became the "very" in God's "very good." What did man bring to the table that allowed God to upgrade His creation appraisal? Before we answer, we need to ask ourselves another question; does the world need man to function properly? While we certainly have the role of stewards or augmenters of God's creation, I argue that the earth would continue to operate just fine without man; the rivers would continue to run, the rain would continue to fall, and sheep would continue to graze. If that's true, what does man add to the world? I suggest that a world without man would be nothing but an empty stage scattered with props—a glorious set with no drama. There would be majestic mountain peaks but no one to bravely climb them, desert sand but no Silicon Valley, and shivering dogs without winter sweaters. Man takes a flower and creates a poem, takes a waterfall and crafts a metaphor, and takes a rabbit and tortoise and writes a fable. Man transforms the good set and props into a very good story.

> And God saw everything that he had made, and behold, it was very good. (Gen. 1:31)

God's use of the "very" modifier was a risk; it opened the door for its misuse, such as "not good," "sometimes good," or "rarely good." God's addition of "very" was a free will gift to mankind.

He calls us to be very good but allows us the freedom to choose to be not good. Animals were different, however, because they were created simply good, incapable of modification with any other adjective. Animals have no concept of excellence or mediocrity, only good.

I asked you before if you considered plants, animals, and mankind to be good or evil. I pointed out you would most likely consider the flora and fauna to be good but would probably hesitate calling man good because you recognize that he also embodies evil. A wonderful illustration of this dichotomy is found in the New Testament story of Jesus' encounter with two demon-possessed men.

> And when he came to the other side, to the country of the Gadarenes, two demon-possessed men met him, coming out of the tombs, so fierce that no one could pass that way. And behold, they cried out, "What have you to do with us, O Son of God? Have you come here to torment us before the time?" Now a herd of many pigs was feeding at some distance from them. And the demons begged him, saying, "If you cast us out, send us away into the herd of pigs." And he said to them, "Go." So they came out and went into the pigs, and behold, the whole herd rushed down the steep bank into the sea and drowned in the waters. (Matt. 8:28–32)

The demons were sent into a herd of pigs that then proceeded to stampede off a cliff. Why did these demon-possessed animals kill themselves? I think the answer goes back to the creation story; animals were created to know only good and were incapable of having good and evil coexist in their bodies, so the pigs' only option was to kill themselves. Adam and Eve, on the other hand, by eating the forbidden fruit, made it possible for good and evil to coexist in humans. This unique characteristic of mankind will ultimately be the source of the conflict in our story. We are the fallen image of God, *The Beautiful Letdown* (Switchfoot), engaged in a cage match to the death between good and evil.

The Apple Doesn't Fall Far from the Tree

If we were created in God's image, there must be specific human characteristics that distinguish us from animals and give us clues as to God's character. What does it mean to be created in God's image? Sacred Scripture gives us the answer in three locations: God's character before the creation of man, God's description of the creation of man, and God incarnate as Jesus Christ.

In the opening chapter of Genesis, before man appeared on the scene, we discover some interesting aspects of God's character that we instantly recognize in ourselves as well. God has a mind; He carefully, sequentially, thoughtfully, and reasonably created the universe. He started big and then progressively became more detailed. God communicated His thought by speaking. God is creative. God has standards and distinguishes between good and not good. God exists in an interactive Trinitarian relationship.

We get even more detail about the image of God in the biblical description of the creation of man. In the Genesis text, just before man was made, God declared that one of the unique roles for a being created in His image would be dominion over the rest of His creation.

> And let them have *dominion* over the fish of the sea and over the birds of the heavens and over the livestock and over all the earth and over every creeping thing that creeps on the earth. (Gen. 1:26, emphasis added)

We already know from the opening verses of Genesis that God made everything; it's all His stuff, so the reference to man's dominion can only mean that the authority allocated to man was subordinate to God's authority. Mankind would be a steward of God's property but not its owner. It would be absurd to think that a God who had meticulously planned and constructed the universe would allow man to do whatever he wanted with it.

It is important to remember that God's command to subdue and have dominion over everything was given before the fall, a time when Adam and Eve were in harmony with God's will. It was only when Adam and Eve rebelled and attempted to be like God that they engaged in the first act of self-promotion, elevating their status from steward to owner and in the process replaced caretaking with exploitation.

God explained what this dominion would look like by defining their garden role. The human steward was assigned the specific task of working and keeping God's garden. God created the labor template by demonstrating His personal work ethic for six days and then sanctifying a day of rest. Work and rest went hand in hand. How often do we start chanting T.G.I.S., Thank God it's Sabbath Day, at the beginning of our work week when we should be spending more time declaring the labors of each day to be good?

Once God began creating mankind, the first thing He did was distinguish them as male and female. I think we too often just blast by the significance of this statement. It appears that the image of God includes both male and female characteristics.

> So God created man in his own image, in the image of God he created him; *male and female* he created them. (Gen. 1:27, emphasis added)

Despite the fact that God is most frequently described in masculine terms and that Jesus was a male, there are times when God gets in touch with His feminine side.

> O Jerusalem, Jerusalem, the city that kills the prophets and stones those who are sent to it! How often would I have gathered your children together as a hen gathers her brood under her wings, and you would not! (Matt. 23:37)

While attributing specific male and female characteristics to God can be a point of contention among well-meaning Christians, I think the most important point the Bible wants to convey is that God is a God of relationships. The intimate bond between a man and a woman imitates the relationship found in the Trinitarian Godhead. The very concept of relationship is the core of God's essence. We know that when God created man, He did so in consultation. God existed in a relationship before the world was created, so anything created in His image must embody this crucial feature. We shouldn't get hung up on God as male or female, but it is absolutely essential we understand Him as intimate relationship.

The second chapter of Genesis gives us even more detail as to how this intimate, man-and-woman, image-of-God relationship can help us understand God as a Trinity. The committed intimacy between a man and a woman is important for understanding the very nature of God.

> So the Lord God caused a deep sleep to fall upon the man, and while he slept took one of his ribs and closed up its place with flesh. And the rib that the Lord God had taken from the man he made into a woman and brought her to the man. Then the man said, "This at last is bone of my bones and flesh of my flesh; she shall be called Woman because she was taken out of Man." Therefore a man shall leave his father and his mother and hold fast to his wife, and they shall become one flesh. (Gen. 2:21–24)

Throughout Scripture, the relationship between God and His people is frequently compared to the bond between a man and a woman. The Bible depicts the ideal relationship between God and man as a marriage union and points out that when it is broken, it's like adultery, prostitution, and divorce. Unfaithfulness toward God is comparable to infidelity with a spouse.

In the New Testament, the church is referred to as the bride of Christ. This marriage language also helps us understand that our relationship with God is not just like that of a master and servant but is rather intimate and personal. God's emphasis on the importance of the committed, monogamous, marriage bond between a man and a woman is crucial for a proper understanding of the nature of God and His relationship with those created in His image. The two shall be one. Paul calls this relationship a mystery.

"Therefore a man shall leave his father and mother and hold fast to his wife, and the two shall become one flesh." This mystery is profound, and I am saying that it refers to Christ and the church. (Eph. 5:31–32)

Earlier, I discussed the idea that the world arose as a thought in God's mind, a thought that was actualized when He spoke. If we each represent a unique thought of God, it seems to me the real purpose of our lives is to understand what God had in mind when He made us. We need to stop trying to be who we think we should be and start figuring out who God created us to be. What type of unique character has He scripted you to be in His cosmic grand drama? You don't want to come to the end of your life and have God look at you and not recognize you as His original thought. We will never be perfect in this life, but we should at least make the effort to conform to His thought as much as possible or we may hear the chilling words, "I never knew you," as we knock on heaven's gate.

While the Genesis narrative alone gives us some clues as to what the image of God looks like, it is only when Jesus arrived on the scene that we were truly able to see the physical manifestation of God's perfect image. In the gospel of John, Jesus was intimately linked with the creation of the world. God had spoken the world into existence, and Jesus was His spoken Word. Furthermore, Jesus was described as the light and life of men.

In him was life, and the life was the light of men. The light shines in the darkness, and the darkness has not overcome it. (John 1:4–5)

Colossians goes further and specifically identifies Jesus as God's image.

He is the image of the invisible God, the firstborn of all creation. For by him all things were created, in heaven and on earth, visible and invisible, whether thrones or dominions or rulers or authorities—all things were created through him and for him. And he is before all things, and in him all things hold together. And he is the head of the body, the church. He is the beginning, the firstborn from the dead, that in everything he might be preeminent. For in him all the fullness of God was pleased to dwell, and through him to reconcile to himself all things, whether on earth or in heaven, making peace by the blood of his cross. (Col. 1:15–20)

For the first time in history, people were able to see God, the very image in which they had been created. He ate with them, talked with them, and ultimately died for them. They were able to compare their personal architectural disasters to the divine blueprint. This image had nothing to do with physical characteristics; in fact, the New Testament doesn't tell us anything about Jesus' physical appearance. The true image of God was concerned with spiritual infrastructure and not biological scaffolding. When you read the New Testament accounts of Jesus' ministry, you quickly see that it was not His physical appearance that made an impact but His presence.

> "I tell them when He was alive He looked like a living man," she says, "and when he was dead like a dead man. I do not tell them what He looked like the last time my eyes saw Him. How could I tell it? I do not tell of the look of His feet, but only the print of His feet in the dust. I do not tell of the look of Him, but only the look of the shadow He cast. I do not tell of the sound of His voice as He spoke, but only of the silence that followed in the wake of His speaking."[89]
>
> —Frederick Buechner

I find it interesting that many people who claim to have encountered Jesus cannot or do not find it useful to describe His appearance. We humans want to know what Jesus looks like, but those who experience Him find His physical appearance meaningless when compared to His overwhelming presence. Let me give you two examples of the difference between the appearance and presence of Jesus.

My father, while awaiting surgery for a lung biopsy to diagnose his ultimately fatal respiratory condition, encountered Jesus in the preoperative area while saying a little prayer.

> The one experience I had during my second hospitalization that I want to relate occurred on the day I went to surgery. I was lying on my side waiting. I said a small prayer asking for help and safety when suddenly I felt the presence of Jesus. It was so real that I looked out from my bed and even reached out my hand to touch him. He was there and it seemed so real. He told me everything would be okay!!! One has to experience such a thing to know what it really is or means. I am not a mystic or given to visions. This experience took me completely by surprise and even now it is as real as it was that early morning.[90]
>
> —D. E. Strandness, Jr.

When I pressed my dad to describe what Jesus looked like, he didn't answer; he was completely uninterested in my question; it was the presence of Jesus that was important to him.

A second example is found in an interview with another physician, Dr. Mary C. Neal, who had a near-death experience in an overturned kayak in Chile in 1999. As she was trapped under the water for fifteen to twenty-five minutes, she had a heavenly experience.

> I feel very presumptuous saying that, but I believe that Jesus was holding me when I was still in my boat and reassuring me and comforting me…he didn't look like the image in my Sunday school books. I would say that I didn't look at him critically in terms of saying, 'what color is that hair?' I looked at him and what I saw was infinite kindness and compassion."[91]
>
> —Mary C. Neal, MD

Why has Jesus made such an enormous impact on human history and culture? I suggest that He wakes the sleeping, image-of-God giant in everyone He meets, and when this giant wakes, he pulls out his sword and engages in some serious soul surgery.

We are fortunate that Scripture has given us a detailed picture of what the image of God looks like, and we are called to clean off the sinful dirt that has long since obscured it.

> Do not think that I have come to bring peace to the earth. I have not come to bring peace, but a sword. (Matt. 10:34)

> For the word of God is living and active, sharper than any two-edged sword, piercing to the division of soul and of spirit, of joints and of marrow, and discerning the thoughts and intentions of the heart. (Heb. 4:12)

We find the one, true image of God a bit intimidating, so we try to cut Him down to size and mold Him into our own personal idol. We make Jesus into a warrior king, wise sage, good teacher, or enlightened being because we find a holy, suffering servant just too darned inconvenient.

His Father's Eyes

Jesus made it clear that once we recognize our family resemblance to our heavenly Father, we will be able to take our place as the children of God. Whether you like it or not, you have your father's ears and your mother's nose, features that distinguish you as Gene's boy or Roger's girl. But wouldn't it be more amazing if someone said, "You must be God's son or daughter?"

> The true light, which enlightens everyone, was coming into the world. He was in the world, and the world was made through him, yet the world did not know him. He came to his own, and his own people did not receive him. But to all who did receive him, who believed in his name, he gave the right to become children of God, who were born, not of blood nor of the will of the flesh nor of the will of man, but of God. (John 1:9–13)

Every time we encounter another human, we are looking into a mirror and reminded we were created in God's image. Did you ever wonder why it's so uncomfortable to look another human being in the eye without turning away? Could it be that when we're confronted with another soiled image of God, we are forced to ponder just how we have spoiled our own?

> And why is that one can look at a lion or a planet or an owl or at someone's finger as long as one pleases, but looking into the eyes of another person is, if prolonged past a second, a perilous affair?[92]
>
> —Walker Percy

People sense this image of God inside them; they have a vague feeling they are spiritually unique. We see evidence of this in the dizzying numbers of religious options available to people all over the world. The tricky thing about God's image, however, is that once mankind gets a whiff of any kind of divinity emanating from his own pores, he immediately confuses it with God Himself—just ask Adam and Eve. Our task is to show the world the true source of that image and help people realize the absurdity of trying to be divine imposters.

When we place this idea of the image of God back into the context of a story, we quickly see this is what distinguishes the characters from the props. The struggle to reclaim this image in a fallen world is what drives the plot. A frequent critique of an actor's performance is that he or she is one dimensional; unable to bring complexity and nuance to their performance. I think that many of us are quite sad because we realize that our personal performances lack depth; our characters appear wooden. We need to accept the fact that we are a thought in God's mind, a unique character in his grand drama. What could be more interesting and multifaceted than the image of God? If we accept the fact that God is the Author and we are characters in His great drama, then our unique attributes all began as divine thoughts. We have to conclude that finding out who we were created to be would give

157

us a remarkable peek into God's mind and empower us to give the performance of our lives.

No Joy in Mudville

Our human drama is rich and nuanced because it is performed by a cast of thousands. Every day, we perform a scene with another person created in God's image; a being that brings divine attributes to the world stage. These are not specific physical characteristics but qualities that distinguish actors from props and make the story possible. We live with a foot in the physical world and a foot in the spiritual world. We seem to have a unique place in the universe, the only creatures capable of uniting heaven and earth; it is an awesome privilege and a daunting responsibility. It fills our lives with hope and fear. Sadly, most people wander the set unaware they are unique characters fashioned by the mind of an Author. We need to help our orphaned brothers and sisters see the family resemblance and claim their places as children of God.

> Oh, somewhere in this favored land the sun is shining
>   bright;
> The band is playing somewhere, and somewhere hearts
>   are light,
> And somewhere men are laughing, and somewhere
>   children shout;
> But there is no joy in Mudville—mighty Casey has
>   struck out.[93]
>
> —Ernest Thayer

Sadly, mankind's "Mighty Casey" potential has been replaced by the God-grieving reality that the "Mighty Casey has struck out." Our story now has a conflict, a problem that must be resolved, and it appears to be a direct result of man carelessly swinging for the divine fences when all he needed was a base hit.

In the last several chapters, we have described the magnificent stage, intricate props, and introduced the characters created in the image of the Author, but something doesn't seem quite right; there's no joy in Mudville, and everybody knows it. So let's put on our Baseball Night in America thinking caps, call in some experts, and analyze what went wrong with our swing.

Chapter Seven

HOUSTON, WE HAVE A PROBLEM

Far out in the uncharted backwaters of the unfashionable end of the Western Spiral arm of the galaxy lies a small unregarded yellow sun.

Orbiting this at a distance of roughly ninety-eight million miles is an utterly insignificant little blue-green planet whose ape-descended life forms are so amazingly primitive that they still think digital watches are a pretty neat idea.

This planet has—or rather had—a problem, which was this: most of the people living on it were unhappy for pretty much of the time. Many solutions were suggested for this problem, but most were largely concerned with the movements of small green pieces of paper, which is odd because on the whole it wasn't the small green pieces of paper that were unhappy.

And so the problem remained, lots of the people were mean, and most of them were miserable, even the ones with the digital watches.

Many were increasingly of the opinion that they'd all made a big mistake in coming down from the trees in the first place. And some said that even the trees had been a bad move, and that no one should have ever left the oceans.

And then, one Thursday, nearly two thousand years after one man had been nailed to a tree for saying how

160

great it would be to be nice to people for a change. A girl sitting on her own in a small café in Rickmansworth suddenly realized what it was that had been going wrong all this time, and she finally knew how the world could be made a good and happy place.[94]

—Douglas Adams

IF YOU WERE TO CONDUCT a man-on-the-street interview and ask people if they thought something was wrong with the world, I suspect you'd get resoundingly corporate yes! If you pushed your respondents to specifically identify what that problem was, you would probably get a wide variety of answers. Your interviewees would most likely blame politics, economics, or religion, but their answers in the end would be just veiled attempts to avoid the uncomfortable truth that the problem resides not in one specific demographic group or organization but in the heart and soul of every man and woman.

If this is true, we need to consider what makes man such a nuisance. The general sense that there's something wrong with this world is the symptom of a *dis*-ease, and our cultural discomfort prompts us to explore every therapeutic option, from self-help home remedies and religious rehab to pharmaceutical potions all in the hope we will experience temporary relief. But like any other disease, it cannot be cured unless we discover its source.

Standard of Care

We need to begin by stating the obvious: we cannot diagnose a disease if we don't know what it means to be healthy. In medical school, I had to take an anatomy and physiology class to understand how a healthy body worked before I could take an advanced pathology class to find out how disease adversely affected it. We can't have a problem unless a no-problem standard exists. The fact that mankind can identify a problem implies an ideal standard by which we can make that determination.

Unfortunately, the mind-altering, postmodern hallucinogens that course through our veins have fooled us into believing that no standard exists. We skip through life blissfully unaware that the disease we denied has gone viral and has begun an epidemic of global proportions.

Postmodernism takes it one ridiculous step further by accusing anyone who attempts to play cultural physician of having atrocious bedside manners for rudely suggesting the world has a terminal disease. For the postmodernist, the problem with the world is the diagnoser, the intolerant determiner of cultural disease, and not those coughing up the infected green phlegm of cultural decay.

The atheist has no choice but to accept evolution as the standard bearer, and chillingly, the only standard evolution acknowledges is survival of the fittest, a survival based on the lucky confluence of random events. The difficulty with this worldview is that randomness is incapable of establishing a norm, and without a norm, a problem cannot be identified. Surprisingly, then, atheists somehow feel empowered to blame religion for mankind's problems. If survival is their standard, why do atheists get so bent out of shape about religion when religion already has an impressive several-thousand-year track record of survival?

Hindus and Buddhists recognize the impersonal Brahman or a nebulous nirvana as their standards. They contend we are but smaller pieces of a larger spiritual reality. The standard is unification with these unfathomable entities, which therefore means that the dis-ease is separation. We are lost in a world of detailed illusion and are trying to find our way back to the blandness of "true" reality.

The difficulty with these two worldviews is not only that their standard is vague and unknowable but also that we humans are stuck in a world of illusion that cannot be trusted to give us any clues about how to get there. It's very difficult to give real-world treatments to those who don't believe they live in a real world. Unfortunately, they view this dis-ease of separation like herpes; it won't kill you, but it will make you exceedingly uncomfortable, and despite all your efforts to alleviate it, it will continue to recur from one reincarnated life to the next.

The Gaia and Mother Earth adherents cannot identify a standard because everything is the standard; the universal spirit cannot be dissected into good and evil. It places them in a very difficult position because they know something is wrong with the world but don't have a coherent worldview foundation from which to identify it.

New Age religion, similar to Buddhism and Hinduism, deals in vague concepts and defines its standard as fulfillment, happiness, and purpose. It treats our discontent as if it was an empty vat that needed to be filled but has conveniently left the dimensions to our own discretion and allowed us to use any toxic material for filler.

Christianity, however, offers an absolute measure of spiritual health and a barometer of spiritual disease. It offers a simple remedy that attacks the source of all your symptoms and has a 0 percent recurrence risk. The Great Physician understood the very good, normal human physiology and the devastating effects of the pathology of evil. The people under His care, however, made a very bad lifestyle choice and swallowed the toxic, evil fruit, which has been eating up their insides ever since.

In a feverish state, mankind began to hallucinate and foolishly concluded his intestinal turmoil was just the birth pangs of a god. Mankind has been found guilty of spiritual malpractice, self-medicating himself with drugs that could only legally be prescribed by the Licensed Healer.

The Chief Complaint

In the practice of medicine, physicians must take several steps to properly diagnose diseases and apply appropriate treatments. The first step is to obtain the chief complaint; the primary reason a patient is seeking medical attention. Next, the physician must obtain a detailed history of the patient's symptom and perform an exam to see if there are any physical signs that can help pinpoint the source of the problem. Once the physician has put all this information together, he or she can make a diagnosis and prescribe the correct treatment. Occasionally, physicians may also need to perform blood work or obtain imaging studies to narrow down or confirm the diagnosis.

If we apply these same sound diagnostic principles to our human dilemma, I believe we can also come up with the correct diagnosis and prescribe the appropriate treatment. Unfortunately, most of the time, we avoid physicians and try to self-medicate. We place Band-Aids on our bothersome symptoms instead of trying to decisively diagnose and treat the problem. We need to take care because our delay or denial may prove fatal.

As is the case with the practice of medicine, every good story also has a chief complaint, a plot conflict or tension that must be addressed. If, as I have suggested, life is just one grand story and we are important characters in it, what's our conflict? What's the chief complaint of our fellow man? In his prologue to *The Hitchhiker's Guide to the Galaxy*, Douglas Adams suggested the problem was mankind's unhappiness. I think this is a fair place to begin.

Unhappiness

During my medical practice, I found the number of pregnant woman who listed depression as one of their medical complaints and were receiving antidepressant medication quite startling. True clinical depression is a medical entity affecting up to 15 percent of the population, but in the neonatal unit, I was seeing it in up to 50 to 70 percent of the cases. As I interacted with these women, it became clear to me I was encountering medicated unhappiness. It signaled a very real problem but one that was cultural, not physiological. Ultimately, we all find chronic unhappiness to be intolerable, but instead of truly addressing the cause, we choose to cover up the symptoms with chemical bandages.

> Man can only endure a certain degree of unhappiness; what is beyond that either annihilates him or passes by him and leaves him apathetic.[95]
>
> —Johann Wolfgang Von Goethe

In the shadows of Stonehenge, at the foot of temples and altars, in town halls, government buildings, schools, churches, and even in small cafes in Rickmansworth, mankind has tried to come up with a workable solution for his unhappiness but time after time has failed to identify its cause. Our human patient has entered the worldview emergency room and told the admitting nurse the reason for his visit is unhappiness. Let's take him back to the exam room and have him take off his cultural street clothes and put on the hospital gown of intellectual vulnerability. We must begin with a detailed history of all his symptoms to determine how his unhappiness has impacted his life. We must then proceed to the physical exam and employ the tools of our trade; an ophthalmoscope to look at the back of his eyes to find out why he's blind to the world around him and an otoscope to see why he's deaf to the truth. We'll push on his cultural belly and try to detect abnormal spiritual growths or enlarged organs of human pride. We'll tap on his knee with the rubber hammer of truth to see if he gives a knee-jerk response or exhibits flaccid indifference. We'll have him say *aaah* and take a look inside because we know that its what comes from the inside that makes him sick and not what comes from the outside. Finally, armed with all this information, we can identify the underlying disease and send him home with the appropriate worldview prescription.

Signs and Symptoms—Misery Loves Company

Most people are generally unhappy and spend inordinate amounts of time and money trying to numb their discontent. Commercial advertisers tell us that if we just had more stuff—a bigger TV, a better sound system, or a cuddly Snuggie—our happiness would be assured. New Age spiritual advocates tell us that if we just unlocked our hidden powers, happiness would be right around the corner. Paradoxically, as we have acquired more material goods and accepted more New Age spiritual guidance, we have become more miserable.

> The surest evidence that evil is not the enemy of meaning is
> this inescapable existential reality: that meaninglessness
> does not come from being weary of pain but from being
> weary of pleasure.[96]
>
> —Ravi Zacharias

You don't have to look very far to find evidence of our unhappiness. The shelves of every bookstore are littered with the feeble attempts of humans trying to rectify this situation. These books all have their fifteen minutes of fame but are quickly placed into the half-price sale bins once our temporary self-help high is over, and we are once again forced to experience the uncomfortable symptoms of unhappiness withdrawal. We frantically scramble for our next self-help fix, prepared to sell anything to score it, even our own souls. We seem to think it better to inject a temporary anesthetic into the painful abscess of our hopelessness instead of draining it of the infection that causes it to fester.

> For what will it profit a man if he gains the whole world
> and forfeits his life? (Matt. 16:26)

In the past, reading self-help books was almost considered an admission of personal weakness, but nowadays, it has become a badge of human pride. Oprah Winfrey made it fashionable to have open discussions about our corporate human angst by sharing the pain in her life and featuring many of these self-help books on her Oprah Book Club. The good news about this trend is that it has taken our human despair out of our stoic closets and encouraged us to wear it on our sleeves, making it fashionable to acknowledge and discuss our shared human unhappiness. It appears that misery loves company after all, but we cannot just stop at the point when we give each other a big hug and cry on each other's shoulders; we must identify the source of our unhappiness and take steps to fix it.

> There seems to be only one area in my life which the
> television camera has not penetrated with its fantasizing
> lens—and that is inside my mind, behind this façade of

my face which I show the rest of you. In here I am not the clever masculine performer I try to be when I am with you. In here I am often alone and uncertain about me and the future and about you and how you feel about me. And since almost all of us know how to appear to be happy and well adjusted from the time we are old enough to sit in front of the tube, any restless sense of incompleteness and loneliness I experience is even more poignant when I look at you.[97]

—Keith Miller

The Blasphemy of Blame

The people on the street who unanimously acknowledged there was a problem with the world would also be quick to offer you a detailed forensic sketch of the perpetrators; the unanimity of the "yes" would soon be dwarfed by the diversity of the possible suspects. In our haste to find the guilty party, we myopically point our fingers at Republicans or Democrats, environmentalists or capitalists, socialists or dictators, the rich or the poor, or even rock 'n' roll or disco.

The problem for mankind is that at the end of every pointed finger is a human being. In his book *God is not Great*, the late Christopher Hitchens tried to lay blame at the feet of religion, boldly proclaiming, "Religion poisons everything." Unfortunately, he dogmatically pointed to all the atrocities committed by the church and neglected to fully disclose those committed by atheists and agnostics. He seemed to think that a body count could somehow be the litmus test for the existence of God, but the only thing I took away from his book was that man is sinful.

> September 11th, 2001 … What should we say? That this merely shows how dangerous "religion" and "spirituality" really are? Or that we should have taken them into account all along?[98]
>
> —N. T. Wright

My last personal computer responded to technical errors by declaring, "It's Not My Fault." How human of us to build self-denial into our technology! Despite our incredible ability to deflect blame, we know the buck has to stop somewhere, but we conveniently place the monetary guilt marker at someone else's feet. Alcoholics Anonymous would be quite proud of our willingness to admit we have a global problem: "Hi, my name is the Human Race, and I'm unhappy," but it would be quite disappointed by our inability to take the next step and assume personal responsibility for our situation.

To minimize our personal guilt, we place a respectable academic veneer on our problem by identifying the consequences of our sinful nature, but we fail to take individual responsibility. We form advocacy groups and institutes to identify the consequences of our fallen humanness but fail to take a deeper look into our own hearts.

Take the Copenhagen Consensus for example; it's a Danish think tank that publicizes the best ways for governments and philanthropists to spend money. They suggest that the ten biggest problems facing the planet are air pollution, conflicts, diseases, education, global warming, malnutrition and hunger, sanitation and water, subsidies and trade barriers, terrorism, and the treatment of women. If you look closely at this list, you will quickly see that man's fallen nature is responsible for each of these issues.

Unfortunately, isolated in our own little social groups, we get all hot and bothered by the sins of others, picking up swords and knives and making a mad dash for them to make them pay for our corporate unhappiness. Our righteous anger has blinded us to the fact that somebody in our own group has forged those weapons in the furnace of their personal anger and unhappiness. If U.N. inspectors were to investigate our little group, I don't think it would be long before they discovered WMDs, weapons of mass depression, hidden in our midst. Instead of honestly looking at ourselves and accepting our personal contributions to these problems, we blame culture, government, religion, and even Twinkies.

I would like, just once, to hear someone say of a man who has left his wife and four fat babies right in the middle of the kitchen floor, not that he's been through a hard time lately, or that his mother was a very complicated woman, or that he's worried about his job, or that he married very young; but simply, "You louse."[99]

—Katherine Whitehorn

You Are That Man

Our postmodern culture recognizes that blaming our fellow man is a very intolerant thing to do, so it blames our culture or society, conveniently shifting Original Sin from the individual to the corporate level. We get ourselves off the hook by creating a straw man to take the fall. When confronted with our sin, we can fashionably blame "some dude." We can survey the world and blame mankind generally without having to look in the mirror individually. The problem with corporate guilt is that it demands a corporate response that ends up looking like endless rules, regulations, and laws. We look to the state to create more boundaries to keep us unruly humans in check instead of having us take personal responsibility and search for the law written on our hearts. Our once-proud identity as independent moral agents created in the image of God is reduced to that of unruly children perilously playing in the day care of the nanny state.

It's interesting how our culture denies sin but is forced to create regulations to curtail its consequences. If we deny Original Sin and ignore personal responsibility, we have only three choices. First, we can try to mop up the consequences of our sinful behavior such as promoting abortion to eliminate the problematic pregnancy of our poorly "conceived" passions. Second, we can elevate bad behavior to majority rule and accept it as the norm, such as providing free contraception to promote promiscuity. Or third, we can replace the really "bad sins" of murder and stealing with the "victimless sins" of gluttony, sloth, and pornography, numbing our guilt with the anesthetic of our carnal desires. If we keep mankind fat and entertained, lounging on the couch, nobody gets hurt.

Unfortunately, this raises a serious question: who foots the bill for our cultural stupor? The government. We already hear rumblings that contraception, drugs, cable TV, and cell phones should be government subsidized. Heaven forbid that a human being go through life without the ability to have protected sex, watch *Toddlers and Tiaras,* or tweet about the rudeness of other people telling them to get a job.

Why do people make such a big deal about government overregulation when micromanaging is the only option left if we deny Original Sin and forgo personal responsibility? It is yet another piece of evidence supporting the Christian notion that godless man is incapable of making things better for himself. If God is left out of the picture, something must take His place for society to limp along, but sadly, it ends up being the ever-expanding laws of government. The fixed moral law that should be written on our hearts is replaced by reams of paper generated by the government to wallpaper over the consequences of our sinful behavior. Until we admit that our inner man is in need of change, we will continue to formulate rules and regulations to minimize the consequences of our outward man.

Ooooh That Smell—Can't You Smell that Smell?

Mankind knows it is flawed but inappropriately uses that knowledge to justify finger wagging and not mirror gazing. Man recognizes sinfulness in a neighbor with a noisy rooster but fails to see it in the mirror when he lies to his spouse or steals pencils from work. We are quite eager to sit in the judgment seat and conduct court, but somehow, we feel we have diplomatic immunity when it comes to our own crimes. G. K. Chesterton put it quite succinctly when he responded to a *London Times* request for essays on the subject of what is wrong with the world.

Dear Sirs:
I am.
Sincerely yours,
G. K. Chesterton[100]

Our keen sense of spiritual smell tells us that something is rotten in Denmark, and we periodically find ourselves downwind of it. We get so overwhelmed by its odor that we indignantly blame our upwind, pungent fellow man, failing to acknowledge our own overpowering contribution. We need to recognize our own dirt and bathe ourselves before we can in good conscience point others to the shower.

Splinters and Logs

> How can you say to your brother, "Brother, let me take out the speck that is in your eye," when you yourself do not see the log that is in your own eye? You hypocrite, first take the log out of your own eye, and then you will see clearly to take out the speck that is in your brother's eye. (Luke 6:42)

Why are we disappointed by the behavior of politicians, pastors, and pop stars? We exhibit our outrage daily on the front page of newspapers, and weekly on the cover of *People* magazine. Why do we care about humans behaving like humans? We seem to have become very comfortable tossing the first stone at the harlot and making someone else pay the price for our corporate guilt rather than taking an honest look at ourselves, dropping the rock, and walking away, convicted by our personal contribution to the general unhappiness of mankind.

> The scribes and the Pharisees brought a woman who had been caught in adultery, and placing her in the midst they said to him, "Teacher, this woman has been caught in the act of adultery. Now in the Law Moses commanded us to stone such women. So what do you say?" This they said to test him, that they might have some charge to bring

171

against him. Jesus bent down and wrote with his finger on the ground. And as they continued to ask him, he stood up and said to them, "Let him who is without sin among you be the first to throw a stone at her." And once more he bent down and wrote on the ground. But when they heard it, they went away one by one, beginning with the older ones, and Jesus was left alone with the woman standing before him. Jesus stood up and said to her, "Woman, where are they? Has no one condemned you?" She said, "No one, Lord." And Jesus said, "Neither do I condemn you; go, and from now on sin no more." (John 8:3–11)

The difference between the response of the stone throwers in this story and our current cultural outrage at the indiscretions of our cultural icons is found in one important detail, the presence of Jesus. Maybe we need a bit more Light of the world to expose the darkness in our own hearts.

Thorn in the Flesh

Why are we so conflicted about our own behavior? Our problem is not just limited to behaving badly but is also found in our inability to exhibit good behavior. We all seem to recognize a standard by which our behavior should conform but find ourselves woefully inadequate to achieve it. We occasionally say and do the right things, but all too often we recognize that our motives are inconsistent and selfish. Even Mother Teresa, despite all the sacrifices she made and all the good she did, was conflicted about her faith and calling.

I do not understand my own actions. For I do not do what I want, but I do the very thing I hate ... For I know that nothing good dwells in me, that is, in my flesh. For I have the desire to do what is right, but not the ability to carry it out. For I do not do the good I want, but the evil I do not want is what I keep on doing. Now if I do what I do not want, it is no longer I who do it, but sin that dwells within me ... Wretched man that I am! Who will deliver me from this body of death? Thanks be to God through Jesus Christ our Lord! (Rom. 7:15, 18–20, 24)

How are we to understand this inner turmoil between wanting to do good and our inability to achieve it? The apostle Paul intimately understood this dilemma and made three crucial observations. First, there is something wrong with mankind; second, we know this because an external standard exists; and third, left to our own devices, we are incapable of changing it ourselves.

Paul was refreshingly candid about the pervasiveness of this problem in his life and didn't hide behind a veneer of holiness. He freely admitted he was no different from his audience because he also experienced a painful thorn in the flesh. God pointed out, however, that it was through Paul's weakness that God's power was made manifest. Paul discovered that the gospel is good news not because it gives us an instruction manual on how to achieve salvation by ourselves but because it tells us that Somebody else did it for us. Despite our intractable sinful state, God intervened on our behalf and did what we could never do for ourselves.

> So to keep me from being too elated by the surpassing greatness of the revelations, a thorn was given me in the flesh, a messenger of Satan to harass me, to keep me from being too elated. Three times I pleaded with the Lord about this, that it should leave me. But he said to me, "My grace is sufficient for you, for my power is made perfect in weakness." Therefore I will boast all the more gladly of my weaknesses, so that the power of Christ may rest upon me. For the sake of Christ, then, I am content with weaknesses, insults, hardships, persecutions, and calamities. For when I am weak, then I am strong. (2 Cor. 12:7–10)

Whitewashed Tombs

The Pharisees tried to solve this problem by putting a shiny, holy veneer on their "particle board" faith. They thought if they could just hide the inner sinful self under a fancy, "holy" exterior, the problem would be solved. Jesus, however, was never about the outside appearance; He was always about the inner motive. He pointed out that their whitewashed tomb-marketing scheme was doomed to failure because they didn't understand the needs of the religious consumer. The Pharisees thought the people just wanted more wax to shine their coffins, but Jesus knew the people needed someone to give their decaying corpses of unhappiness a new life.

> Woe to you, scribes and Pharisees, hypocrites! For you are like whitewashed tombs, which outwardly appear beautiful, but within are full of dead people's bones and all uncleanness. So you also outwardly appear righteous to others, but within you are full of hypocrisy and lawlessness. (Matt. 23:27–28)

God's power was not revealed through deceptive displays of holiness but through the broken confessions of sinners. The Romans crucified Jesus on a hillside so everyone would fear their power. Ironically, this apparent exhibition of Christ's weakness in the face of the Roman state was the most profound display of God's power the world had ever seen. Jesus visibly took on the thorns of weakness in everyone's flesh to demonstrate God's power at work. Perhaps one of the reasons the early Christians were persecuted was because the Roman state was so angry that this small band of countercultural people had the gall to use the cross, a symbol of Roman power, as a banner for their own kingdom.

I will never forget a meeting I had with a forty-year-old developmentally delayed pregnant woman whose fetus had been diagnosed with a congenital diaphragmatic hernia, a disease that carries a very poor prognosis. The purpose of our meeting was to discuss the expected hospital course, potential complications, and the risk of death or impairment to her baby. Her developmental disability was the result of physical abuse she had suffered as a child at the hands of her mother. I tried to help her understand the seriousness of her baby's condition by making my explanation as simple as possible. I asked her if she had any questions, and she dropped a bombshell; her major concern was that she was afraid she would physically abuse her baby as her mother had abused her! She was afraid she would become just like her mom!

I was devastated by her honesty. I have probably dealt with hundreds of parents who came from abusive childhoods, but I have never had one person voice the fear of becoming an abuser themselves even though the statistics suggest that abuse victims are at a higher risk of adopting that sort of behavior.

Her disability had removed any social filters, giving her the freedom to speak what was truly in her heart. How poignantly sad and yet refreshingly honest! This woman knew the source of her problem and didn't want to inflict the same crime on another innocent life. She wore her Original Sin on her sleeve, speaking what most of us think but socially hide. This simple woman had more wisdom than most of us will acquire in a lifetime; she admitted she was a sinner in need of help.

Split Personality

As man has become progressively more clever, he has acquired the uncanny ability to separate ideas from reality. We frequently quote authors and promote their philosophies and yet neglect the fact that those philosophies didn't work out very well for the authors themselves. Nietzsche, who committed suicide, has been elevated to the status of a postmodern philosophical hero. We now conveniently separate the lies and deceit of politicians' personal lives from their ability to govern. When did personal character become irrelevant to philosophy? It happened when we began to deny that sin even existed. We have effectively eliminated the moral yardstick needed to measure the effectiveness of ideas. It's like taking our broken car to a mechanic who has his own theory about how car engines work but has never successfully fixed one. We see his shop full of unrepaired cars piling up daily but see him cling to the unrealistic idea that his car engine theory has merit.

In reality, when our cars need fixing, we go to the most qualified mechanic, one who has demonstrated a philosophy of car repair that actually mends broken automobiles. So why, when it comes to worldview philosophies, do we seem to think results are irrelevant?

> But pastors can be so reluctant to use the word "sin" that in church we end up confessing nothing except our highly developed capacity for denial.[101]
>
> —Kathleen Norris

Horsey Noises

> For my sighing comes instead of my bread, and my groanings are poured out like water. For the thing that I fear comes upon me, and what I dread befalls me. I am not at ease, nor am I quiet; I have no rest, but trouble comes. (Job 3:24–26)

I am a chronic sigher. If things don't go as planned or a new wrinkle is thrown into my carefully crafted agenda for the day, I invariably let out a pained sigh. In the neonatal unit, the charge nurse referred to them as my "horsey noises." She would bring me some sort of bad news, and I would take a deep breath and exhale over vibrating lips, allowing my equine dissatisfaction to be known to all. While my sighs may be more audible than yours, I know I'm not alone; we all sigh to one degree or another. Even creation groans.

> For we know that if the earthly tent we live in is torn down, we have a building in heaven that comes from God, an eternal house not built by human hands. For in this one we *sigh*, since we long to put on our heavenly dwelling. Of course, if we do put it on, we will not be found without a body. So while we are still in this tent, we *sigh* under our burdens, because we do not want to put it off but to put it on, so that our dying bodies may be swallowed up by life. Now God has prepared us for this and has given us his Spirit as a guarantee. Therefore,

we are always confident, and we know that as long as we are at home in this body we are away from the Lord. (2 Cor. 5:1–6, emphasis added)

What do these sighs and groans tell us about ourselves? It implies that life should be better than the way we usually experience it. We have a feeling, contrary to what beer commercials tell us about "not getting any better than this," that life *should* be better than this. Something is missing. We believe there should be peace and harmony in our families, jobs, and the world. The Hebrew word for this is *shalom*, which implies more than just the absence of conflict or war; it suggests harmony on an even grander scale, a sense that everything is right in God's world. The cacophony of our corporate sighs should alert us to the very real danger of the wide path to destruction and motivate us to take out our scriptural GPSs and find the road to the narrow gate of shalom.

> Enter by the narrow gate. For the gate is wide and the way is easy that leads to destruction, and those who enter by it are many. For the gate is narrow and the way is hard that leads to life, and those who find it are few. (Matt. 7:13–14)

Is That All There Is?

> The world is neither fair nor unfair. The idea is just a
>   way for us to understand …
> So some survive. And others die. And you always want
>   a reason why
> But the world is neither just nor unjust [102]
>
> —Robert Smith

Robert Smith ironically formed an alternative rock group called The Cure, but perhaps he should have more accurately called it The Problem, because he is very good at identifying our sadness, pain, and hopelessness but concludes that life has "no rhyme or reason." I have always enjoyed his music because it has helped me express my general unhappiness, a chance to corporately lament with others. Questioning and lamenting are not anathema to our Christian faith; on the contrary, they have been incorporated into Holy Scripture. We find this despair in Psalms, Lamentations, and the prophets. The difference between the angst of The Cure and the angst of the prophets is that Robert Smith accepts it as the norm while the prophets recognize it as an aberration—lamenting despair versus lamenting hope.

Unfinished Symphonies

> In the torment of the insufficiency of everything attainable we come to understand that here, in this life, all symphonies remain unfinished.[103]
>
> —Karl Rahner

Also contributing to our unhappiness is the unrealistic expectation that we can find contentment in this world. We try to ink the final score to our life symphony but are disappointed by our amateurish attempts at composing. We hear Mozart's requiem in our heads but are capable of penning only the score for "Mary had a Little Lamb." Where did we get the idea that life is a symphony anyway? It certainly didn't come from us because we seem incapable of writing one. So what do we hear in our heads? Augustine understood this dilemma when he wrote, "You have made us for yourself, Lord, and our hearts are restless until they rest on you." Most people have probably experienced the brief sensation that everything was right in the world. Christians would describe that sensation as the "peace that passes all understanding." Maybe it's during those moments of serenity that we hear a few more chords of our unfinished symphony, movements we didn't write but that make us long for more. Maybe God has the finished score in His hands, and if we sincerely attempt to find our rest in Him, He will hum us a few more bars.

Our culture, however, has become very adept at telling us it doesn't matter what your personal life song sounds like just as long as you make sure you keep the volume down so others can dance to their own tunes.

The illusion of our musical adequacy is easily sustained when we're surrounded by a group of like-minded, life-symphony-challenged musicians, but it is very difficult to sustain when we are alone and are confronted by our inability to replicate the symphonic masterpiece emanating from the temples of our souls. It is easier to keep the lie alive when we have a media machine pumping in the elevator music of artistic deceit.

> Don't pour "Lie"ter fluid on the embers of despair.
>
> —Jordan Strandness

Big Bang Theory

> Therefore, my beloved, as you have always obeyed, so now, not only as in my presence but much more in my absence, work out your own salvation with fear and trembling, for it is God who works in you, both to will and to work for his good pleasure. (Phil. 2:12–13)

Our unhappiness frequently takes us to the extremes of human experience. We look for the fireworks and listen for the sounds of the carnival in hopes of finding contentment. We want it big, loud, flashy, and exciting because we know our restlessness is so big and all-consuming. We are so mesmerized by the Vegas lights Satan has hung along the way that we fail to see the pathway leads to hell. Deceived by the dizzying array of sound and light, we fail to hear that still, small voice, "Be still and know that I Am God." We seem content to party in the court of the Gentiles instead of taking the risk of tying a rope around our ankles and nervously entering the Holy of Holies to gaze upon the face of God. Is there any more-extreme, adrenaline-generating sport than working out your salvation with fear and trembling?

> Modern persons will never find rest for their restless hearts without Christ, for modern culture is nothing but

the wasteland from which the gods have departed, and so this restlessness has become its own deity; and, deprived of the shelter of the sacred and the consoling myths of sacrifice, the modern person must wander adrift, vainly attempting one or another accommodation with death, never escaping anxiety or ennui, and driven as a result to a ceaseless labor of distraction, or acquisition, or willful idiocy. And where it works its sublimest magic, our culture of empty spectacle can so stupefy the intellect as to blind it to its own disquiet, and induce a spiritual torpor more deplorable than mere despair.[104]

—David B. Hart

Funny How Falling Feels Like Flying ... For a Little While

I was goin' where I shouldn't go, seein' who I shouldn't see, doin' what I shouldn't do, and bein' who I shouldn't be, a little voice told me it's all wrong another voice told me it's alright. I used to think I was strong but lately I just lost the fight. Funny how fallin' feels like flyin' for a little while.[105]

—Jeff Bridges

When you parachute out of an airplane or bungee jump off a bridge, you get the same sensation you would if you were flying— the thrill of the wind rushing past your body and freedom from the constraints of life on land. These experiences are thrilling, however, only when you have a cord tied to your foot or a parachute strapped to your back. Sin is the same way; it feels great when you're experiencing it but gets quite frightening when you frantically reach for a rip cord and find none. The serpent tempted Adam and Eve to experience the thrill of divine flight by assuring them they wouldn't hit bottom: "Surely God did not say you would die." Unfortunately, mortal men cannot take that God-plunge and live no matter how much they flap their feeble human arms.

> Disciplines and restraints, then, liberate us only when
> they fit with the reality of our nature and capacities ...
> In many areas of life, freedom is not so much the absence
> of restrictions as finding the right ones, the liberating
> restrictions.[106]
>
> —Timothy Keller

Why does sin feel like freedom? Why do so many people disparage religion, pointing out all the rules that will surely limit their independence? When you read Genesis, you realize God gave Adam and Eve a tremendous amount of freedom: "Feel free to eat from any tree you want, all I ask is that you avoid just one particular tree, just one single tree." He forbade only one tree! Why did He do that? He did it because He wanted them to have freedom and knew this one tree would curtail that freedom. Once we obtained the knowledge of good and evil, we spent an inordinate amount of time suffering for the consequences of our thoughts, words, and deeds. Satan's promise of knowledge that would allow us to soar to godlike heights has permanently grounded us. While a whole forest beckoned, we chained ourselves to one tree, but even more remarkably, we deluded ourselves into believing that being shackled to that one tree was freedom. We were the victims of a drive-by fruiting. So I ask you, which state is freer?

> To be free does not mean to be great in the world, to be
> free against our brothers and sisters, to be free against
> God; but it means to be free from ourselves, from our
> untruth, in which it seems as if I alone were there, as if I
> were the center of the world; to be free from the hatred
> with which I destroy God's creation; to be free from
> myself in order to be free for others.[107]
>
> —Dietrich Bonhoeffer

I once heard the great Christian theologian R. C. Sproul quote an atheist friend of his who said, "It is good to be an atheist until it comes time to die." Atheists feel free during their lifetimes because they're not beholden to a manipulating deity or a religious institution.

The problem is that once they near the ends of their lives, they find all their years of freedom are powerless to change the totalitarian rule of death. Maybe that's why our culture spends so much time trying to get us to read books and buy products that create the façade of eternal youth. If we could just look in the mirror and see a face without wrinkles or a scalp with more hair, we might be able to hide the symptoms of the only disease without a cure, death.

Why would we evolve the ability to be anxious about something so inevitable? One could argue that fear would be the ultimate manifestation of the drive for survival, but then why, when death is imminent, do we wish we had reconciled with an old friend, been a better parent, or found a way to serve mankind? People on their deathbeds don't ask themselves why they weren't faster, stronger, or more cunning; they end up asking themselves why they weren't more vulnerable. Isn't that odd? Wishing you had been more vulnerable in life sounds like a terrible evolutionary idea!

> You cannot play with the animal in you without becoming wholly animal, play with falsehood without forfeiting your right to truth, play with cruelty without losing your sensitivity of mind. He who wants to keep his garden tidy doesn't reserve a plot for weeds.[108]
>
> —Dag Hammarskjold

The financial statement for your unhindered, sinful lifestyle is coming due, and you are forced to fumble through your pockets for enough spiritual change to pay the bill. You are forced to admit you have insufficient funds, and so you try to take out a second mortgage on your body by undergoing facelifts, tummy tucks, and Botox treatments. Unfortunately, when the bill arrives, you're left with nothing but a shiny plastic credit card that has exceeded its limit, and a collection agency that says, "This very night your life is demanded of you."

> For although they knew God, they did not honor him as God or give thanks to him, but they became futile in their thinking, and their foolish hearts were darkened.

Claiming to be wise, they became fools, and exchanged the glory of the immortal God for images resembling mortal man and birds and animals and reptiles ... because they exchanged the truth about God for a lie and worshiped and served the creature rather than the Creator. (Rom. 1:21–23, 25)

The Shadow Proves the Sunshine (Switchfoot)

It seems that the main thing we have learned from centuries of bad behavior is that we need to be skeptical of the motives of every human being. We have awoken from our utopian dream. Don't get me wrong; man has done many good and wonderful things, but his sinful nature always seems to get the upper hand. We created antibiotics and then in our desire to make a buck overuse them and encourage bacterial resistance. We admirably invent antidepressants to treat depression and irresponsibly use them to medicate unhappiness. Our good intentions always seem to have a dark side, casting a shadow over our human existence.

Every morning you should wake up in your bed and ask yourself: "Can I believe it again today?" No better still, don't ask it till after you've read The New York Times, till after you've studied that daily record of the world's brokenness and corruption, which should always stand side by side with your Bible. Then you can ask yourself if you can believe in the Gospel of Jesus Christ again for that particular day. If your answer is always yes, then you probably don't know what believing means. At least 5 times out of 10 the answer should be No because the No is as important as the Yes, maybe more so. The No is what proves your human in case you should ever doubt it. And then if some morning the answer happens to be really yes, it should be a Yes that's choked with confession and tears and ... great laughter.[109]

—Frederick Buechner

We need to give up our search for the perfect politician, pastor, or pop star and recognize that sainthood is ultimately God's power found in human weakness and not our own personal superhuman strength to resist sin.

> Most people come to the church by a means that the church does not allow.[110]
>
> —Flannery O' Connor

We should not abandon our attempts at becoming "Holy like He is Holy"; we need to redefine what a saint truly is.

> A Saint is just a sinner who is more repentant than most of us.[111]
>
> —Benedict Groeschl

> A new definition for a saint: a "life giver" who makes others come alive in a new way, a garden variety human being through whose life the power and glory of God are made manifest even though the saint himself may be standing knee-deep in muck.[112]
>
> —Phillip Yancey

We need to remember that God's intentions for mankind were good. He created Adam and Eve in His image, designed with a holy architectural plan. The vision went awry when Adam and Eve decided they wanted to get into the divine architectural business themselves. They began making structural alterations that were not up to code, and as their next of kin, we continue to receive citations from the County Planner. Not content to keep their questionable construction company to themselves, they established an architectural school that has graduated many a bad contractor since. We continue to foolishly hire subs that are not holy bonded and licensed. We construct cheap tenements that house cheaters, liars, and prostitutes instead of building temples suitable for the Holy Spirit to dwell. We engage in our own postmodern housing modifications and seem surprised that even an asthmatic wolf could huff and puff and blow them down.

All I Need Is This ... Paddle Game ... Lamp ... That's All I Need

Douglas Adams suggested that even the technological amusement of digital watches could not alleviate our unhappiness. Acquiring material stuff to make us happy is nothing more than failed electro-shop therapy. If you are an atheist, you have no spiritual place to turn for relief and are forced to resort to the only things you say are real, the physical world. Your therapy becomes sex, shopping, and maybe a good cup of coffee. You can momentarily soothe your pain, but once your material pleasure session is over, the overwhelming sadness quickly returns. You passionately chase what you think will make you happy only to find that when you obtain it, it's never up to the task. You continue to climb the peaks of pleasure, but every time you reach a summit, all you get is a better view of the rapidly moving arctic storm of unhappiness heading straight your way. As you take stock of your ability to weather the coming storm, you realize all you have on is a Margaritaville T-shirt, flip-flops, and a bottle of beer. You have a breathtaking view of the coming tempest but tragically little to protect you from its devastating power.

> It is not pain that has driven the West into emptiness; it has been the drowning of meaning in the oceans of our pleasures.[113]
>
> —Ravi Zacharias

The Bible refers to us as strangers, pilgrims, or sojourners in this land, hinting that we need to be mobile, carrying with us only what we need to survive. We need to be attentive to the sights along the way but resist the temptation to buy cheap souvenirs from the shady vendors. If it doesn't feed or clothe our souls, it's ultimately useless and just adds unnecessary weight to our life backpacks.

In the movie *The Jerk*, Steve Martin's character is distraught by a breakup with his girlfriend, and he's forced to leave their shared home. As he makes his way to the door, he keeps stopping to pick up useless objects, reciting the same benediction with each item, "This is all I need." He continues to accumulate useless stuff to the point that he cannot carry any more, and the scene closes with the pathetic shot of a man dressed in his bathrobe, pants indiscreetly wrapped around his ankles, arms full of useless junk, mumbling to himself that he has all he needs.

The Tyranny of Titillation

We all seem to bristle at the demands, rules, and regulations of authority. We don't like being told what to do or how to behave, but we fail to recognize the tyranny imposed on us by pleasure. Our instinctual distaste at being controlled is anesthetized by the deceptive authority of self-gratification. George Orwell, in *Animal Farm*, wrote about the horror of a utopian state controlled by violence. Aldous Huxley, however, in a *Brave New World*, described a utopian state ruled by pleasure. They are both totalitarian rule, but the latter comes with a sensual anesthetic that numbs the painful fact that its citizens are slaves.

We swallow the pleasure pill and become addicts consumed with the need for the next fix. Huxley has in essence described the postmodern worldview—millions of people addicted to their own truths and fed by a government that knows it can keep them under control by establishing a cultural needle-exchange program. Stay stoned but alive. If all members of society are high enough and tolerant enough, they will be indifferent to the irritating behavior of others. Society becomes a crack house filled with stoned pleasure addicts so intoxicated that they couldn't care less about their neighbors. Tolerance works only if you can anesthetize the ability to respond to the bothersome Original Sin found in your neighbor.

Tachyphylaxis

In medicine, we frequently encounter a physiological phenomenon called tachyphylaxis. It is the progressive resistance of the body to the effects of a particular medication that necessitates steadily increasing doses to achieve similar effects. We see this phenomenon most frequently with the use of opiates. Frequently, a labor and delivery nurse would inform me that the mother of one of the babies in my care was requiring doses of pain medication far beyond the norm. The nurse would be concerned that the mother was most likely an addict who had induced her own tachyphylaxis to opiates through narcotic abuse.

Karl Marx once called religion "the opiate of the masses," but I argue that the true opiate of the masses is materialism. Our consumer culture has induced a material tachyphylaxis in our lives that prevents us from ever becoming content with our material possessions. We can't wait to get the next generation cell phone, computer, blender, or backscratcher. We are duped into believing the next technological advance will make us happier, smarter, stronger, or better looking.

I remember many a time heading to the music store to find some new music that would give me some psychic pain relief when I was sad or stressed out. My vast CD collection, however, never was up to the task. Jesus spoke frequently about the dangers of material possessions, and instead of offering us wine on a sponge to kill the pain, He asked us to chew and swallow the bitter, cross-shaped pill of our own sinful lives.

Our culture tries to make the pill of materialism palatable by making it taste like candy, just like the cherry-flavored Luden's cough drop I took as a child. I don't know if it ever worked, but it sure tasted good.

Gag Me!

Our souls cry out to be fed with spiritual food, but we inexplicably try to force-feed it material delicacies such as cars, watches, computers, and phones. Our souls gag! Why, if we are made of material stuff as the evolutionist claims, does such stuff never completely satisfy? Why would material beasts try to find solace in spiritual things if they weren't also composed of spirit? Maybe we need to listen to the words of the great spiritual dietician St. Paul, who recommended an all-fruit (of the Spirit) diet consisting of large portions of "love, joy, peace, patience, kindness, goodness, faithfulness, gentleness, self-control" (Gal. 5:22–23).

We don't have to recklessly gorge ourselves on the world to apprehend this truth because the "stuff will make you happy" experiment was already performed and published in that timeless research journal, the Bible. The scientific paper of interest to us is entitled Ecclesiastes; it was authored by the leading world expert on material possessions, King Solomon. He spent hours tirelessly researching the long-term benefits of wine, women, and song but in the end found them to be statistically insignificant.

> Vanity of vanities, says the Preacher; all is vanity. (Eccl. 12:8)

He concluded his study by declaring that the only thing that will ultimately satisfy is God.

> The end of the matter; all has been heard. Fear God and keep his commandments, for this is the whole duty of man. (Eccl. 12:13)

Hold on! When I channel surf the waves of religious television, I hear preachers telling me God wants me to be rich. They tell me if I just planted a little money seed I would harvest a monetary tenfold crop. Doesn't God want to give me stuff to make me happy? Didn't God reward people in the Old Testament with material possessions? While it's true there were many Old Testament characters with substantial financial portfolios, they were always treading on a slippery slope that usually ended in disaster. Jesus made it clear that wealth was a major obstacle to salvation, and He even had the nerve to suggest it would be the poor who would inherit the kingdom. He praised those who gave away their stuff and declared that we cannot serve both God and money.

When Jesus appeared to his disciples after the resurrection, he revealed the scars of suffering on his wrist, not the Rolex of prosperity. He asks us to wear a crown of thorns and carry a cross on our backs. Jesus didn't come with money, medicine, housing, and food stamps for the poor and afflicted; He did, however, perform physical healings but then left the people in the same social circumstances in which He had found them. Instead of giving them better jobs or more money, He said, "Your sins are forgiven." He knew the only thing that would save them was the forgiveness of sins.

Those who are financially well off walk on treacherous ground and must constantly ask themselves how they can get the huge camel of wealth through the eye of the salvation needle.

Money, however, is not the only excess baggage that can impede our passage through the narrow gate. We also need to be vigilant about how we use our God-given talents and avoid the temptation to supersize our spiritual gifts to God-sized portions and instead seek to be diligent stewards of our own little happy meal talents.

> The tragedy of sin is that it diverts divine gifts. The person who has a genuine capacity for loving becomes promiscuous ... the person with a gift for passionate intensity squanders it in angry tirades.[114]
>
> —Kathleen Norris

Confession Booth

Why do most of us feel guilt to one degree or another? Why do we feel the need to apologize? We act and think as if we have offended someone or damaged a relationship. We ask ourselves why we're not better parents, friends, siblings, coworkers, or human beings. Graham Greene's novel *The Quiet American* concludes with the main character lamenting his life of misery and moral failure: "How I wish there existed someone to whom I could say I was sorry." Our guilt suggests we feel accountable to someone. Maybe we recognize that deep down inside we have tarnished the image of God in which we were created.

In his book *Blue Like Jazz*, Donald Miller wrote a chapter, "Confession," that I think helps us understand some of this guilt. He describes the annual festival at Reed College called Ren Fayre, which was just an excuse to get naked, drink, and take drugs. He and a group of Christian friends wanted to do something special for this event and agreed to set up a confession booth, but it was no ordinary confession booth. Instead of hearing the confessions of the largely pagan student body, he and his Christian friends were the ones who did the confessing. They apologized for the fact the church had not behaved very Christlike and how they had personally fallen short of the example of Jesus. As I read this story, I realized I carry around a lot of corporate and individual guilt for failing to adequately represent Christ. I find myself perpetually embarrassed by the Christian machine and how it fails to live up to the teachings of Jesus.

> The pure clean water of spiritual truth is placed in rusty containers, and the subsequent failings of the church down through the centuries should not be projected onto the faith itself, as if the water had been the problem ... Would you judge Mozart's The Magic Flute on the basis of a poorly rehearsed performance by fifth-graders ... No, a real evaluation of the truth of faith depends on the looking at the clean, pure water, not at the rusty containers.[115]
>
> —Francis Collins

What evidence do we Christians offer to the world that would prompt it for even one moment to consider the gospel good news? If we are perceived as just more clowns in an endless procession of Christian hypocrites, we've done a disservice to the Great Commission. Christianity is not just one more religious information booth; it is a confessional booth, a booth in which we can freely admit the tragedy of our shared sinfulness but gloriously celebrate the possibility of redemption.

> I once thought Christians went through life burdened by guilt, in contrast to carefree non-believers. I now realize that Christians are the very people who can go through life free of that burden.[116]
>
> —Phillip Yancey

One of the interviewees in the "Truth Project" series made an interesting statement: "Truth is the absence of guilt." Is it possible not to feel guilt, to have a clear conscience? Christianity is ultimately the only worldview that even makes that possible.

> This is an illustration for the present time, indicating that the gifts and sacrifices being offered were not able to clear the conscience of the worshiper ... let us draw near to God with a sincere heart in full assurance of faith, having our hearts sprinkled to cleanse us from a guilty conscience and having our bodies washed with pure water ... Pray for us. We are sure that we have a clear conscience and desire to live honorably in every way. (Heb. 9:9; 10:22; 13:18)

We feel the need not only to apologize but also on occasion the need to say thank you. Unfortunately, thankfulness is a much more difficult sentiment to express. We are quite vocal when we don't have enough stuff but are disturbingly mute when we have all we need. Scarcity makes things more precious, while abundance makes us take things for granted.

Why is abundance a problem? Surrounded by abundance, we should be abundantly thankful. I fear we are more thankful when we receive something scarce than when we are blessed beyond our means to comprehend. As the Hebrew people wandered the desert, they complained about a scarcity of food and water and forgot to be thankful that God had delivered them from slavery. We seem to have a very short memory for blessings but like an elephant never seem to forget a perceived wrong.

The Dissonance of Cognition

Our unhappiness is not just dismay at the bad or incompetent behavior of our fellowman. We also have a general uneasiness about our own existence. A fancy term for this psychological phenomenon is cognitive dissonance, a phrase that refers to anxiety caused by the conflict between the way things are and the way we think they should be. Our personal beliefs and the reality of God's world are frequently at loggerheads, and we end up living a contradiction. We live in God's world yet continually try to claim it for our own. We are engaging in the absurd, like scratching da Vinci's signature off *The Last Supper* and signing our own. We spend most of our lives trying to explain God's world on our own terms and cannot stomach the inconsistencies of a worldview created in our own image. We need to drop our spray paint can and stop trying to tag God's creation with our own graffiti.

> What is this despair? It arises from the abandonment of the hope of a unified answer for knowledge and life … Modern man has given up his hope of unity and lives in despair—the despair of no longer thinking that what has always been the aspiration of men and women is at all possible.[117]
>
> —Francis Schaeffer

Innocence Lost

One of the ways our culture acknowledges that something has gone horribly wrong with this world is the way we value childlike innocence. We seem to think it's good to shield our children from the disappointing despair of adulthood. Our society gets extremely bent out of shape when it encounters child pornography, slavery, or abuse. We are moved to tears when we hear about toddlers dying of cancer or AIDS.

I distinctly remember the point in my life when I realized I had left my childlike innocence behind. It was in a movie theater in Omaha during medical school. I went to see the movie *The NeverEnding Story*, about a young boy mythically resisting the oppressive darkness of the "nothing" of adulthood. In the movie, the little boy succeeded, but seated in that dark theater, I realized I had failed. I could no longer cling to fantasy because I had to care for people who were facing the reality of death and disease. It felt like the oppressive weight of the fall had landed directly on top of me, crushing my innocence and leaving me helpless as I watched the life-giving blood of my youth trickle away.

If we are just animals on the playground of life, lobbying the natural selection captain to be chosen for the best team in evolutionary dodge ball, why do we venerate the naïve innocence of the child who has a stick in his hand and is pretending he's a brave knight fighting dragons? Wouldn't it be better if our youth stopped the evolutionarily perilous practice of reading *The Hobbit* and instead picked up some weights and started pumping iron in the "world's" gym to be fiercer competitors? Wouldn't it be a better child-rearing strategy to hand our babies spears and read them excerpts from *Call of the Wild* instead of giving them pacifiers and reading them *My Little Bunny*?

Evolution has no need for innocence, and in fact, innocence is for sissies: "There's no crying in evolution." The fact we recognize a state of innocence that abruptly changes with adulthood seems to suggest an innocent life once existed and we have since become "lost unto this world."[118]

Theophobia

Atheists and agnostics frequently point out that Christianity has too many rules. They cannot in good conscience shackle their freedom to the capricious rules of a judgmental deity. We've all heard this argument before, but let's take a closer look; what exactly are the rules they find so oppressive? I suspect that most people think that don't murder, don't commit adultery, don't steal, honor your father and mother, and rest one day a week are pretty good ideas and that they may even form the backbone of a civilized society, so what's their real objection? The rub comes with the first three commandments; you shall have no other gods, don't worship idols, and use the name of God respectfully.

Mankind is quite reluctant to relinquish the throne to the real King. He has become so accustomed to indulging every whim that the posture of a servant seems quite unappealing. How dare someone ask us to get the knees of our designer deity jeans dirty with the soil of service! Wouldn't life be much better if God were dead?

> Whither is God? He cried. I shall tell you. We have killed Him - you and I. All of us our His murderers ... How shall we, the murderers of all murderers, comfort ourselves? What was holiest and most powerful of all that the world has yet owned has bled to death under our knives. Who will wipe the blood off us? What water is there for us to clean ourselves? What festivals of atonement, what sacred games shall we have to invent? Is not the greatness of this deed too great for us? *Must not we ourselves become gods simply to seem worthy of it?* There has never been a greater deed; and whoever will be born after us-for the sake of this deed, he will be a part of a higher history than all history hitherto.[119]
>
> —Friedrich Nietzsche (emphasis added)

Friedrich Nietzsche, while ultimately thinking that God's death was a good thing, understood that if mankind killed God, the throne could not be left vacant. Man would have to take charge and assume all the divine responsibilities. This raises a very important question: which human being would you nominate for the position of God, someone qualified to be in charge of the cosmos? You're not alone; I can't think of anyone either!

When we empty the heavenly throne room, a power struggle ensues, and without a deity, people, just like you and I, clamor for a spot on the divine seat. We engage in a cosmic game of musical chairs, circling the one remaining divine seat, waiting for the heavenly chorus to stop, and we cringe as we see the chaos that ensues once the music ends. The annals of history are replete with the tragic tales of humans who tried to fill the God void by making themselves divine.

> [Commenting on the Holocaust:] That this was conceived and nurtured in the mind of the most educated nation at that time in history and brought forth on the soil that had also given birth to the enlightenment almost defies belief. But it was atheisms legitimate offspring. Man was beginning to live without God ... the attackers of religion have forgotten that these large-scale slaughters at the hands of antitheists were the logical outworking of their God-denying philosophy. Contrasting, the violence spawned by those who killed in the name of Christ would never have been sanctioned by the Christ of the Scriptures.[120]
>
> —Ravi Zacharias

Poor Reflections

> Man had pre-eminence over all the brutes; man was only sad because he was not a beast, but a broken God.[121]
>
> —G. K. Chesterton

Could the reason we humans are so sad be because deep down we know we were created in God's image but look in the mirror and see only evidence to the contrary? The Darwinist says we should be happy because we are the most highly evolved animals, but instead, we are miserable because we feel more like broken gods.

We all seem to recognize our unhappiness stems from falling short of some internal idyllic standard. We were told in school, however, that we came into this world as blank slates and that we write our stories day by day as we get older. But why then are the entries in my life diary full of angst, fear, and sadness? Why would I fill my slate with things that make me so unhappy? If I am merely writing my own worldview as I mature, why does it feel so inadequate? And how do I know it's inadequate unless a standard exists by which to measure it?

God Complex

We are creatures not content just to forage for food but are passionately driven to do odd things that have no evolutionary advantage at all, such as collecting stamps, painting pictures, and making wine. We frequently step outside of our physical state and assume the role of curator, investigator, or creator; we are compelled to transcend our existence. The Microsoft word dictionary defines *transcend* as "to exist above and apart from the material world." No other creature is capable of soaring to transcendent heights. We all enjoy spending time in transcendent orbit, admiring the view from our lofty position, commenting on the immanent busyness below, but we all ultimately have to undergo reentry. We simply don't have enough oxygen, fuel, or power to maintain orbit very long, so we either burn up upon reentry or try to minimize the damage to the tiles of our personal spiritual space shuttle.

We look for purpose, meaning, and fulfillment in this transcendent state, but instead of being grateful for moments of spiritual weightlessness, we seem to focus more on the pain of reentry; our happiness and satisfaction are burned away by our return to the world of physical immanence.

> Once you accept the existence of God—however you define him, however you explain your relationship to him—then you are caught forever with his presence in the center of all things. You are also caught with the fact that human beings are creatures who walk in two worlds and trace upon the walls of their caves, the wonders and the nightmare experiences of their spiritual pilgrimage.[122]
>
> —Morris West

Conclusion

We have entered the Worldview ER and told the intake nurse our chief complaint was unhappiness. She ushered us to the exam room, where we discussed the symptoms of our discontent such as misery, myopia, sighing, hopelessness, and lack of fulfillment. We identified some of the physical manifestations of our unhappiness such as blame, thrill seeking, self-help book reading, and denial. We have undergone a thorough spiritual and physical exam. We wait nervously for the doctor to return and give us our diagnoses. He sheepishly knocks on the door and hesitantly enters with a handful of lab reports and MRI scans. He looks us in the eye and tells us that our condition is very serious and that we will need further testing to make specific diagnoses and render appropriate treatments. Stunned, we flash back on our diagnostic mountain journey.

We remember the visit to our friendly atheist who told us our desire to climb Mount Transcendence was really nothing but the tickle of neurochemicals and synapses in our brains. He recommended focusing on our material existence and enjoying as many physical "valley" sensations as possible.

Undaunted, we hiked to the top of a particularly steep mountain to consult with a Buddhist monk about our problem. He at least acknowledged a spiritual realm but told us our unhappiness was due to an unhealthy attachment to the valley life below. He told us the sooner we gave up our desires for purpose and meaning in the world, the sooner we would experience corporate transcendence.

As we descended the mountain, we ran into a Hindu who was gracious enough to hear our complaints and offer some sage advice. He told us we had taken some important first steps by recognizing the divine sparks within but told us the real cause of our unhappiness was the guilt we felt because our "divine spark" books were overdue and the "Brahman" library wanted them back. Unfortunately, there were thousands of branches to return them to, but none seemed to know where the central library was.

Tired and frustrated by our inability to get coherent diagnoses, we stopped to rest in a town made of beautiful crystals and pyramids in the foothills of the great mountain. As we sought lodging for the night, we saw a cute little shop that advertised happiness, fulfillment, and purpose. We entered and spoke with the New Age shopkeeper who told us we didn't need to make any more perilous spiritual hiking journeys to find transcendence because it could be found in the safety of our own homes. He graciously offered to sell us his book and video series and told us that when we got back home, we could lie on our couches, crack open some beer, pop in his DVDs, and think positively divine thoughts.

It sounded so appealing at the time, but we remember that when we got back home, the child we had loved with all our heart and soul still died of leukemia, and despite visualizing wealth and prosperity, we were still fired from our job because of corporate downsizing.

Suddenly, we are jolted back to reality by the sound of the doctor clearing his throat. He tells us that this dis-ease was not contracted from the dirty toilet seat of society but is actually a rapidly growing cancer that has metastasized to every organ of our lives and is steadily eating away at our souls. He makes it clear that time is of the essence and we need biopsies to get a specific tissue diagnosis and institute the proper spiritual chemotherapy.

Once the doctor has left the room, we take a deep breath, sit back, and begin to reflect on all the time we wasted with other alternative worldview health care providers. We reflect on all the false diagnoses they gave us and nervously ask ourselves, are we too late?

Chapter Eight

PATHOLOGY REPORT

I T HAS BEEN A WEEK since our biopsy, and the pathology report is ready. We nervously wait in the doctor's office to discuss the final diagnosis. He soberly enters the room and takes a seat. Holding our hand, he looks us in the eye and tells us the tumor is clearly malignant and is of the Original Sin variety. He tells us that if left untreated, it will be fatal and offers the only known cure, Chemo-Christ-Therapy.

Trying to be informed consumers, we impatiently ask for a thorough description of how this "Jesus Juice" works. But our physician, not wanting to get into the therapeutic details yet, first reviews all the past incorrect diagnoses we have received and explains in detail why they fail to cohere with the pathological findings he holds in his hands.

Of Fish and Rabbits

Floored by the seriousness of the diagnosis, we ask ourselves, *how could we have been so deceived? Did we just hear just what we wanted to hear, or were we taken in by a bunch of quacks? We were led down many a bunny trail and tossed many a red herring. What was their appeal?* These are important questions, so let's take a closer look and see why those trails led nowhere and the herring smelled so fishy.

Atheism is of the belief that our signs and symptoms are psychosomatic in origin. They represent our emotional inability to accept the cruel but ultimately wise ways of our evolutionary creator. In our rush to self-medicate, we turn to the "opiate of the masses" and end up even unhappier as religious hypochondriacs.

> We must also confront the fact that evolution is, as well as smarter than we are, infinitely more callous and cruel, and also capricious.[123]
>
> —Christopher Hitchens

Oddly enough, in the opening paragraph of *The Hitchhiker's Guide to the Galaxy*, Douglas Adams implicates the evolutionary process itself as the source of our unhappiness. Random chance had somehow produced transcendent creatures with existential crises, beings capable of stepping outside their creatureliness and critiquing the wisdom of their own evolutionary creator. Mankind quite unexpectedly had evolved the need for a psychiatrist's couch, which is hardly a fitting place to be when the survival of the fittest rages on outside the confines of the doctor's office.

Buddhism identifies the problem as *dukkha*, or suffering, which is brought on by a desire for the illusory permanence of the physical things of this world. Hinduism says that the problem is our failure to recognize the divine spark within, which prevents us from getting off the relentlessly spinning wheel of karma. Dizzy and nauseated we end up losing our divine cookies.

Buddhism and Hinduism share the belief that man is not inherently bad, just deluded. The world becomes a battleground between divine reality and physical illusion. While they both encourage physical acts of kindness and compassion, they recognize they are just tools to facilitate the extinction or absorption of our illusory egos. The "salvation" end points for Buddhism and Hinduism, nirvana and Brahman respectively, don't personally care about what we do in this life because they are both impersonal entities. In both these traditions, "salvation" is optional because we always get another chance.

Proponents of New Age religion share the Eastern belief that man possesses an internal divine spark but differs on where that spark originates. They tend to locate the divine essence in each person rather than connect it to the Hindu impersonal oneness or the Buddhist nirvana. Instead of considering individuality as an illusion that must be extinguished, New Age religion promotes the fine-tuning of our inherent personal divine nature. New agers don't consider humans to be bad but just underdeveloped deities. Pantheism is frequently incorporated into New Age religion, but it spreads the divine spark equally throughout all nature and explains our unhappiness as arrogant attempts to overstep our spiritual bounds, grieving this universal spirit.

It's interesting that all these belief systems ultimately connect the problem to mankind, but instead of insisting on a specific diagnosis, they tolerantly consider every possible second opinion to be viable. They all believe that mankind has the power to fix himself. They fail to recognize the need for targeted therapy and instead just offer a big group-hug over our shared corporate human unhappiness. Mankind has a potentially fatal disease that these alternative practitioners are incapable of properly diagnosing or treating, but does Christianity do any better? Does the Original Sin diagnosis hold up to careful scrutiny?

Help! I've Fallen and I Can't Get Up!

We all recognize this world falls short of some standard; work seems so hard and inefficient, childbirth is painful, and relationships with spouses, children, and neighbors are incredibly difficult to maintain. We see destruction caused by tornadoes, lives lost at the hands of rogue bears, and children sickened by poison mushrooms, but we don't blame nature for the world's problems, we blame mankind. Why?

Christianity recognizes that man is the problem and boldly asserts, unlike the other worldview pretenders, that he is incapable of fixing himself. Christians are called to admit their sinfulness, accept the consequences of their actions, and recognize they cannot remedy the situation without outside help. Christianity cuts through the fog of human deception with the high beams of reason by acknowledging that if man is the problem, he cannot be his own solution.

With great clarity, the Bible tells us what we already know but have conveniently tried to bury. God set the stage and made a good physical creation. He then took His "image of God" blueprint and created mankind. He seamlessly combined the physical dust of the earth with the breath of His own Spirit to create a unique physical and spiritual being capable of bridging the gap between God and His creation. Man is therefore unique for two important reasons: he was created in God's image and he is God breathed.

Walter Brueggemann places a lot of emphasis on the biblical description of God's life-giving breath by implying that mankind can be understood only in relation to God's infused spirit and not as individual biological entities. "The human person is to be understood in relational and not essentialist ways."[124] We became God's chosen intermediary between a spiritual God and a physical universe. We are not a separate body and soul but a unified physical and spiritual essence. Just like the air we breathe is incorporated into every cell of our bodies, so the spirit is inseparable from our physical being.

Atheists spend a lot of time trying to disprove God's existence scientifically, using evidence from the physical world, but they are ultimately dismissed by the majority of people because they can't explain why man acts so darned spiritual. The reason atheism has been adopted by such a small percentage of people and why postmodernism came into being is because people know they are spiritual. Until the atheist can satisfactorily explain away our spiritual nature, the public will continue to indulge its spiritual side by reciting mantras, meditating in monasteries, and joining religious groups. The standard scientific response that spiritual feelings are merely chemicals secreted in our brains just doesn't fly with the vast majority of people. They want a spiritual answer to their spiritual questions.

Mankind was unique because God had created a being that had responsibility for something other than itself. He had commanded the animals to be fruitful and multiply, but it was man He commanded to subdue, have dominion, and work and care for His garden. Therefore, any complaints from the planet could be directed to God's personal representative in the world.

Accountability for the welfare of the planet was placed in the hands of mankind, which was a pretty sweet gig when things were going according to God's plan, but the whole thing went south when man decided to take matters into his own hands. The Bible makes it clear we are experiencing a different type of "global warming." Man placed himself in the hot seat by defoliating the Tree of the Knowledge of Good and Evil, and the temperature continues to rise with each new innovative sin refinery he builds.

The rules of the blame game, however unreasonably we see them currently played out, state that you can implicate a creature only if he has been given responsibility. The fact that the finger pointing we see every day is directed only at man seems to indicate man is unique and uniquely responsible. This proposition is troubling for the atheist and pantheist alike. The atheist clings to the notion that man is nothing more than a highly evolved animal whose personal survival takes precedence over every other evolutionarily inferior life form. But since survival of the fittest is the engine of evolution, it can hardly be implicated as the mastermind behind the crimes against humanity.

Pantheists, believing every physical thing is infused with the same amount of universal spirit, cannot claim the environmental high ground without charging man with the crime of divine arrogance because they then also simultaneously make the universal spirit an accessory to the crime.

As I mentioned before, the pantheist doesn't have the worldview credibility to consider man either the supervillain or superhero in our ecological battles. You can't blame man for ecological disasters and then expect him to fix it unless you recognize he is a unique transcendent being who is somehow in charge.

In their desire to get man to clean up after himself, pantheists have subconsciously assumed that despite his evil tendencies, mankind has the power and responsibility to make things better, or dare I say, very good, which, unfortunately for them has a bit of a biblical ring to it, don't you think?

You Can't Handle the Truth!

> And the Lord God commanded the man, saying, "You may surely eat of every tree of the garden, but of the tree of the knowledge of good and evil you shall not eat, for in the day that you eat of it you shall surely die." (Gen. 2:16–17)

God established the moral law in the garden with one simple prohibition: do not eat from the Tree of the Knowledge of Good and Evil, because that knowledge was reserved for God alone. The whole forest was available to Adam and Eve, so why did God forbid one particular tree? I think He did it for several reasons. First, it was a reminder that their relationship was not one of equals and therefore needed boundaries similar to the distinct rules and regulations we place on our children to maintain the parent-child relationship. We don't put our teenagers in charge of our checkbook or credit cards, we screen the video games they play, and we regulate the books and magazines they read because we, unfortunately, have a working "knowledge of good and evil" and understand the consequences of using it improperly. While our teenagers may perceive these rules to be harsh and oppressive, we know we are protecting their welfare. We know that when these boundaries are chronically violated, the family breaks down, and we may need to call in Dr. Phil to restore order.

The second reason is that God knew that a mortal creature could never completely understand the big "God" picture. Man was incapable of completely comprehending what it meant to be God and as such was incapable of handling the knowledge of good and evil. In the movie, *A Few Good Men,* Tom Cruise plays Lieutenant Daniel Kaffee, an inexperienced U.S. Navy lawyer trying to get to the bottom of the death of a lower-echelon marine, William Santiago. His investigation leads him all the way up to the prominent senior military leader, Colonel Nathan Jessup, played by Jack Nicholson. In a tense courtroom scene, Kaffee pushes Jessup to admit he had ordered a code red, an unauthorized punishment administered outside the judicial system, that led to Santiago's death. Finally, Nicholson's character comes unhinged, and he blurts out the classic line, "You can't handle the truth!" He explains that there are things military leaders such as himself know that puny subordinates such as Kaffee don't know, can't know, and don't want to know, and that this knowledge ultimately keeps our country safe. Kaffee felt he was appropriately pursuing justice, but Jessup made it clear Kaffee didn't understand the larger global safety picture in which this tiny drama was being played out. He declared that Kaffee's lesser rank made him incapable of understanding the bigger picture and comprehending the complexities of the conflict between good and evil. Kaffee wanted to eat from Jessup's tree of knowledge of good and evil but was in such an inferior position that he could never understand the power of that knowledge.

Adam and Eve, just like Kaffee, wanted knowledge they were incapable of handling, and God, just like Jessup, flat-out told them they couldn't handle the truth.

Before you start making pilgrimages to see miraculous images of Jack Nicholson on a burned tortilla, I want to make it clear I recognize this as an imperfect analogy, but it highlights the issues of relationship boundaries and the limits of knowledge in the hands of those who cannot understand its proper use.

Fallout

Unfortunately, despite being warned, our first ancestors disobeyed God's command and took a big bite of forbidden knowledge, and their offspring have been trying to floss ever since. Fruit remnants have become lodged between our teeth, eroding the enamel and leaving us with a mouthful of sin cavities. If this episode represents more than just some kids stealing apples from a tree, what does it mean, and why is it even important in this whole worldview discussion? This event is referred to as the fall, but it begs the question, from what height did Adam and Eve plummet, and why are their offspring still scurrying to climb back up?

God created a beautiful world and declared it to be very good, but in a twist of narrative narcissism, the characters rebelled against their Author and created a manuscript mess. The cartoon characters took hold of the Artist's pen and tried to write their own script without any understanding of the grammar of divinity. Not surprisingly, the characters found the pen too heavy and the brush too unwieldy, and instead of painting a masterpiece, they succeeded in producing only a childish finger painting of their own vision of the world.

> God had written, not so much a poem, but rather a play;
> a play he had planned as perfect, but which necessarily
> been left to human actors and stage managers, who had
> since made a great mess of it.[125]
>
> —G. K. Chesterton

I'm reminded of the time my wife placed a beautiful, animal-shaped cake in front of our eldest daughter on her first birthday. Stunned by the incomprehensible stupidity of her parents for placing it within arm's reach, she paused briefly to lend a respectable air of artistic appreciation to the occasion and then punctured a hole through its artistic façade by submerging her hands in it, squishing it through her fingers, and in a flurry of postmodern inspiration, took the frosting and finger painted her face and hair. My wife's elaborate creation was reduced to a sticky mess that found its way into every crack and crevice of my child's body. In fact, the birthday celebration had to be followed by a ritual purification bath because we knew if we didn't make her ceremonially clean, she would quickly raise an unpleasant aroma to the gods.

We, like our one-year-olds, have taken God's beautiful gift and made an absolute, sinful mess of it and are also in need of a good scrubbing before our pungent pride becomes unbearable.

Whether or not a man could be washed in miraculous waters, there was no doubt at any rate that he wanted washing. But certain religious leaders in London, not mere materialists, have begun in our day not to deny the highly disputable water, but to deny the indisputable dirt.[126]

—G. K. Chesterton

Even in Christian circles, we seem to have an inadequate understanding of what exactly this "indisputable dirt" is. We all know we have ignored and broken many rules and regulations, but we still have a hard time wrapping our heads around how they all fit together under the heading of "Original Sin." Surely, there must be a simpler way of making sense of it all? I think there is, but we have to go back to the garden and carefully walk through the crime scene to better understand exactly what went down on that particular *fall* day.

Adam and Eve broke God's command not to eat of the tree, but it was more than just breaking a rule; at its core, it was really about the first couple saying to God's face they found His idea of relationship boundaries unsatisfactory. The Original Sin was, in fact, a Dear John letter hand-delivered to God. In essence, Adam and Eve said, "We want more! We kind of like the look and feel of your throne and find the lawn chair at your right hand a bit uncomfortable." Once man partook of the knowledge reserved for God alone, the God-man relationship was forever changed, and mankind was foolishly emboldened to look God in the eye and say, "You're not enough for me." All sin, therefore, can be traced to a simple desire to be like God, which in the process severed the only truly loving relationship we would ever know. It was as if Adam and Eve were heaven's country bumpkins content to climb trees, name animals, and farm the land. Then one day, the kid with the motorcycle, leather jacket, and snakeskin boots rides into town, saunters up to Adam and Eve, cigarette dangling from his mouth, and says, "You guys are a pair of dweebs. Don't you wanna be cool like me? C'mon, break a few rules, fight the power, and cut school. It's Ferris Bueller's day off, so go have some fun and do anything you want."

Unfortunately, Adam and Eve's unique opportunity to learn God's 4-H skills was replaced by detention and expulsion before they even had a chance to graduate, and mankind has been half-heartedly trying to earn his GED, God's Eternal Devotion, ever since.

> The Lord saw that the wickedness of man was great in the earth, and that every intention of the thoughts of his heart was only evil continually. And the Lord was sorry that he had made man on the earth, and it grieved him to his heart. (Gen. 6:5–6)

Unfortunately, the seriousness of Adam and Eve's infraction is frequently downgraded to a youthful indiscretion, just two mischievous kids running around the garden of Eden with scissors in their hands and yelling with their outside voices. Sin is not just a minor violation of a set of arbitrary rules such as running a red light; it's far more serious. It's actually more like stealing the keys to God's Ferrari and driving it in a demolition derby. How could God ever trust us with His stuff again?

The Emperor Has No Clothes

"Wow, I really love this garden. We have everything we need. We even get to stroll with God. How great is that? You know what, though, I wish I knew what was going on in His head. I bet if I had the same mind as His, the same knowledge, our walks would be better and our discussions even deeper. I bet He might even like that. I know He said it was a bad idea to eat from that tree, but it possesses the knowledge I need to understand Him. Chomp, chomp. Whoa! I'm feeling rather woozy. What a divine head rush! You know what, His throne looks pretty comfortable. I think I'll try it out. Wow, this is really cushy, and just look at the view! I can see for miles. I bet He wouldn't let me share His throne with Him, so I think I'll send Him on an errand and lock Him out for a while so I can try out this king-of-the-universe thing. Wow, I kinda like this. I feel so regal!"

All of the sudden there's a knock on the door.

"Who is it?"

"It's me—Gabriel. I need to let you know about a developing problem in the kingdom. By the way, your voice sounds kind of weak."

"Yes … well … I have a cold! What's the problem?"

"Well, Sire, people are dying of a terrible plague. They need your help."

"No problem. I just invented antibiotics, and they work great."

"Sire, the people also need energy to play Angry Bird and watch cable television."

"No problem. I just invented atomic energy. That should allow them to see *Gilligan's Island* reruns for thousands of years."

Gabriel flies away, seemingly content with the answers he had received, and the "new emperor," feeling quite emboldened, pats himself on the back for his great success.

His regal rush, however, is interrupted by even more feverish banging on the door.

"What's the problem now?"

"Sire, you remember those antibiotics you invented? They have created resistant bacteria, and now people are dying by the millions. And also, remember that atomic energy you invented? Well, your people have turned it into a nuclear weapon and are threatening to blow up the planet. What are you going to do?"

"Oops. I hadn't really thought about that. Let me get back to you."

Mankind quickly steps off the throne and yells out the window, "God? Where are you? I need your help. I can't do this alone. I tried to do your job and created a huge global mess. I'm on bended knee. Will you help me, please?"

God replies, "I thought you'd never ask!"

The serpent tempts Adam and Eve with knowledge reserved for God alone by convincing them it will make them divine. The problem, however, is that God's knowledge in the hands of mere mortals is dangerous; knowledge of fire becomes napalm, the information superhighway dead ends at the XXX bookstore, and atomic energy becomes atomic weapons capable of destroying the world.

> In all this he suffers from the inevitable knowledge that his time is a time in which it has become possible for man to destroy not only life but also the possibility of rebirth, not only of man but also mankind, not only for periods of existence but also history itself. For nuclear man the future has become an option.[127]

> —Henri Nouwen

We continue to try to scale Mount Holiness and place ourselves on God's throne, but we quickly find that the air's too thin, the weather's too extreme, and the cliffs are too steep. However, we persist in our rebellion and bivouac on the slopes, a pimple on God's holy mountain.

Your Cheatin' Heart

What Adam and Eve may have envisioned as coregency became a cosmic coup. There's room for only one sheriff in town, and instead of accepting our roles as deputies, we took to the hills and became outlaws. We initiated the breakup with God and brazenly posted we were "available" on our Facebook pages. We had the nerve to woo other lovers in front of His face, rubbing God's nose in the excrement of our idolatrous promiscuity. As it turned out, our real sin was breaking up with the lover of our souls. Astonishingly, God wants us back and will go to any extreme to reunite us with Him!

We so often get so fixated on sins as rule violations that we fail to recognize these infractions are just manifestations of a more serious offence, rejecting our relationship with God. Generally speaking, we are not outraged when someone steals a pencil from a large, faceless corporation, but when infidelity poisons a relationship, we become incensed. Consider the media infatuation with the adulterous affairs of church leaders, politicians, and celebrities. It appears that even the secular world finds infidelity an offense worthy of a technological lynching.

Isn't it interesting that long before *People* magazine, the Old Testament recognized the seriousness of infidelity and used it to characterize our broken relationship with God? God is described as being jealous for His chosen people. The relationship between God and man is frequently described as one between spouses, and God's anger is provoked when man is unfaithful. The Bible likens man's rebellion to cheating with a prostitute.

> Therefore say to the house of Israel, Thus says the Lord God: Will you defile yourselves after the manner of your fathers and go whoring after their detestable things? (Ezek. 20:30)

The chosen people have a very difficult time staying faithful to their first love. They occasionally make valiant attempts at relationship reconciliation but end up grieving God's heart even more. The Old Testament is full of descriptions of God's people serially cheating on Him by constructing idols and worshipping in the high places. Even on the rare occasion when they tried to reconcile themselves to God, they did so half-heartedly, extending an olive branch with one hand while hiding the symbols of their infidelity behind their backs with the other. How would you feel if your spouse cheated on you and tried to reconcile over dinner, but he or she was wearing a necklace or a watch that had been a gift from the ex-lover? What if the place you met to rebuild your relationship was the same "High Place" where she or he had begun the affair? What if, after a temporary separation, you move back in together only to find your unfaithful partner wants you to live with your ex-lover's cat?

Sin is a broken relationship. Perhaps we will take it a little more seriously if we recognize we have grieved the heart of the only One who unconditionally loved us in the first place. How can we choose to be eternally entertained in the strip club of idolatry when our true Spouse waits patiently at home for our return? Isn't it remarkable that a God who needs nothing from us and to whom we are incapable of giving anything patiently takes all the grief we can throw His way and still doggedly pursues us?

The Angst of the Arborist

The Genesis account describes two specific trees, the Tree of Life and the Tree of the Knowledge of Good and Evil. God did not forbid the Tree of Life; apparently, its fruit would allow one to live forever. The Tree of the Knowledge of Good and Evil, however, represented the relationship boundaries between the Creator and the created. Adam and Eve didn't like the idea of limits on their relationship and were willing to risk death to be like God.

Once they took that fateful step, the relationship was forever changed. God could no longer take His daily stroll with walking partners who arrogantly blazed their own paths rather than allowing Him to lead them by the hand. They had violated the holy relationship parameters, and God had no choice but to practice tough love, expel them from the garden, and send them to teen boot camp. Just like a tearful parent with a rebellious child, He implored them to "make good choices" as He watched them step outside the garden gate.

> The Lord said to Cain, "Why are you angry, and why has your face fallen? *If you do well, will you not be accepted?* And if you do not do well, sin is crouching at the door. Its desire is for you, but you must rule over it." (Gen. 4:6–7, emphasis added)

Man, a little bit perturbed at being expelled, crossed his arms, turned his back on God, and said, "Fine! I don't need your stinking paradise anyway. I can build my own garden. In fact, I have a little God knowledge of my own, so I'll do it myself."

We have been trying to construct our own garden ever since. Not learning our lesson, we strategically place the knowledge of good and evil in the center, but instead of placing warning signs around it, we make it wheelchair accessible so everyone has the opportunity to drop a coin in the vending machine of evil. Attracted by the glimmering treats inside, we feel compelled to sample every item in the machine, but then we start feeling sick because our brief sinful sugar high has been replaced by the hypoglycemic crash of consequence.

I remember eating one-pound bags of peanut M&Ms before big tests in college and medical school to alleviate my stress. I would get a lovely, one-hour celestial tour through sugar heaven only to endure the painful reentry into test-anxiety purgatory. The stress I had tried to pacify would return accompanied by the added weeping and gnashing of nausea and headache.

As we curl up into our little fetal ball of gastronomical misery, holding our stomachs because of the pain of sinful indulgence, we flash back to a better time in Eden, a time when we would anxiously listen for God's footsteps and like little puppies run to our Master's feet in anticipation of our daily walk.

Jolted back to reality by the harsh conditions we brought upon ourselves in exile, we try to get back at God for barring us from His garden by returning the favor and restricting His access into our own little gardens. We naively place a security force of "idolatrous angels" at our gate, flashing their flaming swords of greed, lust, and power, denying entry to the only One capable of saving us.

> Dear God,
> Why do you allow so much violence in schools?
> —A concerned student.

> Dear concerned student,
> I'm not allowed in schools.
> —God.

Forbidden Fruit

You may ask, "Why would God place a tree that contained the knowledge of good and evil in the garden in the first place? I thought God was only good. I thought He was love. Why was the knowledge of evil allowed to grow in God's garden?" The answer is simple. God knew that for good to exist, there had to be the possibility of evil; in the same way, for love to exist, the possibility of no love had to exist. True relationship can occur only if there is the possibility that it will not be chosen. For God, however, "evil, no love, or no relationship" were only potentialities, not actualities. The possibility for them existed, but God would never manifest them or act upon them because they were contrary to His nature. God didn't create evil, only its possibility. Mankind, on the other hand, lacking divine wisdom, was unable to handle this knowledge and made "evil, no love, and no relationship" realities. Mankind opened the Pandora's box of evil potential and actively released it upon the world.

> [God] created the fact of freedom; we perform the acts of freedom. He made evil possible; men made evil actual.[128]
>
> —Geisler and Brooks

We all struggle with the question of good and evil; we don't have to be Christians to feel this tension. Why do we generally recognize only two choices, a good choice and a bad choice, a right choice and a wrong choice? Why don't we think more in terms of a sliding scale of choices, a continuum of outcomes? We all seem to think in terms of this dichotomy. Choices are consequential. Isn't it interesting that this idea of consequential choice is so quickly identified and thoroughly explained in the opening chapters of the Bible? If we all just evolved, how did we come up with only two basic options? Why not a billion shades of gray?

The basic question confronting man seems to be, "Why do I do bad when I feel deep down I should be good?" Only the Bible really describes this situation; it explains why the world is good, why man makes it very good, and how the two-pronged choices of good and evil, love or no love, relationship with God or no relationship with God, make everything bad.

Even a non-Christian can relate to Paul's anguished cry. We are all plagued with guilt for not meeting certain standards, but standards must be established ahead of time before guilt is possible. A moral standard is a preexisting condition. In the opening chapter of the Bible, God set the bar by declaring the work of His hands to be good. Evolutionary theory suggests that there are no fixed standards, that life is merely the incessant adaptation to ever-changing conditions. Yet it seems that despite the ever-shifting cultural currents, we always seem to try to navigate by an omnipresent North Star.

Atheists claim that God was created in the image of man and offer the gods of the Greek and Roman pantheon as prima facie evidence. They point to the fact that these gods behave just like flawed human beings on steroids. The problem with this theory, however, is that the Judeo-Christian God is nothing like those gods; He represents something that man is not and could never hope to be. So you have to wonder if maybe the Judeo-Christian God came first and established the criteria upon which all "gods" should be judged. He is in fact the preexisting moral standard upon which we base our behavior.

Curses

God's initial warning to Adam and Eve about consuming the forbidden fruit was that they would die. Sadly, they ignored His warning, and God had to elaborate on all the details. He made it clear they wouldn't physically die right away but would suffer the consequences of their rebellion, which He described in a series of curses called down upon each of the guilty parties. He addressed the serpent first.

> Because you have done this, cursed are you above all livestock and above all beasts of the field; on your belly you shall go, and *dust you shall eat all the days of your life*. I will put enmity between you and the woman and between your offspring and her offspring; he shall bruise your head, and you shall bruise his heel. (Gen. 3:14–15, emphasis added)

The serpent would be the most cursed of creatures, restricted to a life that could be nourished only by the physical, the flesh or dust of the world. God created man from the dust of the earth but

215

breathed "Spirit" into him. It appears from this description that the primary way for the serpent to exercise authority over man was through the dust, the physical side of life.

As we are all quite aware, the most powerful force hindering our relationship with God is the temptation to establish our own earthly kingdom and seat ourselves on its throne. The physical acts of self-worship—sex, money, power, and exploitation—get us in trouble. In essence, we struggle with the desires of the flesh. Satan has no true spiritual power to coerce us but seems quite capable of physically manipulating us. You may ask, "But what about Devil worship? Isn't that spiritual control?" I argue, however, that the foundation of demonic worship is based on the glorification of the sins of the flesh.

Another interesting aspect of this idea of the serpent being restricted to crawling in the dust is that God told Adam and Eve they would also return to the dust when they died. Satan, as the dust dweller, exploited this idea because he knew that at death our eternal destiny was fixed, and if he could switch the tracks of our life train, we might end up pulling into Hell's Canyon instead of Grand Central Heaven.

Paul further explained this concept by describing sin as the sting of death. Your eternal destiny train ticket will be marked either with sin or a cross, depending on your travel choice. Sin stings because it determines your eternal destination—no refunds or return trips, and the ticket office at Damnation Station is always closed.

If the serpent can distract us from thinking about death, "Surely you will not die," maybe he can make us forget about the all-important afterlife leg of our journey. If he can deceive us into believing our spirit will be released into whatever nebulous, godlike state we fancy, then we've "got a ticket to ride, but [we] don't care" about the final destination.

Satan, however, conveniently withholds a crucial piece of information: eternal life comes in two flavors—the bitterness of eternal separation from God, or the sweet taste of eternal relationship with the Divine. Satan's proximity to the dust from which we were partially formed and to which we will ultimately return makes us vulnerable to his sting if we don't take precautions.

> There are no ordinary people. You have never talked to a mere mortal ... but it is immortals whom we joke with, work with, marry, snub and exploit—immortal horrors or everlasting splendours.[129]
>
> —C. S. Lewis

To Eve, God said,

> I will surely multiply your pain in childbearing; in pain you shall bring forth children. Your desire shall be for your husband, and he shall rule over you. (Gen. 3:16)

I have been to hundreds of deliveries and can attest to all you males out there that childbearing is a painful experience. While during the delivery, the woman may express fondness for her husband and the obstetrician; she reserves her most heartfelt praise for the anesthesiologist who is the only one capable of temporarily reversing the "curse" with an epidural incantation. God's remarkable blessing upon mankind to populate the earth through the womb of women ends up becoming a curse. The promise to be fruitful and multiply still applied, but it came with the reminder that human birth without God in the delivery room is a very painful experience.

The second part of the feminine curse involved changing the unique complementary role the woman was designed to play next to her husband. Women would be distracted from maximizing their God given feminine potential and attempt the absurd and try to be more like a man. As politically incorrect as it may be to say this, God created man and woman unequally. This inequality, however, was not based on value, rights, or potential but on the unique biological, emotional, and spiritual gifts that distinguish a male from a female. These differences were never designed to separate a man from a woman; they were designed to create a far greater mystical unity than was possible from their individual spiritual parts. A man or a woman in isolation is woefully incomplete, but when the two become one, you can see another manifestation of the "image of God." God made it clear: "It is not good for man to be alone." This was not because man needed a servant; he needed a uniquely gifted partner of equal value to help him understand exactly what a God of relationship is truly like.

While the woman's rights movement has been an important force in correcting the exploitation and repression of woman, it ironically has done it in a way that made men look more superior in the process. Who are the big winners in woman's liberation? You might say the women, but if you look closely, you have to conclude that it is the men. Why would I say that? Let's take a look at some of the attitudes fostered by these organizations and see how they make men the standard. Pregnancy is almost considered a curse that limits a woman's ability to have sex without consequence. It strangely elevates the ability of a man to irresponsibly engage in promiscuous behavior without having to serve nine months of gestational hard labor to the level of some sort of desirable male diplomatic immunity.

Raising a child at home is often looked upon as a menial task foisted on women by their cruel male taskmasters. Where did we get the idea that raising the future movers and shakers of this planet was better done by third-party day cares? Child rearing is considered a hindrance to achieving career potential. Professional ability is measured by success in traditionally male jobs. In the end, victory for woman's lib, oddly enough, is measured by a *man*-ometer. Here you have a movement designed to empower women and yet you set the bar at male achievement. Ironically, women's liberation has been taken prisoner and placed in a man-cave. Shouldn't the empowerment of women focus on that which makes women unique?

How sad to view womanhood as estrogen poisoning that must be treated with a testosterone patch. Personally, I find women far superior to men in most respects. God also seemed to think women were pretty darned important as well since He placed the fate of the human race in their nurturing wombs. Abortion, contraception, and pornography enslave woman; they demonize the womb, promote inconsequential sex, and view anything uniquely feminine as mere lurid entertainment for men.

When we violate the sanctity of the womb, we unwittingly remove the last human safe house on the planet, and every womb becomes a potential tomb. We offer fetal sacrifices to the god of inconsequential sex. Women should be free to pursue any line of work they choose, be paid equally, and have the same opportunity at promotion as men, but equality with man is a far cry from honoring that which makes women special. I think I speak for most men when I say this world would be a much bigger mess if it were composed solely of men.

To Adam, He said,

> Because you have listened to the voice of your wife and have eaten of the tree of which I commanded you, "You shall not eat of it," cursed is the ground because of you; in pain you shall eat of it all the days of your life; thorns and thistles it shall bring forth for you; and you shall eat the plants of the field. By the sweat of your face you shall eat bread, till you return to the ground, for out of it you were taken; for you are dust, and to dust you shall return. (Gen. 3:17–19)

God's words to Adam began by cursing the ground. Fallen man had taken nature down with him. God's mandate to care for the garden remained but would be carried out in a hostile wilderness. Man would be confronted by his fallenness every time he pulled a weed, tilled the soil, or harvested a crop. Caring for the planet would be difficult, and man's dominion would become confused with exploitation. We groan, and nature groans with us because of the consequences of Adam's sin. We desire to enter God's rest but find that the "to do" list grows longer every day.

Who Turned Out the Lights?

It's easy to get frustrated over the apparent inability of the world to accept the truth of the gospel. We get discouraged by the expanding, oppressive darkness but forget that darkness has no real power on its own. Darkness and light cannot coexist; light will always trump darkness, and darkness becomes an entity only when light recedes.

Even the unreligious see the expanding shadow cast by the excesses of our culture. Without Jesus Christ, they try to illuminate their dull lives with the ambient light of their electronic devices, hoping those feeble little LEDs will keep the darkness at bay. Unbeknownst to them, it ends up inviting the shadows of violence, pornography, greed, and power into their homes. The lamp of the Holy Spirit in their souls has been extinguished, and there aren't enough multimedia lights in the world to restore light to their ever-darkening souls.

We Christians tend not to be very helpful to those lost in the dark because we selfishly take the Light of the world and restrict its use to illuminating our personal spiritual homes. We pull the shades so we don't have to see the cultural darkness outside. The only hope for the world is to take the Light outside our homes and watch as the darkness recedes!

Conclusion

You may have found all my talk of serpents, fruits, and gardens a bit hard to swallow. You can quibble with me over temptations and trees, but you still have to ask yourself, "Does this describe my human situation?" The creation and fall of mankind in Genesis 1–3 perfectly describes what we see every day, people who are spiritual and physical, good and evil, people who strive to achieve a certain standard of behavior but seem woefully inadequate to achieve it.

Genesis 1–3 also describes a God who did not create a master-slave or boss-employee relationship but a relationship between a parent and a child, husband and wife, author and character. Sadly, the child rebelled, the wife had an affair, and the character went rogue. In the end, doesn't your unhappiness feel more like a relationship gone bad than guilt associated with a few broken rules?

We have a dis-ease that exhibits a variety of signs and symptoms. We have gone to unlicensed practitioners and become the victims of spiritual malpractice. Our religious medicine cabinets are full of placebos that have done nothing to alleviate our symptoms.

Much to our relief, we have finally found a Christian practitioner who has taken this diagnostic journey seriously. Employing the latest spiritual technology, He ordered the CT scan of Scripture and found, to our dismay, that we suffer from a particularly aggressive "sin" cancer that has metastasized to every organ in our bodies. We have seen the official pathology report and know the prognosis is grim unless we undergo some gospel chemotherapy.

The good news is that this regimen kills only the cancerous cells of sin and leaves the anatomical infrastructure of the image of God intact. All you need to do is allow God to place the IV of salvation and infuse a dose of redemption into your veins.

The cure, however, can be administered only if you sign the treatment consent form. You have a choice: waste your time seeking help from alternative medical soul healers, or agree to the only therapy that has undergone the rigorous scrutiny of salvation science, the transforming power of Jesus Christ. The ultimate soul Surgeon asks you one simple question: "Do you want to be healed?" (John 5:5–6).

> All is of God; the only thing of my very own which I contribute to my redemption is the sin from which I need to be redeemed.[130]
>
> —William Temple

221

Chapter Nine

CONFLICT RESOLUTION

T HE DIRECTOR SLUMPS IN HIS celestial armchair, lets out a
deep sigh, and mutters, "My actors have become a rebellious,
stiff-necked bunch quite content to pursue their own storyline
rather than the one I spent an eternity planning for them. They
have foolishly tried to become their own authors and rewrite their
parts instead of truly appreciating the nuanced characters I created
them to be. They have exchanged my glorious original script for
deceptive improvisation. Instead of looking to Me for their lines,
they have opted to take suggestions from the audience. I offered
them a glorious catered cast party, and they settled for half-priced
drinks and free peanuts at the bar.

"What can I do? I've poured my heart and soul into these
characters, and I feel they're just as much a part of Me as I am of
them. I'm so sad because I see that many of my cherished characters
have improvised their lives to such an extent that they've dug
a personal narrative hole they cannot climb out of, created a
metaphor they cannot escape, and wrote a poem that doesn't
rhyme. How can I get them to remember the good old garden days
when they sat at my feet, spellbound by every word I spoke?

"How can I restore our relationship and get them to see that
every one of them is indispensable to My story? I need to get them
out of their dark, dingy, smoke-filled improv club and back into
my open-air theater. I know that the bright Son shine may initially

hurt their eyes, but once they get used to it, the world will once again sparkle.

"I've got it! I'll add a plot twist that will blow their minds! I'll write Myself into one of the scenes. I'll empty Myself of my author's prerogative and become one of the characters. I will walk among them and tell them little stories that will refocus them on My bigger story.

"I'll go to the poor, suffering, and oppressed because they're the ones who need my help the most, but truth be told, in their broken and contrite state, they probably have more insight than those who have been so preoccupied with guarding the hard copy of My story that they never bothered to read it. They've been so concerned about not dog-earing the pages or writing notes in the margins that they haven't even bothered to take it off the shelf.

"Once they see Me as a character, they'll understand what it means to be written in My image. I will remind them that My story has always been a love story and that like any good love story it will end in a wedding. I will reassure them that it's okay to occasionally muff a line or miss a mark, but they must never forget the storyline.

"Sadly, their rebellious attitude has become so entrenched that it seems almost impossible to expect them to change by themselves. I know that My dramatic appearance alone will not be enough to make them completely change their ways. What they really need is some cosmic, primal-scream therapy. I'll give them the opportunity to pour their entire bitter cups of hatred and darkness upon Me, even allowing them to kill Me, to get it out of their systems. I will stand in front of them as the abused spouse, the spurned lover, the rejected Father. I will take on all their venom, the worst they can possibly imagine, and I'll transform it into the antidote for our poisoned relationship. I'll offer no resistance, just unconditional love. I will take all their wrath and still forgive them; then they will truly see how much I love them and the lengths to which I'll go to get them back on script so we can all share in the glorious wedding feast to come.

"Once I've taken away all their bile, I'll reappear to them alive so they will truly believe I'm the Author. I will show them that the improvisation of the past is forgiven and that a restored story relationship is once again possible.

"Alas, my heart still aches! Some of my favorite characters have rejected my loving invitation to get back on script and continue to improvise their eternal afterlives in that stuffy, hot, smoke-filled improv club, straining to hear suggestions from an audience not particularly interested in their one-man shows anyway. They stand defiant, alone, and free?"

In the last chapter, we identified the ongoing conflict in our grand drama. The characters, created in the image of the Author, persistently struggle with their identity as physical and spiritual beings possessing knowledge of good and evil they're incapable of handling. They have mutinied, tied up the Captain, and thrown Him into the brig only to find out He was the only one who knew how to navigate these treacherous waters and bring them safely back to Port Shalom.

This conflict has made these humans very unhappy, producing a variety of signs and symptoms that point to an Original Sin cancer lurking deep within. The characters want to stop the saber-rattling in their souls and achieve a lasting peace, but they don't know how. How can this plot conflict be resolved?

We recognize this dis-ease in our neighbors and ourselves. We know it shouldn't be this way, and we sincerely look for ways to make this world a better place. Man remains broken despite his desire to fix and be fixed. Man has good redeemer intentions but inadequate redeemer skills. In his desire to fix himself, man has come up with some pretty creative therapeutic options, salvation salves designed to provide relief from the pain and itching of life.

Atheism accepts the fact that man is basically a stinky creature but explains it away as just an unfortunate consequence of the noble desire to survive. Religious movements, on the other hand, recognize that the odor is unacceptable and offer four possible remedies: deny it, cover it up, wash it off, or cleanse it from within. Buddhism tells us that the smell is an illusion and that once we accept the fact, it will go away. New Age religion considers it politically incorrect to tell people they stink, so it recommends the application of heavy doses of spiritual perfume to hide our corporate smell. Hinduism recommends that we should sequentially strip a little bit of dirt off every lifetime or so until we are united with the one great unscented one.

Islam and Judaism generally recognize that mankind smells pretty darned good most of the time but periodically wanders into the muck, necessitating an occasional bath. Christianity, on the other hand, says that mankind stinks all the time and no amount of perfume or baths will change that because the smell originates on the inside and the only option is an internal cleansing.

> Do you not see that whatever goes into the mouth passes into the stomach and is expelled? But what comes out of the mouth proceeds from the heart, and this defiles a person. For out of the heart come evil thoughts, murder, adultery, sexual immorality, theft, false witness, slander. These are what defile a person. (Matt. 15:17–20)

I have to agree with that great philosophical sage, the Joker, who said in the 1989 *Batman* movie, "This town needs an enema." We need an internal cleansing, a Christian colonic, not the deodorant of denial. I'm sorry, people, but you have reached fifty, and it's time for your spiritual colonoscopy.

> Woe to you, scribes and Pharisees, hypocrites! For you clean the outside of the cup and the plate, but inside they are full of greed and self-indulgence. You blind Pharisee! First clean the inside of the cup and the plate, that the outside also may be clean. (Matt. 23:25–26)

Let's take a closer look at some of the philosophical and religious solutions graciously offered us by our surrounding culture.

Bootstraps and Bombs

Atheists and agnostics have a bit of a problem; they know something is wrong with the world, but they lack the worldview

225

credibility to point the finger or offer a binding solution. Their only hope is humanism, a philosophy committed to the notion that mankind is capable of making the world a better place through science and technology. Unfortunately, with man in the engineer's seat, the salvation train always derails.

> This was humanism: the belief in human reason and in man's power, lifting himself by his bootstraps, to better himself and make a better world ...
>
> That doctrine appealed to me for many years as sufficient. Then below the surface of my life a disquiet, born both of reflection and experience, began to set in. I saw that the fruit of the humanistic age of enlightenment was an age of materialism. Man's increasing belief in himself as God did not seem to be making him more godlike. He was becoming more clever. But he had less and less of the sober, uplifting humility of one who has stood in the presence of God. Much of contemporary history seemed to me to indicate how dangerously near the savage state that man, lacking that humility, may be even while he is most advanced materially and technologically.[131]
>
> —Lin Yutang

Despite the horrific evidence of several world wars, weapons of mass destruction, and ongoing genocide throughout the world, many people still cling to the hope that mankind can somehow make things better. Three cheers for man and his frequently noble intentions, an A-plus for the standard he has set, but an F-minus for his ability to consistently achieve it. How do we explain a creature with good intentions but bad behavior? All we have learned about man over the centuries is that he is simultaneously both villain and hero, and yet we continue to naively cling to the notion that man is somehow up to the task of making this world a better place in which to live.

We have failed to recognize that by taking God off the throne, we have blindly abdicated authority to a suicide bomber strapped with enough explosives to destroy the planet and have deflected our attention from this sobering reality by periodically patting him on the back and awarding him the Nobel Peace Prize. The very being who brought us atomic energy also created the atomic bomb; the creature that rubbed two sticks together in some ancient cave and brought fire to heat our homes and cook our meals burned innocent people with napalm.

Why does man always wants to supersize his newfound powers to God-size proportions? We are obsessed with taking human cleverness to godlike levels, fooling ourselves into believing we are divinizing our newest inventions when in reality we're actualizing the very evil we were never supposed to know. We have dreams of immortal power trapped inside sinful, mortal brains. We cannot handle the knowledge of good and evil simultaneously.

> Man's greatness and wretchedness are so evident that the true religion must necessarily teach us that there is in man some great principle of greatness and some great principle of wretchedness. It must also account for such amazing contradictions.[132]
>
> —Blaise Pascal

Perhaps the more interesting question is why we entertain ideas of a better, more-perfect world anyway. If we're just evolution's most-advanced animals and have millions of years of experience in the fine art of survival of the fittest, how can we envision a world without conflict? Evolution is inherently about conflict. How fickle can we be? We ride the coattails of evolution to superstardom but abandon the concept in a utopian world in which we all learn to "sing in perfect harmony."

Evolution could explain the bad behavior as just attempts to outwit, outlast, and outplay our fellow human beings, but it doesn't explain why we'd then vote the liar and scoundrel off the show. How is it possible to be offended when someone just behaves EC, evolutionarily correctly? Pure evolutionary theory has to accept the fact that there really is no problem, that we are just links in the evolutionary chain trying out the latest weapons in our battle to be the most-fit survivor.

If chance be the father of all flesh, disaster is his rainbow in the sky, and when you hear. State of Emergency! Sniper Kills Ten! Troops on Rampage! Whites Go Looting! Bomb Blasts School! It is but the sound of man worshipping his maker.[133]

—Stephen Turner

"Hold on," the atheist says. "I know many atheists who are just as noble, kind, and service-oriented as you Christians, so what does your Christianity add to the world that my humanistic atheism doesn't?" A fine question, but it misses the real point. We accept the fact that everyone is capable of good because we are all created in God's image, but the difference is that the atheist has no worldview street credibility to condemn bad behavior while the Christian does.

Any antitheist who lives a moral life merely lives better than his or her philosophy warrants.[134]

—Ravi Zacharias

The measure of a religion or philosophy is not how much good it does but rather how much evil it allows. It may call us to good behavior but makes no prohibitions on our bad behavior.[135]

—Ravi Zacharias paraphrase

Idols

Most of us toy with religious ideas and piece together some form of rickety idol that makes us feel spiritual and distracts us from the sobering reality of our fallen nature. However, since we have cobbled together a religion with pieces of spirituality that were never intended to go together in the first place, our final product ends up a wobbly, peculiar looking spirituality that constantly falls apart. Instead of finding a more coherent religion, we cling to our patchwork faith, periodically reaching for some New Age duct tape to temporarily hold it together.

In the ancient Near East, the pagans used to fashion idols out of wood, metal, and stone and treat them as if they were infused with the presence of their gods. They would even feed and bathe the idols as acts of worship to curry favor with them. How often do we feed and bathe our idols of sex, money, and power? We need to pause and consider this: if we have to feed, burp, or wipe the bottom of our idols, maybe we should reconsider what we worship.

> He plants a cedar and the rain nourishes it. Then it becomes fuel for a man. He takes a part of it and warms himself; he kindles a fire and bakes bread. Also he makes a god and worships it; he makes it an idol and falls down before it. Half of it he burns in the fire. Over the half he eats meat; he roasts it and is satisfied. Also he warms himself and says, "Aha, I am warm, I have seen the fire!" And the rest of it he makes into a god, his idol, and falls down to it and worships it. He prays to it and says, *"Deliver me, for you are my god!"* (Isa. 44:14–17, emphasis added)

Our self-deception is occasionally brought to light, and we reluctantly acknowledge that our lives are cluttered with idols, but instead of tearing them down, we use them as scapegoats for our bad behavior. We attribute our inability to change to the fact that we are powerless to resist their allure. As I mentioned before, the temptations in life we call irresistible idols are in reality not idols at all but acts of self-worship. We are in essence just appeasing our "godlike" selves with all the accoutrements of divinity such as wealth, power, and promiscuity. Once again, it appears that Adam and Eve's sin of trying to be like God continues to haunt our personal houses of worship.

All That Glitters Is Not God

In his prologue to the *Hitchhiker's Guide to the Galaxy*, Douglas Adams correctly points out that the "little pieces of green paper and digital watches" were incapable of making us happy. Unfortunately, most of us tip our hats to the financial-wisdom literature by reciting mantras such as "money can't buy happiness" or "money is the root of all evil" and then plunk down money for a lottery ticket in hopes that hitting the jackpot will make our lives better.

Financial security is frequently confused with God's blessing. Listen to the prosperity preachers and you will hear frequent references to the Old Testament because there are so many chosen people who are quite rich, but you will hear precious little about the dismal fate of their lives of excess. They focus on the blessing of financial gain but neglect the curse that plagues its improper use.

Even more interesting is the fact they speak so little about Jesus. It seems that a homeless, itinerant preacher with "nowhere to lay His head," who spoke passionately about carrying one's cross, makes a very poor poster child for the health and wealth gospel they preach. Jesus said it was harder for a rich man to get into heaven than it was for a camel to pass through the eye of a needle, hardly a fitting maxim for those who want to "name it and claim it."

Jesus healed illness and forgave sin but never rewarded faith with a better job, a new car, or a bigger house. Is financial prosperity a blessing or a curse? You could argue that somebody needs to pay Jesus' evangelistic bills, but true evangelism is found in the humble service of the masses and not in the checks written by the wealthy few. Service, not acquisition, is the key to happiness. How often have you heard those who have just returned from a mission trip to a Third World country mention how spiritually inferior they felt compared to the poor and destitute people they were sent to serve? Jesus said happiness was found in giving stuff away and being a servant, not in accumulating wealth.

> I don't know what your destiny will be, but one thing I know: the only ones among you who will be really happy are those who will have sought and found to serve.[136]
>
> —Albert Schweitzer

It is so much easier to write a check to the Union Gospel Mission than go there and physically serve. When God extends His hand to greet me at heaven's gate, I doubt He will be very impressed with the stories of the hand cramps I suffered as I signed donation checks; rather, it will be the rough calluses of a life of service that will bring a smile to His face.

Our culture has become infatuated with the strange notion that money is the appropriate compensation for suffering. While it is true that the legal system needs a mechanism to compensate people for financial harm or loss, how did it get to the point that money was the answer to personal pain and suffering? How come when I go to a counselor to discuss my unhappiness, he or she doesn't just give me a new car or a wad of cash? Whatever happened to the adequacy of apologies and forgiveness?

Money may distract you, but it will never be up to the task of emotionally healing you. Unfortunately, Christianity has gone along with this deception and remained largely silent to the blasphemy of the prosperity gospel. Jesus may have been about health, but He was never about wealth. Why would God think it was a good idea to give unhappy people the "root of all evil" and then watch their tree grow and produce bitter fruit?

Hope Springs Eternal

At one time, we were very optimistic about our future. We entertained ideas of a utopian society built on the back of the rapid advances in science and technology. History was relevant because we could take what we learned from our past mistakes and innovatively apply this newfound knowledge to correct them in the future. We were like Chicago Cubs fans tenaciously clinging to the hope that this would be the year the Cubbies would win the World Series. Hope springs eternal. Unfortunately, we, like our pennant-challenged friends, have to accept the fact that things don't always go as planned. Despite our yearly enthusiasm, there always seems to be a Bartman, and instead of entertaining dreams of a championship October, we act as if it's already December and settle in for long, SAD (seasonal affective disorder) winter.

Our hope of using technology to make a better future has been replaced by its use to anesthetize the present. We create exciting virtual worlds to escape from the disappointing one we find ourselves in. We are essentially trying to rewrite the Genesis account in cyberspace, but in this scenario, it is man and not God who speaks, and instead of offering a moral "very good" blessing, we are left with nothing to say but "Cool graphics!"

We have been kicked out of the garden, and instead of trying to find a way back in, we construct our own digital parks in which the Ten Commandments no longer apply. Unfortunately, in this high-tech garden, we constantly step in the excrement left by our dogs of desire as we take them on their daily walks. We deceive ourselves into believing that digital "doo doo" doesn't smell that bad but notice we can no longer see the souls of our human shoes.

Help Desk

It seems every company has an online help desk to assist us with technical difficulties. The website usually begins by directing us to the FAQ page for solutions to commonly encountered problems, a holy screen that instructs us to perform a few digital Hail Marys or Our Fathers to achieve technological absolution. However, when these fail, we are directed into the electronic Holy of Holies to obtain "divine" technical intervention from a member of the hi-tech pantheon.

Similarly, every religion has the common sense to recognize mankind is in need of repair and tries to offer them mystical or spiritual assistance. The problem with most of them, however, is that they are still promoting nothing more than veiled humanism, the deluded notion that if we just give man enough innovative spiritual tools, he will be able to fix himself. Let's listen in on their conversations and see how each religion tackles man's problem.

Pantheism: The belief that everything is God, from the sea to the flea to me. We are all equal manifestations of God.

Mankind:
  My fellow man thinks he's better than everything else,
  constantly overstepping his bounds, acting like he's in

charge, and grieving the universal spirit. What can I do?
Sincerely, Gaia

Technologist:

Dear Gaia, thank you for your inquiry. I suspect you're probably referring to those pesky Republicans, but the best advice I can offer you is to cut your man down to size. He's clearly acting as if he were created in the image of some sort of greater god, exercising dominion over nature. It's tricky because you need to minimize his significance in the order of things but still get him fired up enough to try to fix the world. I know it doesn't make any sense to view him as both supervillain and superhero, but that's the best I can offer. Sorry I can't give you more time. I'm still busy trying to answer the question I received from a customer in Africa who doesn't understand why he feels so disgusted when he sees a lion killing an antelope when they are both supposed to be infused with the same universal spirit. Good luck with your man!

Panentheism: The belief that an impersonal God of the universe exists apart from the world. The world was not intentionally created but just spilled out of the glass of his overwhelming godness. Therefore, everything contains varying amounts of God sparks within that seek to be reunited with their source. This forms the basis of Hinduism.

Mankind:

My man keeps killing other people, fighting wars, and is generally just mean to everyone. He then gives all sorts of excuses. Your instruction manual says he should have a spark of the universal God in him, but it doesn't seem hot enough to start any fires of good behavior. What can I do?
Sincerely, Vishnu

Technologist:

Thanks for asking. It's simple. Your man has forgotten where he came from. All that emanating has made his memory a bit fuzzy, and in the process, he hasn't always acted in the best way. He has taken on a significant amount of karmic baggage and has found it so heavy that the mere thought of trying to be good is just too daunting. Try baby steps by having him drop a piece of karmic luggage every lifetime or so until it's all gone, and he will finally know the goodness from which he came. Unfortunately, you'll have to be patient because it won't happen in your lifetime or the lifetime of your children. As a matter of fact, it may never happen at all. I can tell by the tone of your voice that you should probably spend a little more time shedding some karmic pounds yourself. Good luck kindling that spark.

Buddhism: The belief that the biggest problem in the world is the suffering brought on by desires for things in this life, such as material possessions and personal identities. The goal is to achieve a state in which our desires are extinguished and we are absorbed into the impersonal nothingness of nirvana.

Mankind:

My man continues to want stuff he cannot get. He thinks his life should have some sort of purpose, and it's making him very sad. He wants permanence in a world that is nothing but change. I have told him to stop wanting things and forget about making his life individually meaningful, but he persists. What do I do? Sincerely, Bodi Sattvah

Technologist:

It's a difficult question because the directions on my eightfold pathway FAQ sheet, which some find helpful, can be a problem if taken too seriously. I'd just encourage him to keep erasing his hard drive through meditation and resist the temptation to reboot with the latest operating software. I know it seems odd to prefer a blank screen to a screen saver, but flying toasters are just an illusion anyway.

New Age Religion: This is a diverse lot, but their basic premise is that there is a secret power in mankind that will make him a better person. It's a force that has the power to attract financial rewards, friends, or lovers and create happiness in life.

Mankind:

> My man is badly behaved. He seems incapable of reaching his potential. I have told him to think good thoughts and find his happy place, but his mind all too frequently visits brothels. Please advise. Sincerely, Rhonda.

Technologist:

> The good news is that embedded somewhere deep inside him is a magic power button, but the bad news is that we disagree on its precise location. All the technicians, however, assure me they have personal knowledge of exactly where it is. If you just send in $19.95 per technologist, we will send you all their individual solutions. I vaguely remember reading some old manual that talked about secret, powerful intentions and good thoughts attracting good things. Unfortunately, these manuals stay on our shelves for only about fifteen minutes before they disappear. I'd write more, but I'm too busy working on my own manual. I can send you an advanced copy for the bargain price of $15 if you would like.

The options for the problem of mankind are not limited to religion, and some may be found in philosophies that border on religion such as atheism and postmodernism.

Atheism: The belief that there is no God and that the only real thing is the material world. The only option atheists have for understanding their existence is evolution.

Mankind:

> I'm having a hard time finding any instruction manual, and my man is always fighting and killing others. I think it's

because he's infected with some sort of religion virus, but it seems the unreligious are misbehaving as well. What can I do? Sincerely, Richard

Technologist:

Sorry, but we kind of built mankind on the fly, tinkering as we went, so there aren't any instruction manuals. We just hope one of them works, but if he doesn't, just toss him in the evolutionary scrap heap, and we'll send you a new one. Unfortunately, the chaotic randomness of our organization makes us quite inefficient, so it may take several billion years before he arrives. Your description of his behavior sounds like he's working pretty darned well, actually. Please call us again if you have any real problems.

Postmodernism: There are no universal truths. Authority is bad. Culture is a construct to give power to others. The answer to all our problems is tolerance and relativism, live and let live.

Mankind:

I'm sorry to bother you, but I'm having problems with my neighbor. He's having loud parties, taking my lawn tools without asking, and playing nude volleyball in his backyard. What can I do? Sincerely, Whatever

Technologist:

First of all, I think you're being a bit intolerant by trying to force your neighbor to conform to your personal oppressive cultural narrative. It sounds like he's having a great time, and I don't think you should be a wet blanket. Why don't you just build a bigger fence, close your shades, or put in some earplugs? By the way, when's his next party?

I believe that Christianity offers the only clear solution to the problem. Genesis emphasizes that man was created in the image of God, so we are already hardwired with original factory settings, but every time we deviate from those preprogrammed parameters, we get an error message. How can we ever hope to function as well as we did when we first came out of the box? Let's take a listen to the Christian help desk.

Mankind:

I want to thank you for the incredibly detailed instruction manual, explaining every bell and whistle, but my man keeps taking these cool innovations and using them to do things they were never intended to do. In addition, he has downloaded so many new apps that the operating system is hopelessly confused, and he just doesn't function correctly anymore. What can I do? Sincerely, G. K.

Technologist:

Well, it's clear you cannot fix this problem by yourself, so I'll send out our best Tech. He will scrub all the useless programs, remove all the destructive viruses, and restore him to the original factory image in which he was constructed.

Mankind:

Sounds great! When can He come?

Technologist:

I have good news for you. He's already come and made the necessary repairs, and just for calling, you'll receive a warranty good for eternity, covering all parts and labor. It is finished! Enjoy your New Man.

While I have walked you through a humorous review of these incoherent, man-made "salvation" paths, I want to make it clear that sincere people who truly want to deal with the unhappiness in their lives have constructed these religious strategies. We need to point out the inconsistencies in their worldviews, but we need to recognize these attempts are the outward manifestation of suffering souls crying out for help. Instead of just criticizing their personal solutions, we need to recognize the shared darkness of our fallen nature and take them by the hand and direct them to the Light.

While I have defined these as independent paths of salvation, we must remember that more often than not, people try to combine them in very awkward ways. One of the most disturbing trends is to deceptively reinvent Jesus and incorporate Him into other non-Christian salvation pathways.

All You Need Is Love

Is it true, as the Beatles sang, that "all you need is love"? Many a religious movement has described its higher power as love. Let's think about this. While you may love coffee, pizza, or sports cars, that kind of love is a feeling of delight or amusement, not true love. True love is found only in a relationship, so if we identify our deity as love, it must be a deity that is in relationship. If your deity just elicits the feelings of love, it is infatuation and not true love. Christianity is the only worldview that can honestly say that God is love because it recognizes a God that exists in an eternal Trinitarian relationship. He is a God not of butterflies in the stomach but a God of committed relationship who loves "in sickness and in health."

Allah is generally not thought of as love because He exists as one and therefore is not inherently a relationship. Islam, in fact, considers the Trinity to be blasphemy. I respect Islam's desire to avoid polytheism, but it is only in the Trinity that God can truly be called love.

In light of the true-love Trinity, it's easy to understand why God cares so much about relationships and was even willing to die on a cross to preserve our relationship with Him. Jesus talked the relationship talk.

> Greater love has no one than this, that someone lays down his life for his friends. You are my friends if you do what I command you. No longer do I call you servants. (John 15:13–14)

He also walked the relationship walk.

> For God so loved the world, that he gave his only Son, that whoever believes in him should not perish but have eternal life. For God did not send his Son into the world to condemn the world, but in order that the world might be saved through him. (John 3:16)

New Age religion frequently speaks of the universal life force as love, but if you look closely, you will see that new agers are really talking about the feeling of being in love and not the committed state of true love. The only place you can find true divine love is in a relational deity. We all know that persistently chasing after the feeling of love leaves nothing but a trail of tears. A true love relationship is hard work; it's glorious and gritty, joyful and jagged, but in the end, it will satisfy like nothing else.

True love is not found in a candlelight dinner overlooking the ocean but in a woman caring for her disabled husband, a man holding his family together while his wife is dying of breast cancer, or a mother and father setting aside career ambitions to raise a special-needs child. Love is not a feeling; it is a commitment to another being created in the image of God.

I implore you to give up the thrill of the deistic one-night stands and rest secure in a committed relationship with the only God who truly loves you.

> When you fall deeply in love, you want to please the beloved. You don't wait for the person to ask you to do something for her. You eagerly research and learn every little thing that brings her pleasure. Then you get it for her, even if it costs you money or great inconvenience. "Your wish is my command," you feel—and it doesn't feel oppressive at all. From the outside, bemused friends may think, "She's leading him around by the nose," but from the inside it feels like heaven.[137]
>
> —Timothy Keller

What Do We Do with a Problem Like Jesus?

> For those people mingle Jesus Christ with their teachings just to gain your trust under false pretenses. It is as if they were giving deadly poison mixed with honey and wine, with the result that the unsuspecting victim gladly accepts it and drinks down death with fatal pleasure.[138]
>
> —Letter of Ignatius to the Trallians

While Christianity has many critics, their complaints are rarely if ever directed at Jesus personally. They blame the Christian machine and those who call themselves followers of Christ but want to claim Jesus as their own. This phenomenon suggests that Jesus is incredibly important and cannot be ignored. Atheism denies His divinity but generally acknowledges He was a really kind, smart guy who spoke about "how great it would be to be nice to people for a change."

Other religious movements make Jesus into an enlightened Buddha, a god in the Hindu pantheon, a prophet, or the prime example of a human achieving God consciousness. Unfortunately, they take poetic license and morph Jesus into whom they want Him to be and not who He is. You cannot pick and choose what you want to believe about Him; it's dishonest to portray Jesus in any other way than He was portrayed in the Gospels, the only historically reliable source we have about who He was and what He did.

If you reject Him, do so on the basis of what you know in the New Testament record, but don't pretend He was something different from whom He or His followers said He was. If you treat Jesus as merely a good teacher who lived in the first century, church becomes a history class and the Lord's Supper becomes a Civil War reenactment.

> A man who was merely a man and said the sort of things Jesus said would not be a great moral teacher. He would either be a lunatic—on the level with the man who says he is a poached egg—or else he would be the devil of hell. You must make your choice. Either this man was, and is, the Son of God; or else a madman or something

worse … You can shut Him up for a fool, you can spit at him and kill him as a demon; or you can fall at his feet and call Him Lord and God. But let us not come with any patronizing nonsense about His being a great human teacher. He has not left that open to us. He did not intend to.[139]

—C. S. Lewis

Sadly, despite the fact most people are attracted to Jesus in one way or another, they find it quite easy to speak of Him apart from the church He founded. The rest of the world doesn't see any connection between what they know about Jesus and the way the Christian church talks or behaves. How did Jesus become separated from Christianity? What has the church done to make the secular world draw this conclusion? Isn't it sad that secular people can find more holiness in empty cathedrals than in churches packed to the gills with Christians? They can enter an empty church, feel the fire of God's presence, and have that holy ember extinguished by a brigade of Christian firefighters. If we don't start looking more like the body of Christ, the world won't see any family resemblance with Jesus.

Jesus was crucified for claiming to be God; that is clear. Now that you know the charges, you need to ask yourself, was He guilty? We need to put ourselves in the shoes of the disciples and respond to Jesus' question, "Who do you say that I am?"

> Now it happened that as he was praying alone, the disciples were with him. And he asked them, "Who do the crowds say that I am?" And they answered, "John the Baptist. But others say, Elijah, and others, that one of the prophets of old has risen." Then he said to them, "But who do you say that I am?" And Peter answered, "The Christ of God." (Luke 9:18–20)

Unholy Alliance

While many other religions resort to amusing uses of the Son of God, the more disturbing trend is the tendency of Christians to incorporate other salvation pathways into their own faith. Why do so many people feel that the Christianity they experience in church inadequate? Why tack on New Age beliefs? What does that add to their faith experience? I think what they are trying to do is use Jesus to cover up the consequences of their sins but allow themselves to partake in the Original Sin of trying to be like God and determine their own salvation parameters. They want to hide the collateral damage of their sinful dalliances behind the flowers and shrubbery of God's forgiveness, but continue to play in the enormous crater caused by the bomb of Adam and Eve's Original Sin.

Surprisingly, it appears that the prosperity gospel has captivated even the atheist and the liberal theologian. They have hitched their gravy trains to Jesus. It appears that this failed preacher and prophet who died a criminal's death has made them quite prosperous. Are they being intellectually honest by making money off someone they say is irrelevant and perhaps even the source of society's ills? They spend their lives trying to take Jesus off the throne and place Him in their briefcases like a bunch of poker chips waiting to be cashed in at the publishing house teller's window.

I'm sure that behind closed doors they must be saying veiled prayers to Jesus, thanking Him for the financial blessings he has conferred upon them, His death on a cross having torn not the curtain into the Holy of Holies but the veil into the vault of Mammon.

Deist Deception

As we noted in the first chapter, as many as 95 percent of Americans believe in a God, but unfortunately, that belief alone does not save you. It may make you a more enlightened occupant of hell, but it doesn't guarantee entry into heaven. Recognizing the complexity and beauty of the set and props may lead you to believe in a God, but that knowledge makes you only a deist, someone who believes God created the world like a great watch or machine and sat back and let it run by itself without any divine intervention.

Antony Flew, a prominent atheist became convinced at age eighty that God in fact existed. The evidence he had found so compelling was essentially that put forth by intelligent design theorists. The only problem is that he died a deist. He recognized the need for a God but didn't accept the most important part of the equation, the need for a Savior. You can look at the world around you, admire the plant and animal life, marvel at the uniqueness of man, and conclude that God exists but still remain eternally separated from God.

Christianity is not just about belief in God's existence; it's much more concerned with belief in a Savior. We can point to mountains, lakes, trees, and squirrels and make the case for a creative mind, but we must not neglect the fact that mankind has a problem that requires a solution. Sadly, we Christians are often so eager to carve another converted atheist notch on our Great Commission belts that we set the conversion bar too low. Jesus didn't come into this world to prove God existed; He came to take away the sins of the world. The unfortunate truth is that hell is full of deists as well as atheists; in fact, Satan is quite a deist himself.

Chemical Buddhism

It may be feasible for wealthy Hollywood celebrities to practice Buddhism in the confines of their comfortable homes, but my recovering alcoholic friends at the Union Gospel Mission have already tested this worldview in the real world laboratory and found it doesn't work. They have practiced chemical Buddhism for years and have found the consequences to be catastrophic. They foolishly believed, just like the Buddha, that life was suffering and that their personal attachment to life was the source of their problem. But instead of tedious hours of meditation and adherence to the noble eightfold pathway, they opted for the noble six-pack pathway and accomplished the same goal—personal extinction and detachment from the world around them.

They quickly discovered, however, that adhering to the tenets of Buddhism did nothing but make the suffering worse. Ironically,

243

they found that the only successful treatment was to face the sources of their suffering head-on and not try to extinguish them. They found that denying they were unique human personalities was detrimental and that healing was possible only when they discovered the persons God had specifically created them to be. They found that treating the world as an illusion did nothing but keep them in a chemical fog but that acknowledging the world as a "very good" place made living a joyful experience.

Redemption

We have all at one time or another longed to return to a better time in our lives. We romantically recall happy events in our childhood such as searching the neighborhood swamp for frogs and newts, experiencing our first kiss, or playing catch with our dad. The problem is that each of these events eventually deviates from the idyllic norm. The swamp gets paved over with new construction, we break up with our girlfriend, or our father dies. We know it shouldn't be this way and we long for restoration. Our longing is not restricted to specific life events; it's also made manifest in a nebulous feeling that something is wrong with the world in general and that it shouldn't be that way. We don't feel as if we have just fallen from a great height, as Carl Sagan opines, but rather have fallen from a great divine height. It's not just that we feel guilty for breaking some rules; we feel we have wronged Someone. We feel that our crime is not just violating some physical rules and regulations but is actually a failure to connect our spirit to its source. Even the great evolutionary poet Carl Sagan made the same observation.

> The Cosmos is all that is or ever was or ever will be. Our feeblest contemplations of the Cosmos stir us—there is a tingling in the spine, a catch in the voice, a faint sensation, as if a distant memory, of falling from a height. We know we are approaching the greatest of mysteries.[140]
>
> —Carl Sagan

Our persistent desire for restoration implies two things: that a better original state previously existed and that we have deviated from it. Therefore, to proceed, we must try to identify what that ideal state looked like and understand how it had fallen apart. In the context of our story, we need to identify the original intent of the Author and acknowledge we have gone terribly off script.

I think a better word to describe this process is *redemption* because it specifically addresses our need to transform our fallen state for restoration to occur. Webster's defines *redemption* with words such as *repurchase, liberate, regain, atone for, offset,* and *make good.* We experience redemption everyday of our lives, from the mundane redeeming of store coupons to the exotic redemption of our souls. What actually happens when we redeem something? We reclaim and restore something we have lost or tarnished. The basic idea of redemption therefore is to take something bad and transform it into something good, which seems like a very appropriate solution for a human race that embodies both good and bad behavior.

Redemption is most frequently thought of as a Christian word linked to the atoning death of Jesus Christ, but redemption is not a Christian invention. Redemption has been the default mechanism of restoration employed by man throughout history. Every day of our lives, we are confronted by stories of personal redemption, and we love them.

The Gospel According to *People* Magazine

I find *People* magazine fascinating because it points out bits and pieces of God's truth we have become blissfully ignorant of. Before you label me a heretic and accuse me of reading the Devil's holy book, let me explain. Almost without fail, every issue has a story about suffering—a failed Hollywood marriage, the tragedy of losing a limb, a celebrity cancer, a natural disaster, or a school shooting—but these stories are inevitably followed by restoration. Life is not ruined, but hope is revealed and suffering is redeemed!

245

The Hollywood starlet rebuilds her life after the infidelity of her partner, the public figure overcomes the odds of cancer, or the community comes together to support its members and rebuild after a disaster. A mother forms MADD after the death of her child at the hands of a drunk driver, parents establish the Polly Klaas Foundation after the death of their abducted child. The most heartwarming stories are those in which suffering has been overcome, redeemed, made a blessing, and changed the lives of others. Individual tragedy creates a redemptive community of suffering where none had existed. You could even call it a "redeemed cloud of witnesses."

Why are we so enamored by the selfless service of those whose lives have been touched by tragedy? It could be argued that we are just emotionally enabling the evolutionarily unfit or rewarding those who have escaped the clutches of natural selection, but the vast majority of people recognize that this explanation is absurd. I believe that when we see the amazing fruit of redeemed suffering and the transformation of individual tragedy into community triumph, we receive moments of clarity. The curtain between God's kingdom and earth is temporarily pulled aside, and we have the miraculous opportunity to see God's shalom revealed. When this veil is temporarily pulled aside, common people receive a temporary work visa in God's kingdom, and what they see is so remarkable that they begin to ponder what it would be like to become full citizens.

Once you set foot in His kingdom, you get this feeling you're a stranger, pilgrim, and sojourner in your own world. You realize that you live in a fallen land and that your true home awaits.

Why does the aftermath of a particular tragedy become so much larger than the event itself? A small obituary in a newspaper becomes a nonprofit organization. If you look at these stories on a purely evolutionary level, suffering is just the risk of living, a colander to sift the fit from the unfit. Some people may try to blame God, but then why Mothers Against Drunk Driving and not Mothers Against a Devilish Deity? Maybe the majority of people who get their news from *People* magazine have a better grasp on reality than does the small minority who think truth is found in the depressing philosophical works of Nietzsche.

Why is redeemable suffering such a powerful force? As disturbing as it is, suffering sells; just ask the editors of *People*. The real secret is that suffering sells only if it's accompanied by a generous helping of redemption. Pick up a copy and read the stories of individual suffering transformed by an even more powerful redemptive response. It may be presumptuous to make this connection, but it sure sounds like the gospel to me; the suffering and death of One makes life better for the many. The gospel story of redeemed suffering is presented to people week after week in the tabloids, but they don't see Jesus!

Why are we so enamored by these stories of redemption? Maybe it's because we all know we need redemption and we recognize we have failed to meet a standard and in our own ways are trying to atone for our mistakes. Redemption stories are powerful because they are universal. Redemption, however, is hard work, and we frequently take the easy way out and either bury our heads in the sand and deny there's anything wrong in the first place, or we conveniently pass the redemption buck by blaming our failings on others. This combined strategy of "bury and blame" works for only so long; sooner or later, we have to pull our heads out of the sand to get some oxygen, and when we do, we have to face the angry stare of our fellow man who thinks we should carry our own crosses and not rely on him to carry it for us.

> If we say we have no sin, we deceive ourselves, and the truth is not in us. (1 John 1:8)

Tools of the Trade

Redemption generally requires a third party to accomplish the task. We need a mechanism to transform our weakness into strength, our tragedy into victory, our sin into forgiveness. We are ultimately unable to redeem our own failings. The abduction of a young girl is redeemed by an intermediary organization such as the

Polly Klaas Foundation. A victim of a sexual predator is redeemed by a state regulation such as Megan's Law, which identifies and locates sex-offenders in communities. The tragedy of amputated limbs is redeemed by an appearance in the Olympics. In each case, personal redemption utilizes a third-party platform to take it to the larger world around us. The offended or hurting parties understand that redemption of their personal pain is so much bigger than they are.

My Redeemer Lives

Redemption is not only accomplished through foundations, laws, and sporting events but also through other human beings. The most dramatic examples are those involving a baby or child. The responsibility parents have for new lives inspires them to take the hard lessons they have learned in their troubled lives and use them to protect their children from similar fates. I have seen this repeatedly in the NICU; someone from a dysfunctional family has a baby, and the joy and grace surrounding the event eclipses the troubled, chaotic lives of the parents. For a brief moment, all their pain is set aside, and they see an innocent soul, a chance to peek through the flaming swords into the garden of Eden, an opportunity to get a clearer view of the image of God in which they were created but have long since made unrecognizable.

> So will you tell me the little things?
> What does God look like?
> And angels' wings?
> I don't remember these things.[141]
>
> —Stone Temple Pilots

I find it interesting how these families use their babies as their personal redeemers. They indelibly write their anguished cries for redemption on their babies by giving them names such as Hope, Heaven, Glory, or Angel. You can hear this cry for redemption in the lyrics of many rock stars that have recently become fathers for the first time. Their reckless lives of sex, drugs, and rock 'n' roll have left them broken and keenly aware of their need for restoration. Such births give them the opportunity to redeem their sins by committing themselves to helping their children avoid the same mistakes that caused them to mess up their own lives. A baby represents the chance to do it all over again.

> I wanna hold you
> Protect you
> From all of the things
> I've already endured.[142]

> —Staind

The use of babies and children as tools for personal redemption highlights two very important qualifications for a redeemer. First of all, the most powerful redeemer is one who most closely resembles us. Our little babies possess a piece of our DNA, making them suitable surrogates to redeem our personal failings. They represent the untarnished template that we should have been.

Second, the redeemer must be innocent. Once innocent children cross the threshold into adulthood, once the potentiality of Original Sin becomes actualized, they have taken on too much baggage to successfully redeem our inadequacies. I find it astounding that even the secular world subconsciously recognizes the qualifications for a redeemer but cannot make the connection with the gospel. Jesus is the perfect redeemer because He became one of us, a physical man, and He also maintained his innocence. Redemption is not a uniquely Christian concept, but Jesus is, however, its ultimate manifestation.

> For we do not have a high priest who is unable to sympathize with our weaknesses, but *one who in every respect has been tempted as we are, yet without sin*. Let us then with confidence draw near to the throne of grace, that we may receive mercy and find grace to help in time of need. (Heb. 4:15–16, emphasis added)

Unfortunately, human attempts at redemption are not usually feel-good stories. Many times, people miss the big picture of redemption and myopically focus only on the redemption of their personal pain, inappropriately using other people to meet those ends. Babies and children are frequently the victims of these misguided attempts at personal restoration.

Consider the all-too-common scenario of parents who try to redeem their failed sports careers by forcing their children into the same sports and mercilessly pushing them to be stars, or the stories of couples trying to salvage their marriages by having a child who then becomes a pawn in the parents' failed attempts at reconciliation. Unfortunately, relying on a human to redeem our human failings will always end in human failure. Even if we somehow helped our children avoid the mistakes that we made, they will still ultimately succumb to their own human mistakes and be in need of their own redeemers. Human redemption will always have a human outcome.

Afterglow

Unredeemed suffering may be the reason we fear death. Suffering is not a surprise to any human being. We don't like it, yet we all seem to accept it as an undeniable part of life. We try to blame it on culture, others, and even God, but that doesn't make it go away. If we are powerless to get rid of it, we have two options— grin and bear it or try to redeem it.

The majority of us embrace the latter option in our own ways. We are fixated with the idea of redeemed suffering; we seem to think there must be a happy ending in which pain and suffering are overcome and reversed to produce an even greater healing.

Who is the holiest person you know? I suspect you may struggle with the answer because nobody is absolutely pure. However, I'd guess someone came to mind, probably someone who had gone through some sort of tragedy or conflict and emerged a stronger person; someone whose faith was formed in a refiner's fire of pain and was left with a holy glow that shines like a lighthouse in the stormy cultural darkness. Perhaps it was someone tragically stripped of everything worldly and left with nothing but a face-to-face encounter with God, an encounter that left him or her radiating the glow of God's holiness.

> When Moses came down from Mount Sinai, with the two tablets of the testimony in his hand as he came down from the mountain, Moses did not know that the skin of his face shone because he had been talking with God … Whenever Moses went in before the Lord to speak with him, he would remove the veil, until he came out. And when he came out and told the people of Israel what he was commanded, the people of Israel would see the face of Moses, that the skin of Moses' face was shining. And Moses would put the veil over his face again, until he went in to speak with him. (Ex. 34:29, 34–35)

Conclusion

The idea of redemption has its origin in the image of God, because you cannot regain or restore that which you never had. Everyone has been created in God's image, so everyone has a horse in this race. We all hope to enter the winner's circle but sadly hear gunshots in the distance that announce the fate of those put down because they had broken a weight-bearing worldview leg that couldn't be fixed. We have soiled the image in which we were created, and we feel dirty.

Although most of us don't understand why we feel guilty, we still know we need a thorough cleaning. If we experience guilt for having sullied the image, how much more do we think it breaks the heart of the One who created it? It so grieved His heart that He stepped into the world to make it right.

Sins are not just individual acts of defiance isolated in time; they are cumulative. Every indiscretion brings with it a string of consequence, like someone leaving the outhouse of sin with the toilet paper of regret stuck to a shoe. Sin creates pain and suffering in our lives, so we need more than just forgiveness; we need restoration. Someone must deal with the centuries of pain and suffering we have inflicted on others and ourselves.

Jesus did more than just sacrificially die for our sins; He took on the financial pain and suffering of our sin portfolio, which had been collecting significant amounts of compound interest since our first garden deposit. God could not ignore the trail of tears we left behind in the wake of our expedition into the wilderness of sin. A forgiving God removes our guilt, but a suffering, redemptive God also removes our pain.

The world has a problem, that's no secret. The life of every human being can be understood as a search for the solution, a satisfactory plot resolution. We need to respect the fact that others have put some thought and effort into this conflict, but we need to have the decency to tell them a Band-Aid is hardly adequate therapy for a hemorrhaging soul. We need to get them to look beyond the valleys of their own personal literary devices and look up to hills at God's Golgothan plot twist.

Chapter Ten

CRUCI"FIX"

WE HAVE SEEN THAT THE characters in our grand drama are faced with a serious unhappiness problem. They have been experiencing a variety of symptoms that show no signs of abating. They have pursued every possible therapeutic option the world has to offer, but alas, they discover they are sicker than ever. Is there any hope? Can the story conflict be resolved before the last page of our lives is turned? Yes it can! Jesus made some pretty bold plot-resolution claims, and since He spoke as One who had Author-ity, He can shed some Light on this problem. Let's take a careful look at His life, death, and resurrection to see if He has the literary chops to resolve this plot tension.

> And when Jesus finished these sayings, the crowds were astonished at his teaching, for he was teaching them as one who had authority, and not as their scribes. (Matt. 7:28–29)

> Jesus said to him, "I am the way, and the truth, and the life. No one comes to the Father except through me." (John 14:6)

Crime Scene Investigation (CSI)

Our human dis-ease is intimately linked to Adam and Eve's Original Sin of trying to be like God. Their garden indiscretion not

253

only resulted in the acquisition of knowledge they were incapable of handling but also challenged the loving, committed, monogamous relationship parameters God had intended from the beginning. The place where God courted us became a crime scene.

A garden crime had been committed, and mankind has been doin' time ever since, senselessly pounding the rocks of unhappiness, picking up other peoples' emotional trash along the roadside of life, and making vanity plates for those who motor through life oblivious to the devastation of human suffering.

Since we have a lot of "hard" time on our hands, we can't help but reflect on our situation and get a little peeved that we have to pay the penalty for something our crazy Uncle Adam and Aunt Eve did during their reckless youth. To make sense of it all, we flash back to the crime scene and review the sequence of events in the hope we can gain a better understanding of exactly what went down that fateful day.

Why didn't God make it easier on Himself and hide that tree from them in the first place? Why didn't He baby-proof the garden, put plugs in the outlets and cushions on the table edges, and make sure all the knives and scissors were in the upper cabinet out of their reach? What was He thinking? He put that darned tree in the center of the garden within plain view of everyone and told them not to touch it. Can you think of a worse parenting mistake than placing a cookie jar right in front of your children, instructing them not to eat from it, and then walking away?

God, however, had to do it because He knew that a relationship without choice was a sham. True love was possible only when the option of not loving existed. Therefore, while the Original Sin was disobeying God and obtaining knowledge reserved for Him alone, the real consequence of the sin was subverting the very choice that made a meaningful relationship possible. The tree represented a choice between eternal marital bliss and mortal single life, an everlasting honeymoon or a lifetime of bar hopping. The serpent tried to make the decision all about upward mobility, power, and knowledge, while God intended the decision to be about relationship commitment.

Influenced by the serpent's lie, Adam and Eve were led to believe the relationship could be enhanced by making it one of equals rather than of Creator to created. The result was not just disobedience but also a relationship coup. Adam and Eve declared that God's idea of a relationship was inadequate. The unique bond between Creator and created was forever changed, and that grieved God's heart.

It didn't take long for Adam and Eve to realize their crime. They were instantaneously overwhelmed by "naked" guilt and in typical human-denial fashion thought it was a clever idea to put on some "camo" and hide in the bushes. They were convicted by their inadequacy and ashamed of their mortal hubris in the presence of immortal grandeur. They knew it was no longer possible to stand in His holy presence without covering their newly acquired unholiness.

Unfortunately, in their haste to hide, they forgot that they were the only two people around and that the human teeth marks on the discarded apple core were a "dead" giveaway as to who perpetrated the crime. God, with utmost omnipotence and omnipresence, quickly found them and asked them a very important question, "Who died and made you King?" God took them to task for brazenly trying to be God. What had they been thinking? What were they going to do when the real King showed up?

> He said, "Who told you that you were naked? Have you eaten of the tree of which I commanded you not to eat?" (Gen. 3:11)

After Adam and Eve ate of the fruit, their desire to be God was quickly replaced by the stark realization they were mere mortals and could never be God. They recalled God's warning about surely dying if they disobeyed. The act of rebellion they thought would bring them closer to God actually moved them farther away. God had made eternal life accessible to them by allowing them to eat from the Tree of Life, but their ambitious arrogance took that possibility away. Adam and Eve's dream of acquiring the perks of a Creator turned into a nightmare of losing the basics of the created.

It's similar to those fateful trips to our college professor's office to try to get more points on an exam. Once we stepped into the professor's office, it became painfully clear that instead of boosting our score, he or she was going to take off more points and our illusory intellectual hubris was quickly melted away in the presence of the fire of his far superior knowledge. It turned out that our newly acquired college freshman "omniscience" was an illusion and that there existed one far greater than us who just happened to be the one responsible for grading our papers.

Adam and Eve's attempt to boost their GPAs by trying to "eat" God's answer key unfortunately came back to bite them on the butt. God and His angelic school board recognized the emotional toll of their shameful scholastic rebellion and decided they should be expelled. God mercifully made them leave Garden University before they also ate from the tree of immortal tenure and condemned themselves to an eternity of incoherent lecturing.

> Then the Lord God said, "Behold, the man has become like one of us in knowing good and evil. Now, lest he reach out his hand and take also of the tree of life and eat, and live forever—" therefore the Lord God sent him out from the garden of Eden to work the ground from which he was taken. He drove out the man, and at the east of the Garden of Eden he placed the cherubim and a flaming sword that turned every way to guard the way to the tree of life. (Gen. 3:22–24)

Branded

I vividly remember watching the old black-and-white TV show *Branded*. In that series, Chuck Connors, the sole survivor of a military battle, was accused of deserting his fellow soldiers and leaving them to die. In the opening scene, he marches into the center of a Civil War fort to face a military tribunal. They strip him of his military badges, buttons, and sword and send him outside the gate. The scene ends with him standing in the desert, a broken man, as the fort doors slowly close behind him.

And they say he ran away.
Branded, marked with a coward's shame,
What do you do when you're branded,
Will you fight for your name?[143]

—"Branded"

Similarly, Adam and Eve, after being found guilty of treason, were dressed down and tossed out of the garden. The only way for God to save them from a fate worse than death, an immortality of guilt, was to send them out of His presence. They were forced into the wilderness, where the echo of God's words, "for in the day that you eat of it you shall surely die," reverberated in their brains, their dreams of immortality a faint memory.

Their fate is our fate, and death serves as a constant reminder to us all that we're not God. Adam and Eve's sin prohibited them from standing in God's presence, a situation ultimately unacceptable to God because at His core He is a God of relationship, a value He holds above His divine essence.

God, however, gave them a glimmer of hope before they were expelled. In the curse called down upon the serpent, God made it clear they would be engaged in a battle outside the garden but promised that the "deceiver" would ultimately be vanquished. The serpent would suffer a gaping head wound while mankind would suffer only a bruised Achilles tendon.

> I will put enmity between you and the woman, and between your offspring and her offspring; he shall bruise your head, and you shall bruise his heel. (Gen. 3:15)

It is with these words, often referred to as the *Protoevangelion*, the first gospel, that God set His salvation plan in motion. Man, in his sinful state, would be cast out from God's presence and would be engaged in a lifelong struggle with the serpent, but in the end, he would triumph. But how would this happen? Man had already shown that left to his own devices he would fail, so how could he hope to win this battle and restore his relationship with his Creator?

257

God knew man's limitations, but because His desire to dwell with man was so strong, He inaugurated a plan that in the end would permanently restore their broken relationship. It was clear they needed some divine guidance, but how could they receive it if in their unholy state they couldn't see God's face and live?

> Moses said, "Please show me your glory." And he said, "I will make all my goodness pass before you and will proclaim before you my name 'The Lord.' And I will be gracious to whom I will be gracious, and will show mercy on whom I will show mercy. But," he said, *"you cannot see my face, for man shall not see me and live."* (Ex. 33:18–20, emphasis added)

God began by fashioning garments of animal skin to cover them. Some theologians suggest that the skins God used to cover Adam and Eve were obtained from the first animal sacrifice, which was performed by God Himself. It's possible that this was a precursor to the Jewish sacrificial system designed to cleanse the people and temple so that God could dwell, albeit imperfectly, with them in the Holy of Holies. Mankind and God could no longer be in the same room, but just as in a confessional booth, they could converse with each other through a latticework of ritual purification. God made it quite clear that sacrifice was the only way an unholy, rebellious people could be cleansed enough to periodically meet with a holy, perfect God. God intervenes on our behalf to restore the broken relationship by graciously offering the first and last sacrifice, a skin to cover our acquired unholiness and His own blood to permanently wash us clean.

> And the Lord God made for Adam and for his wife garments of skins and clothed them. (Gen. 3:21)

Why did something have to die because of Adam and Eve's garden infraction? God had clearly warned them beforehand that they would die if they ate of the Tree of the Knowledge of Good and Evil. The possibility of death wasn't news to the first couple; they knew the potential consequences of their decision. God established the rule, it was consistent with His holy character, and it had to be fulfilled. God, however, not wanting death to eternally separate Him from the beings He had created in His image, devised a plan whereby the penalty for the Original Sin could be temporarily satisfied by the death of an animal substitute.

The Bible quite correctly recognizes that blood is the source of life, and when blood is removed, death ensues, so the blood taken from an animal substitutes for the death required of mankind for committing the crime of eating from the Tree of the Knowledge of Good and Evil. God's justice and mercy were on display from the beginning.

> For the life of the flesh is in the blood, and I have given it
> for you on the altar to make atonement for your souls, for
> it is the blood that makes atonement by the life. (Lev. 17:11)

God hoped that man would continue to remember Him and pass on the stories of their wonderful time together in the garden, but unfortunately, man's feeble attempts at story transmission quickly became a game of "telephone" gone horribly wrong.

> The Lord saw that the wickedness of man was great in
> the earth, and that every intention of the thoughts of his
> heart was only evil continually. And the Lord was sorry
> that he had made man on the earth, and it *grieved him to
> his heart.* So the Lord said, "I will blot out man whom I
> have created from the face of the land, man and animals
> and creeping things and birds of the heavens, for I am
> sorry that I have made them." But Noah found favor in
> the eyes of the Lord. (Gen. 6:5–8, emphasis added)

God encountered the worst "sin" infestation of all time and was forced to clean all the world's infected laundry with a "Rid" bath of floodlike proportions. Despite His grieved heart, He still made relationship with man His top priority and graciously promised to continue His pursuit of a restored relationship. He adopted man as His own and placed a rainbow mobile over his earthly crib so whenever he would look up, he would be reminded of the loving commitment of his Father.

Hi, My Name Is Erik, and I'm a Broken Human Being

Why don't you find self-help books used as the curriculum for Alcoholics Anonymous, arguably the most successful addiction treatment program ever created? Why don't the poor, destitute, and addicted practice yoga, meditate, or tap into their inner divine power? It appears that a lot of these New Age movements are designed only for the affluent, those who can afford a personal guru or a seven-part DVD series. The comfortable can place a Band-Aid over their inner pain, but the poor, destitute, and addicted are broken and need repair. If these self-help books are incapable of helping the people most in need of assistance, it would seem to me they've failed in their most important clinical trial.

Maybe we need to look to the recovering alcoholic for the answer to our dilemma. Maybe one alcoholic in treatment has more wisdom than a thousand self-help books. Maybe there's some truth to the notion that we're all broken and incapable of fixing ourselves. While most of us don't suffer from chemical addictions, we have become addicted to the idea that man is capable of alleviating his unhappiness through material novelty or spiritual innovation. Addiction treatment has taught us that hitting bottom is often the only way to strip away that illusion. We therefore need to listen carefully to our afflicted brothers and sisters because they've done the hard work of suffering on our behalf, taking on the pain of our own personal crosses to reveal the brokenness of us all and remind us we are powerless to fix it on our own.

Darrin, one of the men I met at the Union Gospel Mission, put it quite succinctly. He said he would be glad to sell a cardboard box timeshare to any unhappy affluent person to help them understand what it means to be truly dependent on God, and he would even throw in the rats for free.

While man's sinful nature grieved God's heart, He could not give up. A relationship with the unique being created in His own image was far too important to Him. Isn't it remarkable that a pesky bunch of unappreciative, rebellious humans is somehow important to the Creator of the universe?

> When I look at your heavens, the work of your fingers,
>   the moon and the stars, which you have set in place,
> *what is man that you are mindful of him, and the son of*
>   *man that you care for him?*
> Yet you have made him a little lower than the heavenly
>   beings and crowned him with glory and honor.
> You have given him dominion over the works of your
>   hands you have put all things under his feet,
> all sheep and oxen, and also the beasts of the field,
> the birds of the heavens, and the fish of the sea, whatever
>   passes along the paths of the seas. (Ps. 8:3–8,
>   emphasis added)

Message in the Stars

Why doesn't God just appear to everybody and declare He is God and let that be the end of it? If we saw a powerful display of God's power, we would surely repent, believe, and serve, but that's not the point. God doesn't want belief; He wants relationship. God knew divine miracles and signs were ultimately incapable of changing a rebellious people with a god complex. God doesn't want servants, He wants friends. He doesn't want serfs, He wants children. He doesn't want concubines, He wants a faithful spouse. God's grieved heart is not due to mankind's disobedience but to his unfaithfulness. God doesn't need our service; He can do whatever He wants, but He does want our relationship, and that cannot be coerced, only chosen.

The Hebrew people saw God's power in plagues, parted seas, and manna from heaven, so belief wasn't the issue; the real problem was they didn't realize what YHWH wanted was a relationship.

261

The chosen people all too frequently tried to act like their neighbors and appease God because that was a heck of a lot easier than the hard work of fostering a relationship.

In the Old Testament, God's anger is depicted as a jealous anger. God's jealousy, however, is not to be confused with destructive human jealousy; it's rather based on His intense desire to be the only partner in our physical and spiritual relationship and the searing pain of rejection when we choose other lovers.

Frederick Buechner, in an essay entitled *Message in the Stars*, tells the story of a particular day when God chose to reveal Himself. He wrote, "I exist" in the sky. Every day this display changed so the people would never get tired of seeing it but would be in constant awe. Some people repented, dying people were reassured there was an afterlife, and priests and pastors felt vindicated for all their years of teaching and preaching. Finally, the scene shifted to a boy who, with childlike innocence, asked, "So what?" This little boy recognized that a dramatic display of God's existence was just an amusing fireworks show, eye candy that lacked any nutritional value.

If God were just about pyrotechnics, who would care? A Technicolor light show in the sky may make one an enthusiastic spectator, but it would never be up to the task of making one a committed follower.

Your Cheatin' Heart

The Bible variously describes our relationship with God as that between a parent and a child, a lover and loved, a husband and a wife. One of the most powerful descriptions of this broken relationship between God and man is found in the book of Hosea, in which God is depicted as the faithful Husband and the people as the philandering prostitute wife. The main point of this book was that despite the unfaithfulness of the chosen people, God continued to pursue His adulterous spouse.

The Bible frequently calls the chosen people to task for prostituting themselves, whoring around, and being adulterous. Is God obsessed with sex? No, God is obsessed with monogamy, one man and one woman, one Creator and one creature, and One God and one people. He is jealous for our affection and for our ability to freely choose Him. Coercion can never be the basis for a committed, loving relationship. Remember, mankind's ultimate garden crime was not breaking some rules but breaking a relationship with God. It's one thing to steal pencils from a corporation but quite another to cheat on your husband and tell Him you don't love Him anymore.

> You have played the whore with many lovers; and would you return to me? declares the Lord. (Jer. 3:1)

We tend to see the Old Testament as merely a recounting of the mistakes made by God's people, a record of the wrongs they perpetually perpetrated. I think we miss the point if we concentrate too much on our historically documented depravity. It's not a testament to man's perpetual sinfulness but a witness to God's relentless pursuit of a philandering spouse. Why does He care so passionately about us? The Old Testament is really about God's commitment to a relationship He formalized in a progression of covenants between man and Himself. The marriage covenant between a man and woman, described in Genesis 2, served as the template for our understanding of our relationship with God. If mankind's sin had merely been a broken rule, some sort of restitution would seem adequate, but restoring a broken, committed relationship would require some serious work. God had become the jilted lover, the betrayed spouse, and His heart grieved. We became the unfaithful spouse and adulterous partner who continued to prostitute ourselves. The only thing God was powerless to do was to make us say, "I do," to His wedding proposal. God wanted an intimate, chosen relationship, not a shotgun wedding.

The New Testament makes it abundantly clear that God is love. Love just happens to be the glue that holds relationships together. When we reject God, we are not just rejecting some rule maker; we are also rejecting the essence of true relationship itself. Why do you think Jesus boiled the law down to two main commandments that both deal with intimate relationships? That was because God is the manifestation of what a committed relationship should look like.

> "Teacher, which is the great commandment in the Law?" And he said to him, "You shall love the Lord your God with all your heart and with all your soul and with all your mind. This is the great and first commandment. And a second is like it: You shall love your neighbor as yourself. On these two commandments depend all the Law and the Prophets." (Matt. 22:36–40)

The relationship dynamic in a Christian marriage is frequently depicted as a triangle, with the man and woman representing the bottom two corners and God representing the peak. As the partners focus on their love and devotion to God, they find themselves growing closer not only to God but also to one another. God is love, the glue that holds all relationships together and forms the basis of what it means to be formed in God's image.

> Beloved, let us love one another, for love is from God, and whoever loves has been born of God and knows God. Anyone who does not love does not know God, because God is love. (1 John 4:7–8)

How Do You Mend a Broken Heart?

So how does an unfaithful spouse make amends to a partner and reestablish trust when such an enormous wall of anger, resentment, and suspicion has been built up? He or she could begin with gifts and acts of service, a good start perhaps, but in the end, these are merely external acts that may or may not signal a change of heart. What the offended partner really needs is assurance of internal change, a transformed heart. Then and only then will it be possible to restore the relationship.

Sadly, the chosen people quickly made their marriage to God a sham by engaging in a string of idolatrous affairs. They tried to maintain an external façade of respectability by performing heartless acts of "Torah and sacrifice" service, but it was clear to God that they considered the relationship one of obligation and not freely chosen intimacy. How could God restore a marriage when it appeared the other party was unwilling to make any effort at all? While divorce seems to be the cultural default solution for "irreconcilable differences," it was never an option for God. Instead, He chose to do the hard work of reconciliation.

> For I hate divorce, says the LORD, the God of Israel. (Mal. 2:16)

Finally, after thousands of years of education in the school of relationship hard knocks, God stepped in, and despite our ongoing infidelity, "while we were still sinners," took on the hard work of relationship building by offering His Son. God infused a dose of the greatest love of all, the laying down of one's life for another, to make things right. The relationship was reenergized with the ultimate act of love.

We stare at Jesus hanging on the cross and our hearts are convicted. Ironically, that which Rome offered as the most vicious display of worldly power strangely became the ultimate act of God's love. As we look up at that hill and see a God willing to suffer on our behalf, we realize that the ball is in our court. God cannot do any more for our ailing relationship than offer us the greatest act of love possible, and so it's up to us. What's our choice? Will we continue to fool around with other gods, or will we accept a relationship-restoring love that we are incapable of offering on our own? Do we accept the ring and say, "I do," or do we give some weak excuse such as "It's not you, it's me. I'm just not ready for a commitment" and end up as one more spinster in hell? God cannot force the "I do," but He can make it painfully obvious what it means to say, "I don't." Enter Jesus!

> Behold, the days are coming, declares the Lord, when I will make a new covenant with the house of Israel and the house of Judah, not like the covenant that I made with their fathers on the day when I took them by the hand

> to bring them out of the land of Egypt, my covenant that they broke, though I was their husband, declares the Lord. But this is the covenant that I will make with the house of Israel after those days, declares the Lord: *I will put my law within them, and I will write it on their hearts. And I will be their God, and they shall be my people.* And no longer shall each one teach his neighbor and each his brother, saying, 'Know the Lord,' for they shall all know me, from the least of them to the greatest, declares the Lord. For I will forgive their iniquity, and I will remember their sin no more. (Jer. 31:31–34, emphasis added)

What more-profound display of relationship commitment could there be than the willingness of the offended Spouse to completely forgive all the cheating and lying, especially when the rebellious partner persisted in their unfaithfulness?

> For while we were still weak, at the right time Christ died for the ungodly. For one will scarcely die for a righteous person—though perhaps for a good person one would dare even to die— *but God shows his love for us in that while we were still sinners, Christ died for us.* (Rom. 5:6–8, emphasis added)

Heart Transplant

For His plan to succeed, man would need to have his hardened stone heart replaced with a healthy heart of flesh.

> And I will give them one heart, and a new spirit I will put within them. *I will remove the heart of stone from their flesh and give them a heart of flesh,* that they may walk in my statutes and keep my rules and obey them. And they shall be my people, and I will be their God. (Ezek. 11:19–20, emphasis added)

I vividly remember attending a pathology conference at which we passed around the anatomically abnormal heart of a baby who had just received a heart transplant and was being cared for in the NICU. It was an eerie feeling to hold a diseased human heart, noting all its anatomic abnormalities and yet knowing its previous owner was alive with a renewed chance at life. Just like this baby, we need to be able to hold our old, broken hearts in our hands, honestly analyze their defects, and rejoice in the fact we now have new hearts. Reconciliation is possible only with a new heart. God made it clear that perfunctory, outward displays of love and respect such as flowers and chocolates were inadequate for the jilted Spouse. The only possible place to begin the repair of this cosmic "separation" would be a broken and contrite heart.

> For you will not delight in sacrifice, or I would give it; you will not be pleased with a burnt offering. The sacrifices of God are a broken spirit; a broken and contrite heart, O God, you will not despise. (Ps. 51:16–17)

> For thus says the One who is high and lifted up, who inhabits eternity, whose name is Holy: "I dwell in the high and holy place, and also with him who is of a contrite and lowly spirit, to revive the spirit of the lowly, and to revive the heart of the contrite." (Isa. 57:15)

Adam 2.0

> Mary's pregnancy, in poor circumstances, and with the father unknown, would have been an obvious case for abortion; and her talk of having conceived as a result of an intervention of the Holy Ghost would have pointed to the need for psychiatric treatment, and made the case for terminating her pregnancy even stronger. Thus, our generation, needing a savior more, perhaps, than any that has ever existed, would be to humane to allow one to be born; to enlightened to permit the Light of the World to shine in a darkness that grows ever more oppressive.[144]

> —Malcolm Muggeridge

Adam and Eve had committed the mind-boggling crime of divine identity theft, and it could not be ignored; the criminals had to be extradited to the scene of the crime and tried in a court of law. Since God had barred mankind from returning to the garden because of unholiness, He had to provide an alternate mechanism for the legal process to proceed. God compassionately gave them opportunities to settle out of court through sacrificial work-release programs and community-service options, but it was clear their criminal minds were not reformed. They went through the motions but failed to recognize the severity of their crime.

A court date was set, but a suitable representative was needed to make an appearance in the garden courtroom. A New Adam was needed, One who fully understood the motives of the criminal and seriousness of the offense but had never personally committed any crime that would bar Him entry into the courtroom.

> He is the image of God in human form, God's perfect self-portrait and humanity's perfect prototype.[145]
>
> —Gerald Sittser

His credentials were impeccable; He had been tested in the most rigorous wilderness bar exam ever administered. During the oral portion of His exam, He was presented with several scenarios to test His knowledge of the specifics of His clients' case. He demonstrated a thorough understanding of the Law and passed with flying colors.

> Then Jesus was led up by the Spirit into the wilderness to be tempted by the devil. And after fasting forty days and forty nights, he was hungry. And the tempter came and said to him, "*If you are the Son of God,* command these stones to become loaves of bread." But he answered, "*It is written,* 'Man shall not live by bread alone, but by every word that comes from the mouth of God.'"
>
> Then the devil took him to the holy city and set him on the pinnacle of the temple and said to him, "*If you are the Son of God,* throw yourself down, for *it is written*

'He will command his angels concerning you,' and" 'On their hands they will bear you up, lest you strike your foot against a stone.' Jesus said to him, *"Again it is written,* 'You shall not put the Lord your God to the test.'"

Again, the devil took him to a very high mountain and showed him all the kingdoms of the world and their glory. And he said to him, "All these I will give you, if you will fall down and worship me." Then Jesus said to him, "Be gone, Satan! *For it is written,* 'You shall worship the Lord your God and him only shall you serve.'" Then the devil left him, and behold, angels came and were ministering to him. (Matt 4:4–11, emphasis added)

Instead of being tested in a garden, Jesus was tested in the wilderness. While Adam and Eve were tempted when they were fat and happy, Jesus fasted forty days and was tempted when He was at His most physically and emotionally vulnerable. My daughter pointed out to me just how embarrassing for the Devil this must have been because of his inability to successfully tempt Jesus even when He was near death.

Adam and Eve's failure to resist temptation in the garden resulted in their expulsion into the wilderness. Jesus' ability to resist temptation in the wilderness allowed Him to enter the garden. Some would be quick to point out that since Jesus was God, it would have been easy for Him to resist temptation, but I have to counter with the fact that Adam and Eve sought to attain power they didn't have while Jesus resisted using powers He possessed and had every right to use. What is a greater temptation, trying to obtain power you can never get or resisting the urge to use power you already have?

The Final Solution: Death on a Cross

God had made it clear to His chosen people that the only way they could maintain a relationship with Him was to acknowledge their crimes and offer payment. He had established a sacrificial model of justice for His people. But what about the rest of the world? Didn't God say to Abraham that His salvation plan would be a blessing for *all the nations*? How could God link the chosen people to His corporate vision for the rest of mankind? He had to extend the scope of the sacrificial system to include the rest of humanity. To accomplish this enormous task, He had to make the sacrificial system of the chosen people relevant to the sins of the rest of the pagan world.

If the Jewish religious establishment didn't participate, it would not have been a proper atoning sacrifice, and if the Gentiles were not involved, it would not have been efficacious for all. The perfect Jewish sacrifice had to be performed on a secular, cross-shaped altar to ensure the salvation of all people.

> The concept of substitution may be said, then, to lie at the heart of both sin and salvation. For the essence of sin is man substituting himself for God, while the essence of salvation is God substituting himself for man. Man asserts himself against God and puts himself where only God deserve to be; God sacrifices himself for man and puts himself where only man deserves to be. Man claims prerogatives which belong to God alone; God accepts penalties which belong to man alone.[146]
>
> —John R. Stott

On the Jewish Day of Atonement, a specific series of rituals had to be performed for the sacrifice to effectively cleanse the people and the temple from sin. God had already established the protocol; an unblemished animal would have the sins of the people conferred upon it by the laying on of hands, the animal would be sacrificed, and the blood sprinkled on the people and in the temple.

The consequence of the Original Sin was death, which would have meant permanent separation from God, a situation God found intolerable, so He established a sacrificial mechanism whereby man could still maintain a relationship with Him. God could not change the penalty for mankind's rebellion since that would be contrary to His just nature, but He could institute a system whereby someone or something could take the punishment and allow for the possibility of a continued relationship between them. God had made it clear that life was in the blood, so an offering of the blood of another living creature could temporarily satisfy the death penalty warranted by Adam and Eve's divine coup attempt. Sprinkling the blood of the sacrifice on the people and the temple allowed man to temporarily come near God's presence because the crime had been acknowledged and the penalty had been paid.

In addition, blood not only payed a penalty but also preserved life. The blood of the sacrificed lamb painted on the doorposts and lintel of the houses of God's people in Egypt preserved them from the final plague, death of the firstborn. Jesus is also the Passover lamb and His blood not only pays a universal debt but it also paves the way for universal eternal life.

An animal sacrifice, however, was only a temporary solution. It was incapable of permanently eliminating the sins of mankind for several reasons. First of all, animals lacked human DNA; they were poor substitutes for the real criminal, man. Second, the animals knew nothing of sin or the law, and third, they went to the sacrifice unwillingly. Jesus, however, fulfilled all the criteria necessary for a permanent sacrifice; He became a biological man, He understood the significance of the infraction and the requirements of the law though innocent of any crime, and finally, He willingly went to the cross with the expressed purpose of redeeming mankind.

As we mentioned before, the greatest demonstration of relationship commitment is laying down one's life for another. As an unblemished human, Jesus was qualified to have the sins of everyone placed on Him. During His passion, he had the hands of the Jewish religious establishment, the chosen people, the Roman Gentile state, and even His friends laid upon Him in such a way that He truly took on the sins of the world.

> As He feels his friend's lips graze His cheek for an instant, maybe He feels nothing else. It is another of His last times. On this last evening of His life he has eaten His last meal, and this is the last time that He will ever

feel the touch of another human being except in torment. It is not the Lamb of God and His butcher who meet here, but two old friends embracing in a garden knowing that they will never see one another again.[147]

—Frederick Buechner

In addition, the sacrifice occurred not on a Jewish temple altar, which would have been efficacious only for the chosen people, but on a pagan cross-altar, which made it effective for all mankind. While the doctrinal consistencies between the Jewish sacrificial system and Calvary are astounding, we must remember the cross is not just an intellectual argument for the theologian but more important, the sacrificial relationship commitment of a spurned Spouse who passionately desires reconciliation.

Calvary is not a very complex solution to human sin, but it cost God all He had. And Calvary was God's crying place. To change a world is to spend everything and then to wait and weep.[148]

—Calvin Miller

The Burden of Proof

Jesus, as man's legal representative, was obligated to bring all the overwhelming evidence against His client to trial. Unfortunately, there is no statute of limitations on sin. The accumulated hatred, anger, and rejection harbored in the souls of man were focused like a laser beam on the cross. Jesus represented everything the world was not, and the world hated Him for it. He held up a mirror to the world, and what the world saw wasn't a King but an Emperor without any clothes. Instead of covering themselves up, they thought it would be better to destroy the mirror bearer. The cumulative rejection of God by all the people of the world was the darkness and isolation Jesus felt on the cross. The ultimate manifestation of the Original Sin of trying to become like God would inevitably lead to a divine hit job, and there, on the cross, Jesus experienced the impenetrable darkness evoked by the murder of God. Just like cosmic, primal-scream therapy, man effectively cursed God until he was blue in the face, spewing all the venom in his soul upon the cross. Physically spent and dog-tired, mankind slouched and propped himself up against God's tomb to rest, oblivious to the flurry of activity taking place in the celestial courtroom above.

All Rise!

> For Christ has entered, not into holy places made with hands, which are copies of the true things, but into heaven itself, now to appear in the presence of God on our behalf. (Heb. 9:24)

The trial is about to begin, and our defense Attorney has just entered the garden courtroom. As He makes His way to His seat at the right hand of the Judge, we notice a very strange thing—the blood dripping from His wounds doesn't leave a trail of crimson guilt; it makes the garden grass a more luscious shade of green. The crime-scene tape evaporates, and the chalk marks silhouetting the image of the fallen man quickly fade.

> Come now, let us reason together, says the Lord: though your sins are like scarlet, they shall be as white as snow; though they are red like crimson, they shall become like wool. (Isa. 1:18)

A hush falls over the courtroom as the Judge waits for Him to present His case. He reaches into His briefcase to pull out the charges, but His briefcase is empty! He peers up, eyes barely able to see through the blood dripping from His bleeding brow; He holds up His scarred hands and announces to the Judge, "The price has been paid. It is finished!" The Judge bangs His gavel and bellows, "Case dismissed!"

Our Advocate, barely able to contain Himself, quickly leaves the courtroom to report the good news to His clients. When He appears to them, they can't believe their eyes; they thought they had just witnessed the death of all hope, but now He's telling them hope has just been born. It seems too good to be true; how can they be sure He testified on their behalf?

Thomas, the most skeptical client, wants proof, so he asks Jesus to reveal His legal scar credentials that certify His work. But wait! Wouldn't it have been a better story if Jesus' scars were gone, signifying the fact He had conquered their sin and emerged unblemished? No, because then it would have been only a symbolic redemption and not a truly efficacious redemption. Jesus retains His scars to remind His followers there was no easy way to salvation; a cross had to be carried—no twelve steps to holiness, no anointing with holy oil, no conquering messiah, but rather the death of a suffering servant.

His job complete, He instructs His friends to spread the good news verdict to everyone, to tell them the garden, which had previously been roped off with crime-scene tape, is once again open for those who accept Him as their legal representative. The class action appeal has been won, but the benefits of victory are available only to those who sign on. Jesus invites those created in God's image to once again stroll the garden park with Him.

> Only if I AM found in your heart will our relationship be restored. I Am going to do what you are incapable of, I will provide the ultimate guilt offering for you and make all your external acts obsolete. In the process I will dwell in a new temple, your own body! Our vows will be made and the two of us shall be one. All I ask is that you understand how much I love you and the lengths I went to restore our relationship. I have stepped in to take the knowledge that you acquired in the garden and restore it to its proper place, to make evil a potentiality and not an actuality, and rescue you from the consequences of your rebellion. I will, however, take rejection of this gift as an indication that you would rather be unfaithful, and

if you do choose that path, I will be heartbroken, I will weep, because this is your last chance and we will never be together again.

—God as channeled through the author

Freedom of Choice

We go into the world's restaurant to find amusement. We sit down at the table and order the finest sin it has to offer. Once the meal arrives, we dig in and eat until our bellies are full. We sit back, loosen our belts, and relax in our culinary stupor. As our tryptophan rush of sinful gluttony begins to wear off, the waiter presents us with the check. Didn't someone once say there were no free lunches? We realize our appetite has run up a bill we cannot pay, a debt we cannot settle. We rustle through our pockets and pull out a bulletin from a Christmas service we attended six months previously, but the waiter is unimpressed.

Nervously, we prepare ourselves for an eternity in the hot, humid kitchen trying to wash enough dishes to pay off our debt. Our weeping and gnashing is suddenly interrupted by the presence of a holy benefactor. Jesus picks up the bill, crumbles it, and stuffs it in His pocket. He wraps an apron around His waist and heads to the kitchen to clean our dirty dishes. The waiter tells us we're free to go. But as we leave, Jesus' parting words ring in our ears: "Temptation comes with a heavy price. I have paid it once and for all. Don't ever underestimate the cost again."

The great news is that we are given the opportunity to personally rid ourselves of Adam and Eve's Original Sin by once again exercising that most-cherished and God-given gift, free will. Jesus stands in front of us just as the forbidden tree stood in front of Adam and Eve, but this time, the choice to eat the body and blood grants us access back into the garden and not expulsion.

We Christians are accused of being exclusive and arrogant by limiting salvation to those who choose Jesus, but if you think about it, what God offers us is the ultimate free choice—the opportunity to determine our eternal dwelling place. Our culture gets a little peeved when Christians claim that Jesus is the only salvation pathway, but the problem is that the world doesn't know what the dilemma is, for if it did, the answer would make perfect sense. If we have a nebulous understanding of man's problem, any nebulous solution will do, but if we honestly look at what the real problem is, we will clearly see there's only one adequate solution. I don't think our culture is so concerned about the mechanism of our Christian salvation but just mad we Christians don't accept those it has invented for us.

> Anselm was right that only *man should* make reparation for his sin, since it is he who has defaulted. And he was equally right that only *God could* make the necessary reparation, since it is He who has demanded it. Jesus Christ is therefore the only Savior, since He is the only person in whom the *"should"* and the *"could"* are united, being Himself both God and man.[149]
>
> —John R. Stott (emphasis added)

Why are atheists so mad about hell? God doesn't send people to hell; He is far too concerned with our free will to do anything that drastic. He desires that everybody be saved but respects our ability to choose and make decisions that are not coerced. We can choose Jesus and salvation or eternal separation from God. The free will that got mankind into trouble in the first place is redeemed by once again letting it take center stage. This time, however, the consequence for choosing is not "You shall surely die" but "You shall surely live."

> Hell must be an awesome place not so much because of its fires, whether real or metaphorical, but because of its deluded occupants ... Hell is not just other people. It is something, which those who find themselves there have helped to construct. It is not so much the prison of the damned as their chosen domicile.[150]

—Paul Johnson

It's a Mystery!

The apostle Paul, before his encounter with the risen Christ, had spent his life reading the opening chapters to God's story. He was able to see the set, props, characters, and the conflict, but the rest of the story remained a mystery to him. The sentences and paragraphs seemed to offer some clues, but the plot resolution remained unknown to him until he was confronted with the Word Himself.

As it turned out, the story he had spent his life reading had a surprise ending, a plot twist nobody suspected. Paul was stunned as he reread the story because he began to find the clues that had been there all the time. It was similar to our modern experience of seeing a movie with a completely unexpected ending. Once the theater lights come back on, we flash back to those earlier scenes that might have given us clues to the surprise ending. In fact, we may want to see the movie again so we can try to pick up on every detail. Once we leave the theater, we can barely contain our excitement; we start telling everyone about it and encourage them to see the movie as well. Paul's enthusiastic response to God's salvation mystery thriller was no different, except that the ramifications of not seeing this particular drama were far more consequential.

Our witness to this unexpected, good news ending should not be construed as a requirement for Christian club membership or a mere obligation to sell a certain number of boxes of Salvation Thin Mints. Our motivation should be overwhelming gratitude for the surprise, happy ending to our life dramas. Failure to tell others about it should be considered a crime against humanity, a human rights violation of biblical proportions. We are not just publicists trying to drum up sales for the Author but are rather very picky salvation consumers who have just hit the mother lode.

To me, though I am the very least of all the saints, this grace was given, to preach to the Gentiles the unsearchable riches of Christ, and to bring to light for everyone *what is the plan of the mystery hidden for ages in God who created all things,* so that through the church the manifold wisdom of God might now be made known to the rulers and authorities in the heavenly places. (Eph. 3:8–10, emphasis added)

That's Not How I Role

Mankind could never have come up with a magnificent plot twist of the magnitude found in the New Testament; it goes against every fiber in our human bodies. Since it's unlike anything mankind could have devised, it makes us wonder if maybe this idea came from somewhere else.

The great pitfall of Christian art, especially when it tries to portray the birth of Christ, is sentimentalism ... the Incarnation becomes merely a Christmas card with all the scandal taken out of it instead of what St. Paul called 'a stumbling block to Jews and folly to Gentiles', instead of the proclamation that the Creator of the ends of the earth came among us in diapers.[151]

—Frederick Buechner

The Bible consistently portrays a God who doesn't roll like any other god. He is a God unified in character and behavior; He cares so much about people that He gives them the dignity of choice. He repeatedly reminds them they must care for the alien, poor, widowed, orphaned, and criminal. He chooses to associate with those lower on the social scale rather than ally Himself with the powers of the world. He allows His chosen people to be fruitful and multiply through infertile women. He speaks of a kingdom reserved for the poor, grieving, and hopeless, not the rich, type A overachievers. He says they need to be like children and not responsible adults to enter His kingdom. He makes it clear repeatedly that the God-man problem is one of broken relationships and not broken rules.

The just and loving God of the Hebrews was quite different from the selfish, impetuous, power-hungry, sensual, arbitrary gods of their ancient near Eastern neighbors. Since the Judeo-Christian God is so remarkably different from every other deity, why would we expect His solution to our problem be anything but unique?

> But if a man is seen going into a "house of ill repute" without a Bible, he might be mistaken for a customer. And everyone knows the risk of this kind of vulnerability when they see it. But it's the risk that Jesus took.[152]
>
> —Keith Miller

Who Is Your Messiah?

We are all looking for some sort of savior to rescue us from our unhappiness. Unfortunately, we continue to rehearse the Original Sin of trying to be like God and attempt to create our own personal messiahs. The Jewish people were waiting for a powerful king who would overthrow Rome, and the Romans were waiting for the most powerful caesar. Our culture looks for the highest paying job, the best-looking girlfriend or boyfriend, the most accomplished children, or the sportiest car. The only Messiah who will ultimately suffice, however, is the One who calls us to suffer, carry our crosses, die to ourselves, and surrender our delusions of deity.

Of all the religious figures who have appeared throughout history, offering answers to our human dilemma, Jesus has the most street cred. He clearly recognized man had a problem, and He went directly to those most impoverished by it. He didn't look for those who had the resources to pay for His wisdom but rather gave freely to those most in need.

We most often measure the value of a message by the direct experience of the speaker or writer. Drug and alcohol counselors are far more effective if they've had firsthand experience with addiction. People can sniff out insincerity a mile away, but Jesus walked the walk and went to the mat for mankind. The Pharisees were appalled by Jesus' claim that He was God, but is it possible their real outrage was at the type of God He claimed to be? They were looking for a military messiah who would unleash God's power on their foes, but Jesus chose to be a humble teacher. All their foreign neighbors had powerful gods, so claiming a suffering servant God would just be too embarrassing.

Even the disciples struggled with this radical concept. Jesus rebuked Peter by calling him Satan when he tried to deny the possibility that Jesus would suffer and die. Jesus' reference to Satan was designed to remind Peter of the garden temptation and the danger in trying to redefine God in human terms. Peter tried to get Jesus to be the God he wanted instead of the God He was. We, like Peter, also have a bit of garden fruit stuck in our teeth and can't quite get the divine taste out despite trying to be faithful flossers.

> "The Spirit of the Lord is upon me, because he has anointed me to proclaim good news to the poor. He has sent me to proclaim liberty to the captives and recovering of sight to the blind, to set at liberty those who are oppressed, to proclaim the year of the Lord's favor." And he rolled up the scroll and gave it back to the attendant and sat down. And the eyes of all in the synagogue were fixed on him. And he began to say to them, "Today this Scripture has been fulfilled in your hearing." (Luke 4:18–19)

God's vision of a restored creation was a kingdom of shalom in which the evils of poverty, oppression, and physical disability would no longer plague His creation. It would be a kingdom in which all things would work as God had originally intended and would be unlike anything ever conceived or built by man. The world had become possessed by the actualized evil that man had ingested in the garden, and the only hope was an exorcism.

Many of Jesus' healings were depicted as the release of evil spirits. Some would argue that these "demon possessions" were frequently just misunderstood biological diseases; while that may be true, it doesn't change the fact that any disruption in God's plan was still due to introduced evil and needed to be removed.

Puzzles and Parables

> Give ear, O my people, to my teaching; incline your ears
> to the words of my mouth!
> I will open my mouth in a parable; I will utter dark
> sayings from of old,
> things that we have heard and known, that our fathers
> have told us.
> We will not hide them from their children, but tell to the
> coming generation the glorious deeds of the Lord,
> and his might, and the wonders that he has done.
> (Ps. 78:1–4)

I have spent a great deal of time explaining the importance of Jesus' death and resurrection in reestablishing our broken relationship with God, but we cannot forget He came also as a teacher. He not only made a restored relationship possible but also revealed to us what that relationship would look like. God, the Author, chose to come down to earth in the form of man to make personal guest appearances and offer public readings of His grand story.

Jesus' parables served to remind His listeners of the larger God narrative in which they lived. Jesus shifted the discussion from the crowd-pleasing stories of man-made military kingdoms anticipated by the Jewish people and the Roman state to tales of a kingdom best understood in agricultural terms. He preferred to get "back to the soil" and use examples of things directly created by God rather than derivatively fashioned by man. His use of rural metaphors and analogies allowed His parables to work the soil of the heart rather than overtake the ramparts of the will. He declared that the kingdom would begin like the smallest of seeds and not by the conquest of the largest army. The kingdom would arrive slowly, like a crop, and not be won overnight in battle. The kingdom would not be forced but would be chosen and belong to those whose soil was conditioned to receive it. The kingdom would not be built on a clear-cut field but would grow up through the weeds. The kingdom would be full of vulnerable sheep, not brave lions. The Ruler of this kingdom would care more about the one clueless lost sheep, the one reprobate son, than all those who followed the rules. Finally, the borders of this kingdom would not be protected by military outposts but by the shed blood of a crucified Jewish criminal.

> The harlots who have no imagined righteousness to protect will be dancing into the Kingdom while you have your alleged virtue burned out of you! Hear me well: I have come to announce the dawn of a new age, and era of incredible generosity. Allow yourselves to be captivated by joy and wonder at the surpassing greatness of my father's love for the least; set its life grounded against your own joyless, loveless, thankless, and self-righteous lives. Let go of your impoverished understanding of God and your circumscribed notion of morality. Strike out in a new direction. Cease your loveless ways and be compassionate. Celebrate the homecoming of the lost and rejoice in my Father's munificence.[153]
>
> —Brennan Manning

To most of Jesus' listeners, these stories were intriguing but probably didn't make much sense. Like the pied piper of parables, His little story tunes took them to the foot of the cross, where they must have scratched their heads and asked, "Is this where the kingdom is found?" And after His crucifixion, they would have walked back to their homes and families, marveling at the mighty works of the Roman kingdom that surrounded them on all sides and feeling sorry for Jesus. He seemed so well intentioned but so out of touch with reality.

Three days later, however, they would be stunned by reports that Jesus had risen from the dead and had promised to send a Helper to explain everything they had previously thought was folly. When the Helper arrived at Pentecost, He guided them into all truth, and they began to connect the dots of God's grand narrative. The parables and Scripture suddenly made sense in the context of Jesus' life, death, and resurrection.

The clues had been there all along. The crucifixion of Jesus allowed the people to take their rebellious storyline to its ultimate conclusion, the death of God, but as it turned out, the story didn't stop there; God hadn't died, and man could now have eternal life! Mankind's ultimate crime against God was transformed into God's ultimate act of forgiveness. Stunning! Empowered with this knowledge, they began one of the most amazing publicity tours ever mounted.

> The Biblical view of things is resurrection—not a future that is just a consolation for the life we never had but a restoration of the life you always wanted. This means that every horrible thing that ever happened will not only be undone and repaired but will in some way make the eventual glory and joy even greater.[154]
>
> —Timothy Keller

I Still Feel a Bit Queasy

The ending to God's salvation story is unexpected, edgy, and full of gnashing and weeping, joy and fulfillment. If we understand what Jesus did for us and know it all ends in a wedding feast, why are we still anxious? It makes sense that our sins have been taken away and we are now eligible for an extended eternity kingdom cruise with God, but why do we still take every opportunity to lower ourselves overboard into the dingy of despair? Why are we still embroiled in the plot conflict if Jesus resolved it? It's important to remember that we have been given important literary insight into the set, props, and characters, we understand the story conflict and have witnessed the most remarkable plot twist resolution, but we haven't yet read the last chapter of our personal stories. So what are we supposed to do until the promised wedding feast? We're excited about the weekend party to come but still feel as if it's a Monday.

God wants the wedding feast of the Lamb to be the biggest blowout party the universe has ever known, a party to which everyone is invited, but not everybody has RSVP'd. The people must decide whether they want to piece together their own illusory kingdoms or take up residence in a room in a mansion already prepared for them.

Our job is to deliver wedding invitations to as many people as possible so every seat in the sanctuary will be filled. Many will decide not to attend because they never really bothered to take time to get to know the bride or the groom. God will be quite sad when He declares the couple to be husband and wife and looks out to see a sanctuary of empty seats. Our mission is to make sure God doesn't look out on a half-filled house.

Don't you think the final chapter to God's Book of Life would be quite unsatisfactory if every carefully crafted character didn't have the opportunity to respond to the Author's wedding invitation?

> So when they had come together, they asked him, "Lord, will you at this time restore the kingdom to Israel?" He said to them, "It is not for you to know times or seasons that the Father has fixed by his own authority. But you will receive power when the Holy Spirit has come upon you, and you will be my witnesses in Jerusalem and in all Judea and Samaria, and to the end of the earth." And when he had said these things, as they were looking on, he was lifted up, and a cloud took him out of their sight. (Acts 1:6–9)

Jesus took the punishment for our sin, but our rewards cards aren't activated until we die; until we check into God's kingdom hotel, we don't need a key to the room. The good news, however, is that when we arrive, Jesus will be waiting for us key in hand.

I Believe! Help My Unbelief!

> The Lord knew it was going to be hard for me to change into the person he wanted me to be, because I was so used to living the total opposite. He had a lot of hell to squeeze out of me, and believe me—when the hell leaves you, sometimes it screams at God on the way out. And when the pain from your past leaves you, sometimes you have to feel it again on the way out.[155]
>
> —Brian "Head" Welch

Brian "Head" Welch, the lead guitarist of the rock group Korn, wrote *Save Me from Myself,* a book in which he discussed how he became a follower of Christ. He pointed out that his initial joy of being saved was followed by a very difficult period of transition into the Christian life. This is a common scenario for many new Christians. Why is this transition difficult? New Christians are often the most on-fire followers of Christ you will ever encounter; their enthusiasm is infectious. They have suffered dearly for living lives characterized by sinful self-worship. They reached bottom and saw no hope for themselves until they met Jesus. Finally, they found someone who loved them unconditionally and was willing to redeem the pain and suffering they could never redeem themselves. Once the high of knowing God's love receded, they were left with a closetful of sinful junk that needed to be cleaned out. In human fashion, they systematically sorted through each piece of sinful behavior and tried to fit it into their new lifestyle instead of backing the dumpster up to the closet and emptying it out in one shot.

> In childhood I thought of each of my sins as a brick filling in a space that walled me off from God. My guilt feelings blinded me to the truth that I was busily constructing a wall God had already destroyed.[156]
>
> —Philip Yancey

Conclusion

Every character in God's story is exceptional; each one is special in his or her own way, but despite these unique differences, there's a common thread that runs through each of their lives; they were created to be in a relationship with God. Unfortunately, we have all in one way or another been accomplices to Adam and Eve's divine cosmic coup. We continue to be a bunch of unrepentant insurrectionists, yet remarkably, God still extends us His grace despite the severity of our crime. His grace is based on potential and not pity. He created us in His image; He stamped us with His divine seal of approval, identifying us as members of His posse, and tearfully watched as we defaced it by spray-painting it over with human gang signs.

The problem with man was not the craftsmanship but the application, like finding a rare Ming vase and using it for a spittoon. God recognized that underneath the saliva and tobacco stains of sin was a beautiful, one-of-a-kind Ming vase that if properly cleaned would once again be suitable for display in His prized creation gallery. God's rare vase collection, however, was incomplete. Many of His most prized pieces had been lost or stolen, so He sent His one and only curator Son on a mission to restore His collection. He poured all His resources into Him and told Him to spare no expense, to even risk His life in the darkness of the antiquities black market to make sure His collection would be complete.

Every good story has a powerful ending that resolves conflict and ties up loose ends. Unfortunately, the plot tension in every other worldview story is incompletely addressed, leaving those who peruse them confused, disappointed, and angry that they wasted so much time reading them in the first place.

Buddhism declared that the book had an interesting cover but declared that reading it and getting too engrossed in the storyline was actually the problem. Hinduism encouraged us to read the story, but instead of resolving the conflict, it left us hanging until the next poorly made sequel. Atheism offered a final chapter but concluded that there never was a plotline in the first place and that the reader should just feel fortunate to have made it until the end of the book. New Age religion, strangely enough, decided to avoid the messiness of finding a specific solution by declaring that the plot conflict was the solution. New agers in effect asserted that trying to be like God wasn't a bad thing after all and then offered mankind all sorts of new opportunities to take up a seat in God's throne room, vaguely promising them there would be enough divine chairs for everyone.

Each of these other worldviews naïvely clings to the notion that man is somehow up to the task of fixing himself. The Christian worldview, however, is the only one that has the guts to admit what we already know deep down inside, that we are broken and cannot fix ourselves, and then offers us a most glorious remedy.

A crucified Jesus hangs from the cross in view of us all and presents us with a choice: accept the ultimate offer of relationship restoration, a cruci-"fix," or continue to "look for love in all the wrong places."

> In him we have redemption through his blood, the forgiveness of our trespasses, according to the riches of his grace, which he lavished upon us, in all wisdom and insight making known to us the mystery of his will, according to his purpose, which he set forth in Christ as a plan for the fullness of time, to unite all things in him, things in heaven and things on earth. (Eph. 1:7–10)

Chapter Eleven

THE CAST PARTY

O NE DAY, YOUR STORY WILL come to an end; your character in this grand earth drama will have recited his or her last line. You will hope you have given the performance of your life but wonder if the many years of hard work you put into your personal character development weren't just a cosmic waste of time.

What happens next? If you are an atheist, you can pat yourself on the back for giving life the good old college try but must accept the fact that "school's out forever" and you won't be invited to any future homecoming games. The contract for your one-man improv show has expired, and there is very little interest in the video retrospective of your brief, unremarkable career.

If you believe in reincarnation, you have another shot at the big time. Unfortunately, appealing to your past-life performances as a pharaoh or a queen doesn't guarantee a future as a headliner because some of the mistakes you made along the way may relegate you to the level of a mere prop in some other karmic overachiever's life story. Perhaps you will experience spiritual release, jettison your illusory biological character prison, and reunite with a great, nameless, faceless cosmic force, or maybe, just maybe, you will be reunited with your fellow actors at the cast party for the greatest story ever told. It will be a chance to reminisce with other life thespians about your shared past performances and corporately anticipate the day when the curtain will once again be raised and a new Broadway run will begin. This cast party won't be just a bunch of old people sitting around talking about their bowel habits or what they had for lunch but will be characterized by youthful, pant-peeing exuberance in anticipation of the wedding feast to come, a second chance to perform your part with all the nuance and subtlety the Author had originally intended.

Our life, like any good story, must have a final chapter in which all the joy and sadness, doubt and certainty, and failure and accomplishment are conclusively resolved. I suspect you'd be disappointed if you spent hours reading a book and arrived at the last chapter only to find that the author hadn't tied the plot lines together or provided a satisfactory resolution to the dramatic story tension. Why should it be any different with our own stories? Don't you think that it would be odd if, when you turned the last page of your life, it still didn't make any sense? If, as our atheist friends opine, our lives are the result of purely random forces, then any ending will do whether it makes sense or not. If, however, we are characters in a larger story, we would be justified in expecting a satisfactory conclusion to all the drama we experienced in our lives.

Since only the Author is omniscient, our roles in His drama may make sense only once we've reached the concluding chapter and have looked back on the events of our lives with enough perspective to finally recognize the glorious characters we were created to be.

Unfortunately, for the majority of us, our best panoramic view is uncomfortably found on cemetery hill. I don't mean morbid speculation on how we will die but rather reflection on where we have been and what lies beyond. It's a steep climb we approach with trepidation because we're afraid of what we might see from the summit as we look back on the circuitous trail we have trampled through the valleys of our lives. We will most likely wince when we see how we had veered off the yellow brick road of God's plotline and engaged in impertinent improvisation in the poppy fields of pleasure or got lost in the dark forest of sin. We will see the places where the flying monkeys of desire carried us off to the castle of despair, and we will regret the opportunities we missed to douse the wicked witch of sin with the holy water of faith.

I suspect that almost all human beings, if they were honest, would tell you they had regrets about the way they had lived their lives. Maybe it was a lack of courage to pursue their dreams, a mechanical inability to love and mend relationships, or even disappointment at the times they behaved as if their brains were made of straw. How is it possible to have regrets if no life storyline standard exists?

As we contemplate our thespian missteps, we are even more ashamed because the road paved with gold bricks was always only a mere stone's drop away from the trail we had carelessly blazed.

> "Let him who is without sin among you be the first to throw a stone at her" ...But when they heard it, they went away one by one, *(dropping their stones)*, beginning with the older ones, and Jesus was left alone with the woman standing before him. (John 8:7, 9, my addition)

It Ain't Right

We have all had moments when we've thought, *Life shouldn't be like this. Something just doesn't seem right.* Why would we entertain thoughts like these unless we knew there was something better? Maybe it's in those moments that our stopped-up ears are briefly opened and we hear the distant echo of God's voice: "It is good, it is good, it is good." Why do we know life on earth doesn't function as it should but don't come to the conclusion that it should be scrapped and rebuilt in a new way? We don't want destruction; we want restoration. We sense an underlying goodness to the world that has been concealed because we catch glimpses of God's beautiful hardwood floor hidden beneath the pink shag carpet of man's sinfulness. The solution is not to destroy the beautiful hardwood floor but to get rid of the ugly, smelly carpet. Restoration is in fact what God promises us in the Bible.

Buddhism and Hinduism suggest that both the carpet and the wood are the problem and that the sooner we detach ourselves from the physical illusion of a floor, the better off we'll be. I think, however, if we were honest, we would probably not be all that thrilled with a disembodied spiritual existence after death but would prefer to live in a physically restored earth. Deep down inside, we know the earth is a "good" place that occasionally even borders on being a "very good" place.

Regardless of how we view the afterlife, we don't really want to die because we find this planet quite amusing. We recognize there's something special about this world despite all the pain and suffering but cannot quite put our finger on it. It would appear that Christianity provides the most satisfactory explanation for this desire for restoration. God was always calling the chosen people to remember His earthly work. God's sovereign power is most often illustrated in the Bible by references to His physical creation. God created a physical world and made physical covenants with His people. He met them in a physical temple. He remarkably chose to become a physical man descended from an earthly lineage to make things right on this physical planet. Why would we expect a God who has so much physical investment in this world to scrap it all for cloud condos?

Graveside Gazing

Death raises so many questions, but the topic is rarely if ever raised in polite conversation. Along with birth, death is one of the few topics mankind completely agrees on. We will absolutely gush at the one and yet run for cover from the other. Why do we avoid the topic of death? I suggest that a discussion of death forces us to momentarily exit the highway of life at our personal scenic lookout points, vistas where we are afforded a clear view of our past, and we cringe as we read the historical markers bluntly critiquing the points of interest below. Unfortunately, the rationalizing, justifying, and excuse making of our inner press secretary has entered the "no spin zone" and finds the podium exceedingly uncomfortable. Death is where your worldview rubber meets the road!

> I sit beside my empty grave and peer at the blank headstone. I wonder to myself what words will be inscribed upon it? Will my life be worthy of elegant poetry or an actuarial table? Will my tombstone direct the attention of the mourner to the decaying corpse below, or offer a forwarding address to the glorious new home that I spent my whole life saving up for? Will it be marked with a gleaming cross pointing others heavenward or will it be littered with junk mail still eagerly offering me solutions for a happier life.
>
> —Author's lament

Every worldview has to confront this blank, gray tombstone, and it's frequently there that many a worldview ends up attending its own funeral. If there is no God, the only hope for meaning in this life is to somehow create a memory that will outlive your puny insignificant existence. The problem with that scenario is that the world has serious short-term memory issues, and the impressive array of earthly accomplishments adorning your gravesite will quickly be blown away by the indiscriminate winds of time. Your tombstone of temerity will one day topple, and as that monument falls, so will your last vestige of significance.

Jesus, on the other hand, quickly demolishes the absurd idea that our significance can somehow be permanently impressed upon the world by awarding posthumous honorary diplomas. Jesus instead says something absolutely shocking, that people who warranted a glorious afterlife are buried in a pauper's grave—no fancy mausoleums, no golden urns of sacred human ash, and no elaborate headstones poetically serenading them off to a better life. Their graves are marked with two twigs that form a cross instructing the passersby to look elsewhere for significance. Confused, nonbelieving graveside mourners will look about for any evidence of human accomplishment; they will search through the *Who's Who* of human significance and find no entries.

Surprisingly, as they strain their ears to hear echoes of any human worth, they are deaf to the party that's rockin' above as another saint enters heaven. In *The Great Divorce*, C. S. Lewis described a glorious procession passing through heaven that honored one particular woman. The main character asked what famous person she was and received a surprising answer.

> It's someone ye'll never have heard of. Her name on earth was Sarah Smith and she lived at Golders Green ... Aye. She is one of the great ones. Ye have heard that fame in this country and fame on earth are two quite different things ... But already there is joy enough in the little finger of a great saint such as yonder lady to waken all the dead things of the universe into life.[157]
>
> —C. S. Lewis

Portrait Sitting

Isn't it interesting that the only time we're able to sit still for our life portraits is when we're dead? Instead of carefully painting them ourselves, we end up handing the brush and palette to a pastor, family member, or friend. It's just like when we attended elementary school and were asked to write papers on how we spent our summer vacations, but this time, the papers are about how we spent the last eighty years of our lives. We procrastinated too long, our papers are due, and the date just happens to coincide with the day we die. So there we are, dressed in our Sunday finest, lying flat on our backs, unable to gather enough breath to blame the dog for eating our homework.

We spent a lifetime carefully forging our identities and then abruptly ask others to create a eulogistic masterpiece in several short days, a lifetime of poetic nuance reduced to Cliff's Notes. Perhaps one of the most difficult tasks for a pastor is to give a eulogy for someone whose life is by any standards a failure. The good news for the Pastor is that He knows SomeOne who sacrificially loved the deceased to death but whose love sadly went unrequited.

> You may go to hell unsaved but you won't go unloved.[158]
>
> —Jack Graham

I was honored to give the eulogy at my father's funeral. I had only a week to compose it, and I think I did an adequate job, but I have since realized his portrait continues to paint itself. Over the years, I have had the opportunity to talk with family, friends, and colleagues about the impact my father made on their lives. I continue to reflect on our relationship and wonder what he would have thought of the changes in my life. The eulogy I gave for my father is continually being rewritten in my mind as I learn to appreciate the complexity of his life. Humans are just too darned complex to reduce to simple, short eulogies.

Maybe some of the sadness we feel at a funeral is a reflection of our inability to pay proper tribute to the dead. It's quite reassuring to know that the door to my father's memory gallery is always unlocked and that I am permitted if not encouraged to periodically stand at the foot of his portrait, pull out a paintbrush, and lovingly daub in a few more details.

I suggest that all other worldviews lack substantial-enough foundations to construct adequate eulogies. They are forced to steal words from the Christian lexicon that speak of meaning, purpose, uniqueness, and hope. An atheist eulogy must applaud a life of foraging, dominating, and procreating. Buddhists cannot speak about any accomplishments in this life because every accolade they receive is one more bit of suffering; eighty years of blood, sweat, and tears are reduced to pathological desires.

The Hindu eulogy may recount the deceased's former life OS 3.0 but will remain uncertain if the next will be the new and improved OS 4.0 or merely an obsolete beta version of Pong. New Age religion will have some nice things to say about the departed but then can offer only an afterlife in which the deceased becomes more voltage for the world's spiritual power grid.

Higher Ground

As we discussed in chapter 3, we are obsessed with overarching stories or metanarratives because we recognize there has to be a better vantage point from which to view life. We buy every book we can on transcendental rock climbing, we outfit ourselves with fancy, spiritual pitons, and we make our ascents up the holy mountain to get panoramic views of our lives.

Our postmodern friends implore us to stay in the valley of our personal narratives, warning us of the danger lurking in the transcendent cliffs that surround us. They point out how thin the air is and that the lack of oxygen might just cause us to hallucinate and see omnipotent apparitions. They not only warn us of the personal dangers but also point out that our climbing may place the valley dwellers in harm's way because we may dislodge some "delusional" rocks of truth, which could tumble down and disturb the peacefully tolerant polytheistic orgy in progress below. Unfortunately for our postmodern friends, humans cannot help themselves, and despite repeated warnings, the valley dwellers look up and see the surrounding cliffs littered with spiritual rock climbers.

> For a scientist who has lived by his faith in the power of reason, the story ends like a bad dream. He has scaled the mountains of ignorance; he is about to conquer the highest peak; as he pulls himself over the final rock, he is greeted by a band of theologians who have been sitting there for centuries.[159]
>
> —Dr. Robert Jastrow

Many spiritual mountaineers will be unprepared for the arduous climb and will settle for base camps where they will be momentarily invigorated by the refreshing spiritual wind blowing on their faces but will continue to be restless, haunted by the dream of one day making the final ascent.

Some will find the climb so difficult that they will turn back and resume their unsettled valley existences, dodging the rocks of truth dislodged by the more experienced climbers. The few who are mentally and physically prepared for the climb will reach the summit and enjoy views of the valley below as well as panoramic views of the heavens above.

Fear of Death

> As a matter of fact, the sense of lack of meaning and
> purpose in life (which is at present so widespread that it
> may be considered as one of the characteristics of modern
> man) seems only rarely, if at all, to be connected with
> an awareness of mortality. The main problem appears
> to be what one ought to do with one's life, what to do in
> it … It would seem then, that it is not so much the fact of
> having to die in itself as the regret of not having 'lived' or
> of having wasted one's life, or of having made "a mess"
> of it, that is the main cause of their mortal distress.[160]
>
> —Jacques Choron

Why are we so afraid of death? Why do we spend so much
time and money trying to stay youthful and ward off the demons
of old age? Why do we try to hide the ravages of time with nips,
tucks, and potions? What do we fear? Death forces us all to answer
important questions: Is this all there is? Does my lifetime of pain
and pleasure, joy and sadness, love and hate, accomplishment and
failure all just end? I put a lot of work into my life; shouldn't there
be a gold watch commemorating eighty long years of service to the
company of man?

One of the most profound differences between man and animals
is the fact that man knows he will die, but he takes this unique gift
and buries it in the backyard only to be dug up when he lies flat
on the ground awaiting burial. Animals have no such awareness.
Doesn't that seem like an extremely profound distinguishing
feature? Atheists try to put an evolutionary spin on it by declaring it
to be a protective mechanism allowing humans to avoid dangerous
situations, but why does every religion create an afterlife scenario
to helps it deal with this fear? Once again, our atheist friends
would suggest it's a way of avoiding the psychologically paralyzing
notion of death and preventing us from asking ourselves the only
question of atheistic philosophical significance, "Why don't I
commit suicide?"

> There is but one truly serious philosophical problem, and
> that is suicide. Judging whether life is or is not worth
> living amounts to answering the fundamental question
> of philosophy.[161]

> —Albert Camus

Let's turn the question around. Why are we so passionate about life? Why do we care about living if we're all going to die? Why do we get excited about the healing of a relative's cancer only to have him or her die of heart disease ten years later? Why praise the doctors and nurses who treated your life-threatening infection when they're powerless to prevent you from dying of Alzheimer's disease when you're older? Why have a celebration for cancer remission when death still ultimately crashes the "life" party?

We do so because we know that death is not a friend but the enemy. Millions of years of animal and human life have taught us one very important lesson—we all die, so why, armed with all this evidence, do we think death is such a bad idea? Why do we try to outrun the inevitable?

> And the Lord God commanded the man, saying, "You
> may surely eat of every tree of the garden, but of the tree
> of the knowledge of good and evil you shall not eat, *for
> in the day that you eat of it you shall surely die.*" (Gen.
> 2:16–17, emphasis added)

God created man in His own image because He wanted to make a creature with which He could have an actual relationship. It was not meant to be a one-day stand but rather an eternal friendship. It all went wrong, however, when mankind decided he wanted to change the relationship rules and strike out on his own divine publicity tour. The gracious audience of One was exchanged for a fickle audience of millions. Adam and Eve's sin separated them from the Tree of Life, and because of that, death became a reality. Man, however, could never shake the feeling that despite its 100 percent predictability, death just didn't feel right.

If you're an atheist, you have no choice but to view death as evidence that the natural selection machine is operating perfectly well. The theory of evolution tells us that our existence is predicated on the death of other inferior animals. If this is true, why do we feel sad when we see a dead deer on the side of the road? Shouldn't it be a happy reminder of just how superior our truck technology is compared to evolutionarily inferior roadkill?

> For God so loved the world, that he gave his only Son, that whoever believes in him should not perish but have eternal life. (John 3:16)

What does God promise through His Son? He promises eternal life! Eternal life isn't a new promise; it was an ancient garden reality. Eternal life was always the default plan; it was death that messed things up, so our fear of death is based on deviation from the norm.

> When the perishable puts on the imperishable, and the mortal puts on immortality, then shall come to pass the saying that is written: "Death is swallowed up in victory." "O death, where is your victory? O death, where is your sting?" (1 Cor. 15:54–55)

Next Stop

Every competing worldview has an opinion on the matter of death, and there seems to be two basic categories: death is either a final destination or a stopover. Maybe our ecumenical discussion needs to begin at the grave and work forward and backward because at least we all agree things will radically change from that point on.

For atheists, death is the end, and all they can do is mourn the loss of the past or say good riddance to lives that were never very kind in the first place. Hindus gets mulligans and just hope they have earned enough brownie points to avoid coming back as slugs. Buddhists view it as the final moment of a Houdini-like escape from the physical illusion of life. New agers like to keep their options open by accepting all possibilities except the nasty one that involves hell. For Christians, death is the starting point for a new life in which the broken relationship between God and man is once again restored. For the secular world, death is a closed door beyond which none shall pass; for the Christian, however, death is an open door to eternal possibility.

The whole afterlife discussion presents a serious problem for atheists because the concept runs rampant throughout the world. Despite their persistent attempts to convince us that it's just neurochemicals and survival strategies, mankind continually tries to make reservations for an afterlife holiday. If, as atheists would say, heaven is just wishful thinking, how did we evolve wishful thinking anyway? How could a purely material being even evolve the idea of a realm that is not physical? How could we envision or hope for something that goes beyond DNA, chemicals, and foraging for food? Atheists cannot invoke transcendental speculation one moment and then say the transcendental ground they're standing on doesn't exist. As soon as you step outside of purely material evolutionary processes and pontificate about mankind's spiritual search, you violate the rules of your own materialistic worldview.[162]

I've been present at the deaths of many babies during my neonatal career—babies too premature, too sick, or too malformed to survive. Usually, the room is very quiet, but the air pulsates with thoughts of meaning, regret, God, and the afterlife. If you cut the heavy atmosphere with a scalpel, it would bleed a torrent of metaphysical questions. The atheist has to conclude that it's merely stage blood created by years of evolutionary denial and deceptive spiritual wishful thinking. I can assure you, however, that this spiritual blood is very real because the people in that room may spend the rest of their lives trying to stop the bleeding because if they don't, they will barely have the energy to get on with their anemic, pale lives. A little spiritual bloodletting now and then may actually drain us of some of the pent-up evil humors that if left unchecked could destroy us.

Walking a family through this process is never an easy task, but I have consistently found that Christians best cope with the death of an infant while the families with no religious convictions are frequently the most broken and difficult to deal with. For Christians, death is the beginning of a better life; for nonbelievers, it is the end of the only life they will ever know, a life reduced to a miserly allotted number of breaths and heartbeats that have been exceeded, signaling game over.

> We trivialize the body in our indulgences. We treat it as a means to other ends. But when death comes, we grasp at it and cling to it because it is all we have left.[163]
>
> —Ravi Zacharias

I was present at the death of my father and grandfather. I remember holding their hands and suddenly feeling them go cold when they died. Death is clearly a physical event, and even though we don't see a soul fly from the body or a light ascend to heaven, we get this feeling that something more has just happened. We get the sense that they have moved on and not been annihilated.

In the movie *Temple Grandin*, Temple, a woman with autism, is twice confronted by death, once with a cherished horse and the other with one of her schoolteachers. In each instance, she quite dramatically asks, "Where did they go?" Even with her autistic limitations, her inability to grasp abstract concepts, she recognized that something as complex as a human life doesn't just end, that it must go somewhere.

When we witness a death, we can't shake the feeling that something else must be going on. We aren't experiencing the death of just a biological machine, just some broken cogs and gears that have worn out, but rather the relocation of a spirit. If it is true that our spirit goes somewhere, how do we prepare for that journey?

Carnival Styx Cruise

What will be on your bedside when you die? What will accompany you into the afterlife? The day my father died, he was listening to an Enya CD and reading a historical account of the duel between Alexander Hamilton and Aaron Burr. The last things my dad did were listening to Celtic pop music and reading history. My father was about to die and become history himself but continued to be intrigued by historical figures and modern Celtic music.

The Egyptians made elaborate preparations for the afterlife by filling coffins with jewelry, trinkets, and books. Burial chambers were filled with dead relatives, pets, boats, snacks, and gold to make sure the deceased didn't starve or experience a second death by boredom in the afterlife. How sad that their understanding of the afterlife was so depressing that the only way they felt they could tolerate it was to make sure they had something nice to wear and some cash to bribe the maître d' to get the best seat in the house. Unfortunately, the deceased would quickly realize that the bags they had meticulously packed for their afterlife cruise never made it on board. The crew of the SS *Eye of the Needle* could not accommodate their bulky camelskin luggage.

> And Jesus looked around and said to his disciples, "How difficult it will be for those who have wealth to enter the kingdom of God!" And the disciples were amazed at his words. But Jesus said to them again, "Children, how difficult it is to enter the kingdom of God! It is easier for a camel to go through the eye of a needle than for a rich person to enter the kingdom of God." And they were exceedingly astonished, and said to him, "Then who can be saved?" Jesus looked at them and said, "With man it is impossible, but not with God. For all things are possible with God." (Mark 10:23–27)

Are we really that much different from the pharaohs? We embalm ourselves with material excess in the hope that we'll look marvelous for our afterlife premiere. We even try to bypass the heavenly "camel through the eye of a needle" clause by conveniently storing our possessions in the cloud, where they won't be subject to rust, moths, or thieves, the only caveat being that our harp-playing cloud is connected to the Internet.

Christians, however, won't have any worries when they die because they will have already stored their heart-shaped treasures in heaven and can access them any time without having to remember a username or password.

> Do not lay up for yourselves treasures on earth, where moth and rust destroy and where thieves break in and steal, but lay up for yourselves treasures in heaven, where neither moth nor rust destroys and where thieves do not break in and steal. For where your treasure is, there your heart will be also. (Matt. 6:19–21)

I'm Not Dead Yet. I Feel Happy!

Atheists have a real problem on their hands because most people believe in an afterlife. Some of the best-selling books are those that deal with NDEs, near-death experiences. Why do people care about what happens to them after they die? Is it because they want some sort of assurance that death isn't the end?

The majority of NDEs have some very common characteristics such as seeing an overwhelming light, feeling peace and love, desiring to remain in that place, and being disappointed at having to return. The people touched by these experiences are convicted to tell others about them but are frustrated by the limitations of human language to adequately describe what they saw.

> But now that I have been privileged to understand that our life does not end with the death of the body or the brain, I see it as my duty, my calling, to tell people about what I saw beyond the body and beyond this earth ... I had a duty not just as a scientist and a profound respecter of the scientific method, but also as a healer to tell that story. A story—a true story—can heal as much as medicine can ... what had happened to me was healing news, too. What kind of healer would I be if I didn't share it?[164]
>
> —Eben Alexander, MD

> Regardless, it is impossible for me to adequately describe what I saw and what I felt … the appropriate words, descriptions, and concepts don't even exist in our current language.[165]
>
> —Mary C. Neal, MD

These near-death experiences have been reported by a broad cross section of people and cannot be attributed to just those who are superstitious and uneducated. Two books have been recently written by accomplished physicians describing their personal near-death experiences. It appears that we have some thoughtful, well-educated, near–eye witnesses to something beyond this life, a place glorious beyond description.

> My arrival was joyously celebrated and a feeling of absolute love was palpable as these spiritual beings and I hugged, danced, and greeted each other. The intensity, depth, and purity of these feelings and sensations were far greater than I could ever describe with words and far greater than anything I have experienced on earth.[166]
>
> —Mary C. Neal, MD

Why would a physically dying human whose very existence was based on physical functions encounter a spiritual reality when those functions stop working properly? It seems to suggest that we are in fact physical and spiritual entities that encounter a dilemma at death. If the body is just material stuff, why do those who return from NDEs have this overwhelming notion that their physical bodies have unfinished spiritual business to attend to?

These near-death experiences are just too consistent and universal to attribute merely to failing neurons and neurotransmitter depletion. In fact, the neurosurgeon Eben Alexander I quoted above meticulously examined his experience scientifically to assure himself that what he had experienced was not merely some neurochemical event.

I find these experiences fascinating, but we need to be careful about formulating our theology around them. While they do not answer all our questions about the afterlife, at a minimum they give us some assurance that there is something after this life that by most accounts is glorious.

Who Turned Out the Lights?

> We were traveling down a path that led to a great and brilliant hall, larger and more beautiful than anything I can conceive of seeing on earth. It was radiating a brilliance of all colors and beauty ... I felt my soul being pulled toward the entry and as I approached, I physically absorbed its radiance and felt the pure, complete, and utterly unconditional absolute love that emanated from the hall.[167]

—Mary C. Neal, MD

The majority of those who have had near-death experiences report encountering a welcoming, bright light that seems to embody absolute peace and love. Why a bright light? Why not the smell of flowers or a vision of a tropical beach? I think the Bible gives us some clues. In Genesis 1, God created light before He created the sun, moon, and stars. Jesus is described as the Light of the World. The book of Revelation describes the New Jerusalem coming down from heaven as being filled with God's light. Coincidence? I think not.

> And the city has no need of sun or moon to shine on it, for the glory of God gives it light, and its lamp is the Lamb. By its light will the nations walk, and the kings of the earth will bring their glory into it, and its gates will never be shut by day—and there will be no night there. They will bring into it the glory and the honor of the nations. But nothing unclean will ever enter it, nor anyone who does what is detestable or false, but only those who are written in the Lamb's book of life ... They will see his face, and his name will be on their foreheads. And night will be no more. They will need no light of lamp or sun, for the Lord God will be their light, and they will reign forever and ever. (Rev. 21:23–27; 22:4–5)

Atheists have no choice but to believe death is the end—game over, lights out. They keep trying to turn the afterlife light switch off only to have it rudely turned back on by somebody encountering a beautiful, bright light during a near-death experience.

Now that we have some assurance that something happens after we die, let's take a closer look at some of the afterlife packages offered to us by our friendly worldview afterlife cable network.

Th ... Th ... That's All, Folks

If you're an atheist, death is the end. If all life is just material substance, death is annihilation. You are born with a capital L on your forehead, a loser from the moment of birth because you can never beat the undisputed heavyweight champ, death. It doesn't matter how much money you make, how many companies you own, or how many lives you temporarily save with your medical knowledge; in the end, all your work will turn to dust.

You can say you lived a good life, were a good parent, and loved animals, but no matter how you try to decorate your life journey, death still has the final word. Your life, while possibly interesting, will have ultimately been nothing more than marinating your corpse for some worm family fiesta. If you were lucky, perhaps some of your hard-earned selfish genes could be used as the ingredients for some future worm entrée.

For atheists, death becomes the prerequisite for evolutionary progress and the arbiter of physical value. Simply stated, the well adapted survive and the inferior die. If you're lucky enough to survive to the age of reproduction, you can fulfill your evolutionary role and pass on your genes to the next generation no matter how stupid, ugly, or uncoordinated they may have made you. The purpose of life becomes proliferation before annihilation. As unpleasant as it sounds, natural selection has only one measuring stick, the number of dead and dying left along the evolutionary trail of tears.

Predominantly secular countries tend to have birth rates lower than the rate necessary to maintain their populations. While atheists may spin this as a generous act designed to prevent overcrowding, they may have made the evolutionarily unfashionable decision to place themselves on the pathway to extinction. Uncomfortable with the harshness of this evolutionary truth, many of our atheist friends have turned to a "kinder, gentler" scenario.

> The Cosmos is all that is or ever was or ever will be. Our feeblest contemplations of the Cosmos stir us—there is a tingling in the spine, a catch in the voice, a faint sensation, as if a distant memory, of falling from a height. We know we are approaching the greatest of mysteries.
>
> The size and age of the Cosmos are beyond ordinary human understanding. Lost somewhere between immensity and eternity is our tiny planetary home. In a cosmic perspective, most human concerns seem insignificant, even petty. And yet our species is young and curious and brave and shows much promise ... They remind us that humans have evolved to wonder, that understanding is a joy, that knowledge is prerequisite to survival ...
>
> The Cosmos is rich beyond measure—in elegant facts, in exquisite interrelationships, in the subtle machinery of awe.
>
> The surface of the Earth is the shore of the cosmic ocean. From it we have learned most of what we have learned. Recently, we have waded a little out to sea, enough to dampen our toes or, at most, wet our ankles. The water seems inviting. The ocean calls. Some part of our being knows this is from where we came. We long to return. These aspirations are not, I think, irreverent, although they may trouble whatever gods may be.[168]
>
> —Carl Sagan

I think Sagan is saying your decayed remains will become divine fertilizer for a questionable world spirit. All your great human contributions such as saving rare species, cleaning up the environment, or random acts of compassion will be compensated for by the opportunity to be cosmic compost for some vague universal mind. This kind of poetic language may temporarily make you feel better about your life, but sooner or later, you must face the scathing reviews of the cruel, literary natural-selection critic who has no sympathy for your beautiful prose. You can soothe yourself with an elegy of evolution or you can face the unpleasant fact sheet of your materialistic worldview.

> In a universe of blind physical forces and genetic replication some people are going to get hurt, other people are going to get lucky, and you won't find any rhyme or reason in it, nor any justice. The universe we observe has precisely the properties we would expect if there is, at the bottom, no design, no purpose, no evil and no other good. Nothing but blind pitiless indifference. DNA neither knows or cares. DNA just is. And we dance to its music.[169]
>
> —Richard Dawkins

While Sagan's description of life is beautifully written, none of his word choices are found in the evolutionary lexicon. He has appropriated the language of transcendence to describe a purely immanent physical process. Richard Dawkins, while not as gifted a writer as Sagan, is honest about the ramifications of a purely materialistic evolutionary worldview. Dreamy adjectives and clever metaphors are nothing but the evolutionary opiates of the masses, helping relieve the pain of the wounds inflicted by the bloodied hand of natural selection. We need to call some of our atheist friends to the carpet, ask them to be honest about the implications of their worldview, and prevent them from sneaking out the transcendental backdoor.

Groundhog Day

Reincarnation—now that's a creative solution to the death problem. Add a cup of divine spark, a sprinkle of morality, and stir with the wheel of samsara and voilà! Unfortunately for our chefs, this basket contains ingredients that don't complement one other particularly well, and despite repeated attempts to transform them into unique culinary creations, the cruel karma critics of reincarnation cuisine are forced to chop them! The benefits are that you never have to worry about extinction and that you don't have to feel guilty about overfilling the human landfill with another smelly corpse because you've done your part and recycled.

As we sit at the bottom of our human recycling bin alongside millions of other empty generic human water bottles, we try to make ourselves feel good by telling our neighbors that we used to be Perrier. The only relevant question left is, "Does the numerical moral code at the bottom of my earthen container qualify me for useful recycling?" Hindus, some Buddhists, and many New Age followers have found reincarnation to be a useful way of distracting themselves from the harsh reality of death. Life becomes a lovely carousel endlessly revolving to a happy circus tune. Reincarnation reduces the fear of death to just some minor apprehension about where we will begin our next life.

We seem to prefer the proposition that life is a linear story with a beginning and an end. We aren't really that thrilled with the idea of a life replayed over and over. We want finality, consummation, and resolution. Remember the movie *Groundhog Day* with Bill Murray? Every day, the same events repeated. The main character was initially scared by his situation but became intrigued by the repeated opportunities to get the girl of his dreams. In the end, however, despite his success at getting the girl, they never grew old together, they never shared a full story, just an opening chapter. A cyclical life cheapens all our experiences because they no longer become unique moments but just generic life scrimmages.

Extinct Species

Buddhism teaches us that life is characterized by suffering brought on by the desire to make the transient permanent. Death is welcomed because it allows us to detach ourselves from the desires of the things in this world. We are then free to blend into the great nothingness of nirvana. Doesn't it seem odd that humans who are so obsessed with purpose, finding their true selves, and maximizing their potential would think extinction of the self was an appropriate response to a life spent defining their personal identities? You cannot laugh off suffering.

> Life is suffering Tee-hee, ha-ha …
> Smile on little Buddha, smile on …
> It's only illusion then it's gone.[170]
>
> —Toad The Wet Sprocket

Feel the Electricity

Those in the New Age community borrow the best afterlife scenarios from every other worldview. They offer the largest spiritual cable package available, with thousands of afterlife channels to choose from. The problem arises when the power for your worldview television is about to go out and you're still channel surfing, trying to find the most appealing final image to accompany you into the next life.

Probably the most popular New Age afterlife scenario involves a return to an indifferent psychic energy source of some kind. If I were God, I would be a little peeved that my people cared so little about my personal commitment to them that they ended up treating me more like a Tesla coil than the relationship-seeking Creator of the universe I truly was.

The New Age way of viewing death is appealing because it allows you to do whatever you want in this life and still be welcomed into the afterlife with open arms. You can confidently say, "What happens on earth stays on earth" and be welcomed to the afterlife by the Great Oz who conveniently allows you to hide your humanity behind his curtain of human denial and then lets you pull the levers controlling a smoke-and-mirror show of self-deceptively divine proportions.

The New Age universal energy source is frequently described as being composed of unconditional love. If you carefully analyze the kind of love it offers, you will quickly see it's not true, committed love but emotional puppy love. New Age religion basically promises a divine, nameless prostitute who welcomes everyone into her brothel, a free shuttle to the spiritual red-light district where the divine harlots of desire await you. The afterlife becomes *The Joy of Sex* and not *Love Story*, an eternity of carnality, not an eternity of commitment.

The Christian God, however, is a jealous God whose heart is grieved because we have broken our relationship with Him. He desperately wants us back but recognizes that relationship must involve choice. He didn't wait for us to come to Him but descended to our level, came face-to-face with us, and in the act of ultimate love, hung on a cross and asked, "Do you love me now?"

How do you respond? I find an afterlife of eternal relationship with the lover of my soul much more appealing than a series of one-night stands with a cosmic whore. Temple prostitution may be a thing of the past, but we have since replaced it with spiritual prostitution.

All Roads Lead to God

We have looked at some of the more popular answers to the afterlife question and found that each worldview has a unique conclusion. Our postmodern culture, however, adopts a poorly informed yet profoundly tolerant stance by boldly proclaiming, "All paths lead to God!" How is that possible? At one time, I held that belief, but once I engaged my brain and asked some hard questions about where each path led, it became clear to me they were simply incompatible. Not everyone can be right, so who is?

The concept of many paths leading to the same God raises three serious issues. First, it implies the object of our spiritual search is ill defined, nebulous, and inconsequential. I return to my sentiments from the earlier chapter; if God is not universally relevant and consequential, He is not God. Nebulous cosmic energy sources, remote divine essences, diffuse universal spirits, or divine vacuums that suck out personality are inconsequential because they're all optional and I'm free to believe all or none of them. Just because our tolerant postmodern spiritual marketplace says it's okay for everyone to set up all kinds of religious booths doesn't guarantee they're not offering just "God junk."

Second, many paths implies that mankind, not God, sets the rules for God engagement. If we're talking about ultimate meaning, purpose, and salvation, I get a bit of a cold chill thinking that people will invest their spiritual lives in the divine pretensions of some guy across the globe who just happens to like his personal scenario because it floats his spiritual boat.

Finally, when you look carefully, you will see that each religious path does end on a summit, but the problem is that all these summits are on different mountain peaks. We can get out megaphones and congratulate each other for reaching the top of our respective peaks, but let's put aside the silliness that they all represent the same mountain.

I'm actually giving these different peaks more credit than they deserve; in reality, they're nothing more than mounds of mystical human refuse on which we have defiantly stuck our spiritual flags. We admire the rolling hills of the religious landscape while in the distance, Holy Mount "God" Everest looms, daring us to climb its cliffs of consequence.

To make ourselves feel that we have somehow reached the thin air of divine significance, we place religious oxygen masks over our noses and mouths to make it appear as if we've scaled a mountain of consequence when in reality the masks are just protecting us from the smell of our own mystical poop.

All this talk of many pathways to the same god reveals something quite interesting. It assumes that there should be only one peak or god in the first place. So where did mankind get the idea there was only one reality upon which all religions converge? It sounds as though most people believe an ultimate truth exists after all, but they seem content to play in the safety of the valley below rather than scaling God's holy mountain with "fear and trembling."

A New Creation

> Then I saw a new heaven and a new earth, for the first
> heaven and the first earth had passed away, and the sea
> was no more. And I saw the holy city, New Jerusalem,
> coming down out of heaven from God, prepared as a
> bride adorned for her husband. And I heard a loud voice
> from the throne saying, "Behold, the dwelling place of
> God is with man. He will dwell with them, and they will
> be his people, and God himself will be with them as their
> God. He will wipe away every tear from their eyes, and
> death shall be no more, neither shall there be mourning
> nor crying nor pain anymore, for the former things have
> passed away." (Rev. 21:1–4)

In the past, I tended to view heaven as a blender in which saved
souls were homogenized into a spiritual smoothie. Individuality
was lost, and each of those souls ended up as just one more voice
in the heavenly choir. I have since realized that heaven will be the
opposite, that our individuality will become more distinct.

Randy Alcorn, in his book *Heaven,* makes the case that many
Christians misunderstand what heaven will be like. He shatters the
myth that heaven is just a bunch of Christians sitting on clouds playing
harps and singing hymns by pointing out that the Bible promises a
resurrected life in a new heaven and new earth. The ultimate afterlife
will not be a place inhabited by floating, disembodied spirits but a
restored earth inhabited by resurrected humans. It will be an earth
that deep down we all knew should have existed all along.

Revelation describes the New Jerusalem as a beautiful city with
rivers running through it and trees bearing fruit on either side. It
will be God's kingdom; He will sit on the throne in the midst of
His people unshielded by a temple because Christ's atoning work
cleansed us from all sin and made it possible for us to once again
live in God's presence.

> Then the angel showed me the river of the water of life,
> bright as crystal, flowing from the throne of God and

of the Lamb through the middle of the street of the city;
also, on either side of the river, the tree of life with its
twelve kinds of fruit, yielding its fruit each month. The
leaves of the tree were for the healing of the nations. No
longer will there be anything accursed, but the throne of
God and of the Lamb will be in it, and his servants will
worship him. (Rev. 22:1–3)

Why would we think that God, who made such a big deal out of
making everything and then declaring it to be very good, would scrap
His creation for cheaper, low-maintenance cloud dwellings inhabited
by a bunch of ethereal, couch-potato spirits lounging around and
singing hymns? Wouldn't it make more sense for Him to restore the
unique physical and spiritual place He had created in the first place?
If you owned a damaged Rembrandt, I doubt you'd throw it in the
trash; I'd guess you'd painstakingly try to restore it to its original state.

Genesis begins with man dwelling with God in a garden and
ends in Revelation with him dwelling with God in a city. Since
cities reflect man's innovation, it would seem that God embraces
man's role in culture building as an aspect of a restored creation. A
city is a complex entity that requires a variety of specially talented
and trained individuals to run and maintain, so it wouldn't be
surprising that the unique gifts God gave us all would be put to full
use in the New Jerusalem; it would be our opportunity to fulfill
the roles God had intended for us from the beginning.

Inauguration Speech

> The time is fulfilled, and the kingdom of God is at hand;
> repent and believe in the gospel. (Mark 1:15)

Jesus portrayed the coming afterlife as a kingdom that operated
by a different set of rules, a kingdom of shalom, of harmony and
unity, where everything would be right in God's world. So what
does this kingdom look like? Jesus gave us clues through His
earthly words and deeds. His healings revealed that it would be a
kingdom free of disease and death; His parables revealed that it

would be the best thing anyone could ever hope for. It would start small and grow big, it would be ruled by the King, who valued the least and the lost, and it would be governed by love, not power.

Jesus had a hard time trying to get His followers to understand the significance of what He was inaugurating because they had been so steeped in the world's idea of kingdoms dominated by power, special interest, and greed. They had a difficult time wrapping their minds around a kingdom in which the less gifted and less fortunate would be the prized citizens.

Our situation is no different from that of Jesus' early followers; we too live in a world dominated by governments that are similar to the mighty Roman kingdom. It's hard for us to imagine the kingdom Jesus offers, but we get the sense it's the kingdom we need. We have a choice to put our faith in His kingdom or scramble to reapply for citizenship in an endless succession of failed earthly kingdoms whose only legacy is the archeological debris of human pride.

Jesus' accentuates His kingdom argument with a cross-shaped exclamation point. The crucifixion death machine that was the symbol of Roman power had been strategically displayed on the hillsides to make people tremble at Roman might, but ironically, it became the power symbol for God's kingdom. We all must gaze up at that hillside and ask ourselves, which king we will serve, the King of sacrificial love or a king of crushing power?

Success in this world is measured by power, money, and fame. In God's kingdom, it is measured by anonymity, poverty, and service. By every earthly standard, Jesus and His kingdom were failures, so why has His message survived for 2,000 years? There must be something enduring about His kingdom that has allowed it to outlive some of the most powerful kingdoms ever. What is it about His kingdom that somehow makes it feel like home? Why are we so eager to exchange our world work visas for the true citizenship papers of God's coming kingdom? I think the reason may be that God's kingdom economy runs on the currency of love, and not on gold. Jesus' lucre of love is not subject to the whims of the market and is of greatest value when the cultural market crashes. God's kingdom is so different from anything the world has ever offered that it screams for an otherworldly source. Do you really think that mankind is capable of devising such a radically different idea of a kingdom?

Weeping and Gnashing

> But nothing unclean will ever enter it, nor anyone who does what is detestable or false, but only those who are written in the Lamb's book of life. (Rev. 21:27)

Citizenship in God's kingdom is open to everyone, but many fail to file the proper paperwork. We are all invited to this glorious kingdom wedding feast, but many of us seem too busy counting the meager pennies of our earthly treasures to enjoy the lavish heavenly party God spared no expense, even the life of His Son, to throw.

> And again Jesus spoke to them in parables, saying, "The kingdom of heaven may be compared to a king who gave a wedding feast for his son, and sent his servants to call those who were invited to the wedding feast, but they would not come. Again he sent other servants, saying, 'Tell those who are invited, See, I have prepared my dinner, my oxen and my fat calves have been slaughtered, and everything is ready. Come to the wedding feast.' But they paid no attention and went off, one to his farm, another to his business, while the rest seized his servants, treated them shamefully, and killed them. (Matt. 22:1–6)

The characters who chose to go off script and improvise their lives somewhere else find that their jokes have become tired and their routines predictable. They find that living without a script means they get the same in the life to come, an unending improvisational show in a hot, stuffy theater of their own creation. It's a theater with a massive stage but only one audience chair occupied by the harshest satanic critic of all, and between performances, they're forced to read the scathing reviews he crafted for them with his poison pen. They never stopped to think what would happen when they ran out of material and the audience no longer wanted to hear their recycled routine. They hear laughter and singing coming from the cast party and vaguely remember being invited to attend. Rifling through their pockets, they pull out crumpled invitations and desperately scurry off to the party. They knock at the door but are unfortunately turned away. Irate, they ask to speak to the Author, who patiently listens as they pull out their pristine, never-opened copies of the script and point to their names in the pages. The Author lifts up His eyes, tears streaming down His cheek, and says, "I created you to be unique. I thought long and hard about the character you were to be, but I no longer recognize you."

> Not everyone who says to me, "Lord, Lord," will enter
> the kingdom of heaven, but the one who does the will
> of my Father who is in heaven. On that day many will
> say to me, "Lord, Lord, did we not prophesy in your
> name, and cast out demons in your name, and do many
> mighty works in your name?" And then will I declare to
> them, "I never knew you; depart from me, you workers
> of lawlessness." (Matt. 7:21–23)

Thought Experiment

The goal of the educational system is to get students to rethink the teachers' thoughts. To verify this thought exchange, a test is administered. If the information was successfully transmitted, the students pass; if not, they fail. Similarly, we also began as original, unique, and glorious thoughts in the mind of God, and when we reach the end of our lives, we will also be tested. When we die and stand before His throne, will He see us as His original thoughts or will we be unrecognizable?

Animals are incapable of rethinking God's thoughts, so when they die, there's no difference between the thoughts God had of them in the beginning and the thoughts that return to Him. Man, however, is the only creature capable of making himself unrecognizable to his Creator, which leaves us with a very serious question, what will you do with God's thought?

> And when I sit alone at night, your thoughts burn
>   through me like a fire
> You're the only one who knows, who I really am.[171]
>
> —Thousand Foot Crutch

While none of us will ever perfectly represent God's thought back to Him, we know the sacrificial death of His Son will remove the sinful human "upgrades" we have nailed to our human temples and reveal the architectural plan He had envisioned for us from the beginning allowing us to be welcomed back into his heavenly-gated community. But for those who stand defiantly unrecognizable before God, the scene will be quite different. They will be denied entry because their personal remodeling projects won't have met God's building code. Sadly, outside of God's heavenly housing project, there are no planned communities and those who fail to meet His standards will be forced to live eternally isolated because, as it turns out, even their fellow eyesores who were also denied entry won't be very fond of their avant-garde architectural improvisations either.

Resurrection

> Death, be not proud, though some have called thee
> Mighty and dreadful, for thou are not so ...
> One short sleep past, we wake eternally,
> And death shall be no more; Death, thou shalt die.[172]
>
> —John Donne

God seems intent on redeeming our planet and restoring it to its original condition. God is about rebuilding what was broken, not about giving up and trying something new. The life, death, and resurrection of Jesus made this abundantly clear. The earth was a sinful mess, but God cared enough to empty Himself and become a physical man to fix His broken creation. The problem was not a defect in God's vision but rather in man's ability to carry it out. God didn't need fixing, man did, so like any great problem solver, He went to the source of the problem and adopted a three-prong approach to planet restoration: remind, remediate, and reboot. He reminded His characters of His kingdom story and their roles in it. He disposed of all old, incomprehensible, redacted scripts and handed out new copies of the original script so they could again see the characters they were intended to be.

Jesus announced the coming kingdom; He suffered and died so everyone could be a citizen and then showed us what living there would be like. Jesus' resurrection appearances made it clear that God's ultimate afterlife plan didn't involve disembodied spirits but a restored physical and spiritual unity. If God had intended for the afterlife to be just a spirit realm, wouldn't it have made more sense for the disciples to have had an Easter séance and mystically called the ghost of Jesus forward instead of encountering the physically resurrected Jesus? If Jesus' resurrection was just a spiritual event, what would be the point of telling the inconvenient story of a doubting disciple who wasn't happy until he touched the physical wounds of Jesus.

If God had meant death to be the release of our spirits from physical shells, why would he drag His Son back to earth for a fish bake with his followers? It appears that we have two very important points to consider. First, God considers His physical universe to be very important; second, He values the people who have made a mess of it. The solution: redeem mankind and redeem the planet.

Yes, yes, that's all very interesting, but will my favorite dog or cat be there with me in heaven? The answer, given by most people, is usually predicated on a second question: do animals have souls? This suggests that if animals don't have souls as humans understand them, they won't be included in the afterlife plan. If God's plan, however, is for a restored physical creation, the real question is not whether animals have souls but if God created animals "good." Animals were important to God's drama, so it would make sense that a restored story would have a restored set and props. Remember that God didn't consider His creative endeavor to be "very" good until man arrived on the scene. Therefore, it would seem to me that for God to once again restore the planet back to its very good state, He must also restore that which He first created good, which I understand to be both Spot and Whiskers. Why else would Paul speak of nature groaning to be set free from its "bondage to decay" if it had no part in the afterlife?

Even those who have encountered near-death experiences describe a place that looks very much like earth, with landscape, plants, animals, and humans—a theater with a set, props, and a reunited cast.

> I was flying, passing over trees and fields, streams and waterfalls, and here and there, people. There were children, too laughing and playing. The people sang and danced around in circles, and sometimes I'd see a dog, running and jumping among them, as full of joy as the people were.[173]
>
> —Eben Alexander, MD

Labor Pains

> Galaxies revolve and dinosaurs breed and rain falls and people fall in love and uncles smoke cheap cigars and people lose their jobs and we all die—all for our good, the finished product, God's work of art, the Kingdom of Heaven. There's nothing outside heaven except hell. Earth is not outside heaven; it is heaven's workshop, heaven's womb.[174]
>
> —Peter Kreeft

The metaphor Paul uses for creation restoration is one of childbirth. Babies are born with characteristics quite similar to those of his or her parents. Similarly, if creation is in the throes of childbirth, it implies that the old creation is giving birth, and we would suspect its offspring would look just like its parent. A human baby would have its father's eyes or its mother's toes; a reborn creation would more than likely have its mother's trees and its father's lions. Eben Alexander also describes this sensation of birth in his afterlife experience.

> Brilliant, vibrant, ecstatic stunning ... I could heap on one adjective after another to describe what this world looked like and felt like, but they'd all fall short. I felt like I was being born. Not reborn, or born again. Just ... born.[175]

> —Eben Alexander, MD

Great Gig in the Sky

For musicians, the heavenly story ends pretty nicely. The band never breaks up, the gig is eternal, and there's no fighting over who leads the group. The alternative hell story, on the other hand, is quite different. You end up going solo and due to a lack of popularity end up driving a dilapidated van from show to show 365 days a year. You have to load and unload your own equipment, and you play in front of crowds that chant "Stairway to Heaven!" when all you really want to do is play your own songs.

Dejected after every show, you clean the tomato stains off your guitar, look into the tip jar, and find you have barely enough gas money to make it to the next gig. You pack up your van and head off into the stormy, gray night, unaware that the torrential rain hitting your windshield is in fact the tears of a God who desperately wanted to hear every note of your original material.

Hell is a place we choose for ourselves, so before you get all bent out of shape about a cruel, malevolent God sending people somewhere to suffer, remember that Christ did everything in His power to help you avoid that fate except the one thing He was incapable of doing, and that was to force you to say, "I do." I believe that hell is an uncomfortable place to live eternally because without a healthy slathering of Jesus Sin Block 1000, your sin will be like baby oil, scorching your skin under heat of the holy Son. Your sins will be exposed to the absolute goodness of God, and without the cabana of Jesus' atonement, your sin will sear like a third-degree burn in His presence. Your divine pretension brought on by the Original Sin of trying to be like God is like a mote in your eye blinding you to the larger God reality around you. Unless you remove that log, you have no other choice but to spend an extended miserable vacation at the Mote-Hell California, where you can "check out but never leave."[176]

Illustrated Man

> Now Thomas, one of the Twelve, called the Twin, was not with them when Jesus came. So the other disciples told him, "We have seen the Lord." But he said to them, "Unless I see in his hands the mark of the nails, and place my finger into the mark of the nails, and place my hand into his side, I will never believe." Eight days later, his disciples were inside again, and Thomas was with them. Although the doors were locked, Jesus came and stood among them and said, "Peace be with you." Then he said to Thomas, "Put your finger here, and see my hands; and put out your hand, and place it in my side. Do not disbelieve, but believe." Thomas answered him, "My Lord and my God!" Jesus said to him, "Have you believed because you have seen me? Blessed are those who have not seen and yet have believed." (John 20:24–29)

When Jesus appeared in His resurrected form, He bore evidence of His physical life. We need to once again ask ourselves why Jesus was resurrected with the scars of His earthly ordeal? Wouldn't it be better evidence for God's victory over suffering and death to have an unscarred Jesus appear to His disciples? Why would God do that? Thomas, despite his skepticism, gives us some important insight. If Jesus hadn't physically suffered and died, His mission would have been a sham. Only a real physical sacrifice and resurrection could solve man's real physical problem.

The scars of Jesus are like the signed copy of the Author's book. He has written His Word, His personal signature, inside the cover of His God story. You need to ask yourself, is Jesus a forged signature or a divine autograph? Are His scars the climax to the God story, the resolution of the plot tension? You have a choice; write your own ending in the "hot" pink of your own divine pretension or accept a complimentary copy of your life story autographed with the crimson blood of the Author of your salvation.

When we are resurrected, we will retain the scars of our physical lives, vivid reminders of the salvation path we shared with Christ. I distinctly remember the old 1960s movie *The Illustrated Man*, a story of a man whose body was covered by tattoos, each representing a specific event in his life. When others looked at one of his tattoos, they were magically transported into a story.

Just like in this movie, we too will see the scars of our fellow castmates and be reminded of the stories of our shared redeemed lives. We will be struck by how frequently we see the same scars and recognize that it was at those moments our lives intersected. The cast party will be our opportunity to finally see how all the smaller subplots were intertwined in the larger God story. I believe that heaven will be comparable to those magical, organized reunion moments where the stories of our friends and family like asphalt will fill in the memory potholes of our bumpy life roads. And as we look back, we will realize that our rides could have been much smoother had we known that each pothole was the story of another person intersecting our lives that we should have taken the time to notice.

Been There, Done That

Well, all this talk of heaven is very inspiring, but what if after a few millennia we get bored and start sinning; do we have to go through the same old painful process yet again? If God seems to think our ability to choose is so important, won't we also be able to choose in heaven? If we were capable of a rural garden crime, won't we also be capable of big city crime in the New Jerusalem? I believe the answer is no for three main reasons: Jesus drained the evil swamp, innocence will be replaced by righteousness, and the ability to choose the knowledge of good and evil will become irrelevant.

In Eden, you will recall, evil was only potential, a potential that had to exist for meaningful choice to be possible. Adam and Eve opened the Pandora's box of potential evil and unleashed a torrent of actual evil that has plagued mankind ever since. In the new heaven and earth, we will still have the ability to choose, but there will be no evil left to choose because Jesus, through His sacrificial death and resurrection, effectively drained the evil swamp. Mankind's past, present, and future evil was reduced to nothing. The worst evil man could ever do was completely spent on the cross, eliminating the possibility of choosing it in our future heavenly existences.

Adam and Eve's existences prior to the fall were characterized by innocence, but our future states will be characterized by righteousness. "Innocence is the absence of something [sin], while righteousness is the presence of something [God's holiness]."[177] Adam and Eve's initial innocence was characterized by the absence of sin and was therefore always in danger of being filled with something like sin. For us, however, that absence has been filled with righteousness because of the work of Christ, so there's no longer any potential hole to fill with sin; Jesus left no room for it. The world wants innocence, but what it needs is the righteousness only Christ can supply.

Perhaps the strongest temptation argument Satan made to Adam and Eve in the garden was that God was holding out on them. He tried to convince them that God wanted to keep the divine perks to Himself. Adam and Eve had no way of knowing whether that was true, but in heaven, we will be in the presence of the Lamb who was slain, and we will never be able to think God was holding out on us again. In fact, every time we greet Jesus in the New Jerusalem, we will feel His rough scar brush up against our palms and will be reminded that God didn't hold back anything but instead gave everything. He emptied Himself and became a suffering servant so He wouldn't have to walk alone. In addition, we must remember that the tempter is ultimately exiled to sulfur hot springs and will no longer be available for consultation.

The choice presented to Adam and Eve by the Tree of the Knowledge of Good and Evil will cease to be an issue in the new heaven and earth. In fact, the description of the New Jerusalem found in Revelation contains no mention of that troubling tree at all. The only tree mentioned by name is the Tree of Life.

Conclusion

If Jesus inaugurated the kingdom, registration has begun, but it's a limited-time offer, and the enrollment period ends at your death. After this point, death either stings with the burn of sin or soothes with the aloe of forgiveness. Your life then becomes what C. S. Lewis would refer to as an immortal horror or an immortal glory. It's your choice. Join in the greatest amnesty program ever offered by a kingdom or forever longingly peer over the carefully guarded border fence into the land of milk and honey.

Chapter Twelve

LINGUA DEI

Lingua Franca

I SUSPECT THAT MOST OF you were forced, as part of a well-planned work-release program from the purgatory of youthful indiscretion, to perform the unspeakably harsh penance of sitting through a class on world history. As you sat there, butt numb from the incessant spanking delivered by the hard wooden seat of school justice, you may have heard the phrase *lingua franca*. It describes a common language that allows people of diverse cultures and ethnicities to communicate with one another in the marketplace of life.

As I have discussed throughout this book, we share a world with our fellow man that has a remarkable unity, a world that looks surprisingly like timeless, classic literature penned by a transcendent Author. The script for this remarkable story is in fact a lingua franca, or more accurately a *lingua Dei*, a language of God that everyone is capable of understanding but most consider too crude to utter in public.

Deceived by the "sophisticated" lilt of the language of academia, we have neglected the majestic soliloquy of the King's speech. The divine Author continues to patiently read His classic literary work to anyone who will listen but sadly finds a world content to shuffle along with cultural earbuds securely in place, humming along to the music of the pied piper of deception. God's clever use of word and phrase is drowned out by the Devil's slang.

The good news is that His words are recited day after day, and those willing to do the hard work of relearning the common language spoken into existence long ago will be rewarded with a personal screening of *The Greatest Story Ever Told*.

Sadly, instead of becoming fluent in divine discourse, we choose to translate the world into our own forked tongue, and the original meanings formulated long ago have been transformed into sixty-second sound bites. We transform God's vernacular, a language that should seamlessly be spoken in both secular and religious circles, into our own Christian*ese* and the rest of the world scratches its collective head because it doesn't understand a word of it. We have become divinely illiterate and are in desperate need of a remedial class in Godspeak.

If you accept the premise of this book, you will see our Christian task is to regain fluency in the one, true, cosmic language so we can tutor a world that has rendered God's words unintelligible, a world that despite possessing a keen sense of hearing and sight doesn't hear or see.

> For this people's heart has grown dull, and with their ears they can barely hear, and their eyes they have closed, lest they should see with their eyes and hear with their ears and understand with their heart and turn, and I would heal them. But blessed are your eyes, for they see, and your ears, for they hear. Truly, I say to you, many prophets and righteous people longed to see what you see, and did not see it, and to hear what you hear, and did not hear it. (Matt. 13:15–17)

We need not be intimidated by the thought of learning or teaching this language because we have already acquired a significant vocabulary through divine immersion. We read it every day of our lives; it's written into our DNA. Most people subconsciously retranslate God's speech into beautiful poetry, paintings, or song but neglect the creative etymology of the objects they serenade. Our problem is that we hide God's words under the cover of our personal quiet time and neglect the commission to make them public reading. Our culture seems to think truth is found only in the extremes and the talking points. The winner in the cultural debate is frequently the one who argues the loudest. As Christians, we are not called to yell and be argumentative but to gently whisper God's truth through our speech and actions.

> And the Lord's servant must not be quarrelsome but kind to everyone, able to teach, patiently enduring evil, correcting his opponents with gentleness. God may perhaps grant them repentance leading to a knowledge of the truth, and they may escape from the snare of the devil, after being captured by him to do his will. (2 Tim. 2:24–26)

Under Construction

We all live in God's world; God doesn't live in ours, so we have only two choices: accept that reality or live a lie. I ask those of you who think Christianity imposes too many rules and regulations that you consider to be roadblocks to true freedom a question: which is more freeing, sitting back and enjoying a world you didn't have to build, or laboring twenty-four hours a day, 365 days a year to erect and maintain an exceedingly fragile worldview façade just to perpetuate the illusion that you're in charge?

> Come to me, all you who labor [constructing your own worldviews] and are heavy laden [with the burden of constantly remodeling them to fit your ever changing desires], and I will give you rest. Take my yoke upon you, and learn from me [because I made it all], for I am gentle and lowly in heart, and you will find rest for your souls [once you accept the fact that you are honored guests in my world]. For my yoke is easy, and my burden is light. (Matt. 11:28–30, my additions)

Puddle of Mud

In chapter 2, we discussed modernism and postmodernism as the two most significant philosophical obstacles to the spread of the gospel message. As I pointed out, they offer contrary worldview perspectives but are surprisingly mixed in the blender of our relativistic cultural consciousness. We trudge through it with our Christian waders on but can't avoid getting this philosophical mud all over our clothing.

It's astonishing that some of the smartest people on the planet, those who have spent lifetimes tacking letters of scholastic achievement to their names, are frequently those who ardently support the notion that man is just a smarter animal. These academically gifted human beings who are arguably the most intellectually different from every other animal on the planet make the incredible claim that they are just fine-tuned apes. The multiple PhDs of human transcendence have somehow convinced these brilliant people that they are nothing but the ABCs of immanence. They speak of evolution as if it were a series of collegiate weeding-out classes crafted to prepare us for the graduate school of humanity.

The problem, however, is that there is no good evidence our primate ancestors ever graduated and left the *Animal House* fraternity. The absurd modernist idea that man is just the smartest monkey is exposed when it tries to justify poop-throwing as moments of individual artistic brilliance or considers the ability of a monkey to learn the sign language for banana as a precursor of human intellect. Mere animal instinct without refined overarching truth sounds more like *The Call of the Wild* than poetic license to me.

While we may share 99 percent of our DNA with the ape, we surprisingly do not share 99 percent of our intellect; this fact screams for an explanation, and the Genesis creation account clarifies this reality perfectly. Man is taken from the common dust of the earth and personally animated by the divine, life-giving breath of God, which results in an absolutely unique physical and spiritual being created in the image of God.

Despite the best efforts of materialists to restrict our souls to chemicals and cells, they remain frustrated because mankind just won't give up the "ghost in the machine." They can't understand why people won't accept evolution's explanation for the origin of life but then hypocritically behave as if it weren't true either. They make financial contributions to save endangered species that have clearly failed evolution 101; they collect beautiful artwork that makes for very poor weapons in the battle for survival. They detect apricot tones in a glass of wine exquisitely cultivated by a skilled vintner instead of just getting drunk to drown out the harsh reality of life. They attend fundraisers to generate money for starving children in Africa but then have their conversation turn to why a "rat is a pig is a dog is a boy."[178] How absurd is that?

As we have already seen, my life, your life, and the life of the planet are all part of a greater story, a grand drama. We humans are hardwired to hear and tell stories to make sense of life. We are metanarrative-seeking beings; we can't help but try to connect the dots of the world around us.

Postmodernists, as we have discussed, demote all our stories to mere historical curiosities; they allow the dignity of relevance by telling us we must tolerate everybody's attempts at individual narrative but make it clear we must avoid trying to make it universally significant. We treat the concept of tolerance like a life raft that keeps us individually afloat after the forced evacuation of the sinking good ship "postmodernism" that's breaking up into tiny, individualistic pieces on the jagged rock of relativism.

I think that deep down most people are quite terrified that if we take this God thing too seriously, we may run into a deity of consequence who will ask us to take responsibility for our lives. To avoid accountability, we pay homage to the idea of being "spiritual" and make sure that every god trail is well groomed. We speak of a common holy mountain we all climb but dare not look up in fear we may actually see the one true God and be annihilated. We don't dare lift our gaze above the spiritual paths meandering through the valley of tolerance because we may lock eyes with a God of consequence.

Those of us who claim one God and one salvation path will be called intolerant bigots, but we must respectfully ask our accusers if they aren't being a bit hypocritical to intolerantly beat us over the head with their hammer of tolerance. They can't have it both ways; they either tolerate or they don't. A hierarchy of tolerance in the end is just intolerance. While the strange bedfellows of modernism and postmodernism are disturbing, the good news is that most people don't behave as if either is true and the resulting hypocrisy and inconsistency are glaring.

We will always be ridiculed for our beliefs. Our critics will continue to parade a seemingly unending line of religious hypocrisy in front of us, rubbing our Christian noses in the excrement of our own insincerity. The interesting thing, however, is that God already wrote the exposé on religious hypocrisy. The Bible spends much more time on the failings of God's chosen than on the sins of those outside the church. When the secular world speaks out against religion, it's drawing its breath from God's Spirit. The big difference is that while the secular world is interested only in tearing down religion, the Bible is concerned with purifying and restoring it.

The criticism we have heard from our detractors is nothing new because we have already heard it from God's own lips. Our worship should begin by acknowledging our shortcomings and then going to God with a broken and contrite heart, stepping into the joy of forgiveness and renewal. Our critics are correct in telling us to walk around in sack cloth and ashes, but they can never prevent us from putting on the pure white gown reserved for Christ's bride and dancing at the wedding feast.

Tragedy

God created a magnificent set sprinkled with marvelous props and then, in a stroke of literary genius, transformed a planet into a theater by populating it with a unique array of characters created in the image of the Author Himself. The amazing thing about this story is that while the Author had an ideal plot in mind, He gave His unique characters the choice of performing or not. Unfortunately, they chose to write their own scripts and create an entirely new genre, tragedy. Can you imagine creating something you're passionate about, sitting back, and declaring it very good, only to have it talk back to you and tell you what a terrible job you've just done? Like the painting telling the painter His use of color and texture is primitive, the novel telling the Writer His characters lack depth, or the music telling the Musician His song isn't catchy enough.

The story now has a conflict; the mortal characters repeatedly try to write their own immortal screenplays but find their divinely challenged narrative skills result only in pulp fiction. They are forced to live the rest of their lives as tortured artists perpetually unhappy because their work never reaches the literary standard of the divine image in which they were created.

The good news is that the Author never gave up on His original plot. The tension created by the characters had to be resolved, so in a stroke of creative genius, He introduced a plot twist that mankind could never have envisioned. He employed a unique literary salvation device that has kept His characters' heads spinning for two thousand years. The Author entered His own story and got impaled by the bloody pen of a literary imposter. It looked by all accounts that the rebellious characters had finally eliminated the divine obstacle to their self-publishing ambitions, but they failed to see that their little foray into the literary world was but a tiny subplot that was all but eclipsed by the narrative twist that began to take center stage. The Author edited mankind's clunky narrative, bad poetry, poor grammar, and misspelled words with His cross-shaped pen and transformed mankind's feeble attempt at personal narrative into timeless, classic literature.

Have you ever wondered why the most on-fire Christians are frequently those who come from no religious background? I believe it's because their sinful lives have led them from one disaster to another, a reality they couldn't conceal behind a façade of respectable religiosity. The avalanche of sinful consequence that had buried them and left them gasping for air was completely lifted, and they could once again breathe, but this time with the pure air of the Spirit. How could they contain their enthusiasm? They'd just experienced the startling, unexpected, and overwhelmingly gracious resolution to a plot conflict that had plagued them their entire lives, and their overwhelming gratitude left them with no choice but to share it with others. It's just like seeing a movie with an unexpected ending; you can't contain yourself, and you feel you have to tell others about it because you want them to share the same mind-blowing experience. You don't spread the word in hopes of getting a movie promotion commission but because you feel it would be a cosmic catastrophe if others never saw it.

> The kingdom of God? Time after time Jesus tries to drum into our heads what He means by it. He heaps parable upon parable like a madman. He tries shouting it. He tries whispering it. The Kingdom of God is like a treasure, like a pearl, like a seed buried in the ground. It is like a great feast that everybody is invited to and nobody wants to attend. What He seems to be saying is that the Kingdom of God is the time, or the time beyond time, when it will no longer be humans in their lunacy who are in charge of the world but God in His mercy who will be in charge of the world. It's the time above all else for wild rejoicing - like getting out of jail, like being cured of cancer, like finally, at long last, coming home. And it is at hand, Jesus says.[179]
>
> —Frederick Buechner

Setting the Table

We discussed earlier just how amazing it is that the set and props in our life stories somehow provide soothing balm for our souls. It's a truth subconsciously played out every day when we go out for walks, pet our cats, plant gardens, or take vacations in the tropics. We all somehow seem to know that the best escape from the stress of life is an exquisitely placed furry prop or a soothing stroll through a quiet forest. Maybe it's there that we're best able to hear the echo of God's words lovingly spoken into creation long ago. The need for peaceful escape, however, begs the question, why is the world so noisy? Why does our day-to-day life frequently sound like a bad elementary school orchestra recital? Why do we sneak out the backdoor of the "world" gym during the performance and seek aural relief in the soothing sounds of babbling brooks or chirping crickets? The orchestral performance, while well intentioned, grates on our ears. We can't blame the score or the instruments, so who's at fault? We have no choice but to call the musicians and conductor to task. There's something wrong with the performers. It appears they have the drive and dedication, they can hear the music in their heads, but they are incapable of replicating it, and instead of performing a timeless classic end up composing their own edgy "sin-ata."

Character Assassination

Our culture, by trying to reduce mankind to the level of an evolved animal, has engaged in the ultimate act of character assassination. As we sit in our balcony, trying to see how our lives fit into the great play around us, a postmodern assassin has snuck into the theater and is creeping up behind us, ready to fire bullets of insignificance into our apelike brains. The gunshots reduce the great literature of our lives to the level of a nature documentary. We need to get over all this silliness, because in the end, no human being truly behaves as if he or she was just an ape upgrade. We need to publicly acknowledge what we all privately think: human beings are unique beings on this planet! We must never forget that we bring characteristics to this world that cannot be found in nature, qualities that demand an explanation. The Author strategically established this crucial narrative detail at the very beginning of His Book by revealing that the characters were based on a divine blueprint. Think about this: whenever you read a book you are walking the halls of the author's mental art gallery. Every character he created is a painting hanging on the walls of his personal essence, a unique window into the soul of the Author, and

He would find His collection quite incomplete if the spot reserved for your portrait was empty.

> The Lord is not slow to fulfill his promise as some count slowness, but is patient toward you, not wishing that any should perish, but that all should reach repentance. (2 Pet. 3:9)

The reason God wishes that none should perish is because it is only when we are able to see His entire body of work that we can truly appreciate the full breadth and depth of who God is. We cannot just disregard the people who annoy us, because when we do, we deprive ourselves of one more unique opportunity to view God. It is certainly true that many people have forgotten they are unique windows into the mind of the Creator and fail to keep themselves clean with the Windex of God's truth, but if we can help them wipe off the dirt of deceit, we may be able to allow one more entirely new ray of light to enter the world and one more dusty corner of darkness to recede. My wife likes to call these aesthetically challenged people "divine sandpaper" because while initially quite abrasive, they ultimately help polish our own lenses for optimal God viewing.

Man is the only physical/spiritual unity on this planet, and as such, he has a unique responsibility and privilege. Our ability to enjoy, respect, and care for God's "good" creation is what takes it to the heights of the aesthetically pleasing "very good." Since we are all created in the image of God, we need to respect every human being, but we cannot ignore the fact that many of us have desecrated that image with our own poorly conceived remodeling projects. We need to encourage our fellow man to pull back the dirty, stinking carpet of human innovation and reveal the beautiful hardwood "image of God" floor beneath.

Tabloid or Tennyson

Why do we humans have such great literary potential but end up writing grocery-store tabloids? We recognize this fact and try to employ every means possible to make our literary output look dignified. We try to change our physical limitations by taking performance-enhancing drugs or undergoing plastic surgery. We create clubs, organizations, and religions of like-minded, spiritually unhappy people to praise each other's work even when the air hangs heavy with the unspoken thought that it sucks. We try to overcome our spiritual limitations by wearing crystals or learning how to tap into the cosmic energy source.

Unfortunately, in the end, our butts still sag, every commune turns into a cult, and our attempts to harness cosmic energy end up electrocuting us. Frustrated by the failure of each of these strategies to make us better, we end up making excuses for our human frailty by playing our evolutionary get-out-of-jail-free cards. They represent a chance to excuse our bad behavior by blaming it on the animal residue that has stuck to us from our evolutionary journey. Maybe we should take the common-sense approach and recognize that this is a huge problem that thousands of years of human effort has failed to fix and surrender our admirable but prideful ambitions to the One who had the perfect plan for us in the first place.

God's Grieved Heart

I hope I've made it clear that the problem facing our planet is not just a human incapable of being good but also a human who has rejected a relationship with the One who lovingly created him. The answer is not acquiring a new power or skill but becoming reconciled to God. Our infidelity has been so pervasive and our unfaithfulness so perverse that we could never alone make amends with the lover of our soul. Thankfully, the One we have so grievously offended is still passionate about making this relationship work. He made the ultimate sacrifice for our relationship by giving up any moral superiority He had certainly merited in light of His patient faithfulness, and He has extended His emotionally scarred hands to embrace us despite our ongoing infidelities.

For while we were still weak, at the right time Christ died for the ungodly. For one will scarcely die for a righteous person—though perhaps for a good person one would dare even to die— *but God shows his love for us in that while we were still sinners, Christ died for us.* Since, therefore, we have now been justified by his blood, much more shall we be saved by him from the wrath of God. For if while we were enemies we were reconciled to God by the death of his Son, much more, now that we are reconciled, shall we be saved by his life. More than that, *we also rejoice in God through our Lord Jesus Christ, through whom we have now received reconciliation.* (Rom. 5:6–11, emphasis added)

All Good Stories End with a Wedding

A good friend told me, "All good stories end with a wedding." The story of our broken relationship with God doesn't end with a nice handshake and a promise to be nicer; it ends in a wedding! Sadly, many eligible bachelors or bachelorettes get cold feet because they find the promises of a marriage covenant just too frightening. Instead, they try to find contentment in a series of religious one-night stands where they can conveniently sneak out the backdoor before the rising sun exposes the ugliness of the deity they had just slept with the night before. I'm sure you've had friends who hopped from one relationship to another because they were in love with the feeling of love and not the object of the love. It's the same situation when dealing with spirituality; most humans are in love with religious feelings, but when one divine partner fails to excite them anymore, they move onto the next deity.

True fulfillment will be found only in a committed, monogamous relationship. Accepting God's proposal will be the most glorious thing we can do, but it will also be one of the most difficult. We will be asked to carry the cross of relationship commitment but are promised an unending wedding feast. What's truly amazing is that despite a checkered past of pervasive unfaithfulness, the bride can still wear white because the blood of the Groom has completely washed her clean.

> Then I heard what seemed to be the voice of a great multitude, like the roar of many waters and like the sound of mighty peals of thunder, crying out, "Hallelujah! For the Lord our God the Almighty reigns. Let us rejoice and exult and give him the glory, for the marriage of the Lamb has come, and his Bride has made herself ready; it was granted her to clothe herself with fine linen, bright and pure" for the fine linen is the righteous deeds of the saints. (Rev. 19:6–8)

The world should rejoice because the invitation has gone out to everyone. The question is not "Am I invited?" but "Do I know the bride and groom well enough to want to attend?" It will be a glorious affair. The relationship man squandered in the garden will once again be restored.

> Then came one of the seven angels who had the seven bowls full of the seven last plagues and spoke to me, saying, "Come, I will show you the Bride, the wife of the Lamb." And he carried me away in the Spirit to a great, high mountain, and showed me the holy city Jerusalem coming down out of heaven from God, having the glory of God, its radiance like a most rare jewel, like a jasper, clear as crystal ... And I saw no temple in the city, for its temple is the Lord God the Almighty and the Lamb. And the city has no need of sun or moon to shine on it, for the glory of God gives it light, and its lamp is the Lamb. By its light will the nations walk, and the kings of the earth will bring their glory into it, and its gates will never be shut by day—and there will be no night there. They will bring into it the glory and the honor of the nations. But nothing unclean will ever enter it, nor anyone who does what is detestable or false, but only those who are written in the Lamb's book of life. (Rev. 21:9–11 and 22–27)

Weeds and Wheat

Our task will not be easy. Jesus warned us that the kingdom would grow among the weeds and evil would exist alongside the good. We may get so frustrated that we throw our hands up and declare the world is lost. Before we get too frustrated, we need to remember that restoration can begin only after the decay has stopped. We are called to be salt to the world. We frequently think of salt as a seasoning to enhance flavor, and while we certainly do add the spicy "very" to God's "good," our most important function may very well be as a preservative. It may just be that our most important task for now is to prevent any further decay. Without a Christian presence, our world would be nothing but decomposing sin.

We all too often think of a disembodied spiritual reward for a faithful life, but we must never forget that God's ultimate plan was not a distant heaven but a new creation on earth. Jesus performed His work in a physical form on a physical cross to redeem a physical creation. The plunging of the cross into the ground was a thorn in the side of the planet to remind us that the work of redemption begins here on this planet and that spiritual withdrawal from this world is not an option.

> Now when they heard this they were cut to the heart, and said to Peter and the rest of the apostles, "Brothers, what shall we do?" And Peter said to them, "Repent and be baptized every one of you in the name of Jesus Christ for the forgiveness of your sins, and you will receive the gift of the Holy Spirit. For the promise is for you and for your children and for all who are far off, everyone whom the Lord our God calls to himself." (Acts 2:37–39)

Fair and Balanced

> The church is a hospital for sinners, not a museum for saints.[180]
>
> —Timothy Keller

All of us, Christian and non-Christian alike, must be fair in this discussion. Judging a religious tradition by the behavior of some of its adherents is fraught with difficulty. We have already established that something is wrong with man and that he doesn't always behave consistently or morally, so we need to be careful when we judge someone's deeply held philosophy or religion by his or her behavior alone. We must first look beyond their personal behavior and scrutinize the core philosophy or doctrine that drives their particular worldview. Any worldview worth its salt will have hypocrites because then at least we know it stands for something tangible. It's at this point that we must dismiss postmodernism, because if you stand for nothing except that all truth is relative, then it's impossible to be a hypocrite. A lack of hypocrisy among the followers of a particular religion or philosophy should be a red flag signaling they stand for nothing and have automatically disqualified themselves from the worldview roundtable discussion.

Postmodernism has eliminated the possibility of hypocrisy because everything is acceptable; you can't violate a moral or aesthetic code when there isn't one. A faith tradition can only be considered valid if it has built into its structure specific criteria to condemn bad behavior. If a worldview has no foundation for making such determinations, it's incapable of policing itself or calling others to task, and it quickly falls apart as a consistent system of thought or belief. If postmodernism was honest with itself, it would have to admit its improvisational free love and free thought are performed on a solid stage that was already built by God.

When you come right down to it, you will see that every other worldview is in fact just another club, an exclusive gathering of like-minded people with a shared vision informed by their narrow personal preferences, a group that loves to make its own rules, chant its own slogans, wear interesting uniforms, and pass out merit badges to the most zealous in their ranks. These clubs are exclusive, require letters of recommendation, and seek to enroll those of good social standing. Christianity fails on all these counts. It's not exclusive—no need for good social standing. In fact, Jesus has the gall to invite everybody to join and welcomes those who smell bad and have behavior issues into the kingdom first. While other worldview clubs want you to make a case for why you're worthy to join, Christianity forces you to admit you'll never be worthy, and the only hope for entry is a broken and contrite heart.

Members of the Christian community are not necessarily known for their better behavior because all sin, but they can be easily identified because they are joyfully forgiven. While there are certainly Christians who treat their faith like an exclusive club cruise, they end up missing the whole Jesus boat. The church should not be appealing because it has a cool "cross" logo, snazzy "choir robe" uniforms, or catchy "praise song" chants because every other worldview club offers those. No, the church should be appealing because it's the last refuge for a people dying from sin, a people who finally recognize that marching under a club banner, dressed in their finest club attire, and singing the club fight song only covers up the cancer of sin eating away at their souls; they realize what they need is to be admitted into the church hospital for a round of Jesus chemotherapy.

> And when Jesus heard it, he said to them, "Those who are well have no need of a physician, but those who are sick. I came not to call the righteous, but sinners." (Mark 2:17)

Heartburn

> That very day two of them were going to a village named Emmaus, about seven miles from Jerusalem, and they were talking with each other about all these things that had happened. While they were talking and discussing together, Jesus himself drew near and went with them. But their eyes were kept from recognizing him ... And he said to them, "O foolish ones, and slow of heart to believe all that the prophets have spoken! Was it not necessary that the Christ should suffer these things and enter into his glory?" And beginning with Moses and all

the Prophets, he interpreted to them in all the Scriptures the things concerning himself ...

So they drew near to the village to which they were going. He acted as if he were going farther, but they urged him strongly, saying, "Stay with us, for it is toward evening and the day is now far spent." So he went in to stay with them. When he was at table with them, he took the bread and blessed and broke it and gave it to them. And their eyes were opened, and they recognized him. And he vanished from their sight. They said to each other, "Did not our hearts burn within us while he talked to us on the road, while he opened to us the Scriptures?" (Luke 24:13–16, 28–32)

The men on the road to Emmaus exemplified our modern situation. We all encounter Christ everyday of our lives in our daily walk. We constantly bump into a Christ who causes our hearts to burn, who convicts us of our thoughts and behavior, and who gives us hope for shalom. Our fellow man is constantly faced with the annoying fact that something is wrong with the world; he knows it and feels it. The symptom of our dis-ease is the pain we experience as the cancer of Original Sin gnaws away at the image of God imbedded in us. And as Jesus, the true image of God, walks beside us on our life journey, we catch glimpses of Him out of the corners of our eyes and—get this—sense that we know Him from somewhere but are either unwilling or unable to recognize Him.

On the road to Emmaus, the two men didn't initially recognize the resurrected Jesus, so He began the process of revealing Himself by retelling God's story. Authors are known by their stories, and on that particular dusty road, accompanied by two of his unique characters, the Author of our salvation retold His story. The men had read the first book in the series and anticipated the second installment, but their "hearts burned" as they realized they were witnessing a plot twist they never could have anticipated. They had to hear more, so they invited Jesus to dine with them, but once they broke bread with the Bread of Life, they realized they were having an audience with the Author Himself.

As the body of Christ, we are also called to walk alongside our fellow travelers and tell them the great God story so their hearts will also burn and we can then alleviate their spiritual hunger pains with the Bread of Life and quench their thirst of despair with living water.

Knock Knock! Who's There?

> Behold, I stand at the door and knock. If anyone hears my voice and opens the door, I will come in to him and eat with him, and he with me. (Rev. 3:20)

> You can believe in Christ intellectually and admire him; you can say your prayers to him through the keyhole (I did for many years); you can push coins at Him under the door to keep Him quiet; you can be moral, decent, upright and good; you can be religious; you can have been baptized and confirmed; you can be deeply versed in the philosophy of religion; you can be a theological student and even an ordained minister—and still not have opened the door to Christ. There is no substitute for this.[181]

> —John R. Stott

The evidence is everywhere, and Jesus awaits our response. The story has been told, the conflict revealed, and the mind-boggling solution offered. Do we answer the knock at the door or deny that the door exists? Do we accept the final chapters or improvise our own endings? Jesus stands in front of us; the Author come in character flesh and asks, "Have I been with you so long, and you still do not know me?

> Thomas said to him, "Lord, we do not know where you are going. How can we know the way?" Jesus said to him, "I am the way, and the truth, and the life. No one comes to the Father except through me. If you had known me, you would have known my Father also. From

now on you do know him and have seen him." Philip said to him, "Lord, show us the Father, and it is enough for us." Jesus said to him, "Have I been with you so long, and you still do not know me, Philip? Whoever has seen me has seen the Father. How can you say, 'Show us the Father'? Do you not believe that I am in the Father and the Father is in me?" (John 14:5–10)

Look to the Hills

The scene of Jesus hanging on the cross flanked by the two criminals is a snapshot of our human situation. God is revealed as a suffering Son who hangs in the company of sinners on a cross strategically placed on a hill overlooking the valley of our lives. We can't look away. We have to make a decision about what we see. Jesus doesn't make any demands; He just hangs there, suffering in His innocence. The two criminals represent the choice we must make. Do we choose to see God's power made perfect in weakness, or do we see the power of the world made perfect by imposing death? One criminal is angry because Jesus seems incapable of changing His fate and is forced to accept death as the ultimate power in the world. The other criminal recognizes that the death of the innocent Man next to him is ironically the actual antidote to death. How is that possible? Jesus makes it clear that if you are not at peace with the paradise to come, the fear of death will be the ultimate power in your life. Jesus is at our side, feeling the sting of our own nails, hearing the derision of our own critics, and gasping for breath along with us as we try to inhale the Spirit in a world choking on the smog of sin. He understands and feels our suffering but, in the most horrible of situations, speaks of paradise.

Where Do I Sign Up?

If Jesus is the sacrificial Lamb that takes away the sins of the world, how do we get in on that deal? First, we have to accept the fact that Jesus is the only qualified legal representative to represent us in God's court of law. The evidence for our sinfulness is overwhelming, but to our astonishment, Jesus generates a class action suit in which the blame is focused on Him instead of us. All we need to do is put our signatures in His Book of Life legal documents, and He will take care of the rest.

The biggest difference between Christianity and other religious movements is that we acknowledge we are incapable of being our own legal counsel. The others suggest if you read a couple law books and are a good orator, you can make your own case. Unfortunately for our legally ambitious friends, all these attempts at legal self-representation are inadequate in the highest court in the land. The choice is quite clear: surrender, sign on, and let Jesus do the work, or enter the courtroom and hope the Judge is having a good day.

> This stage is the "final satisfaction" because we discover in the moment of surrender that the God who is on our trail is also the God we seek. In a strange manner, as we seem to be defeated, it dawns on us that we are in the only possible way, victorious! For we are free from having to run from God (who is everywhere), and we can turn and embrace him.[182]
>
> —Keith Miller

The Red Letters

> Truth decay? Try brushing up on the Bible.
> —A sign on a local church billboard

The Bible is a fascinating book. It has been browbeaten, burned, and buried, and yet it hasn't disappeared. Many have tried to rid the planet of it, yet it survives. Christian critics attribute its survival to the fact it was written by the religious power brokers to maintain their rule. The problem with that argument is that it does the opposite; it consistently calls the religious elite to task for being hard-hearted and oppressive, and it reminds the rich and powerful that they will be the ones living with an eternal, unquenched thirst while the poor feast in paradise. It tells stories of a stiff-necked chosen people who repeatedly cheat on their first love, a people who were more frequently punished for their unfaithfulness than rewarded because God chose them. They were chronic covenant breakers.

It's a book that speaks of a God who works through stubborn sinners, outcasts, infertile women, and reluctant prophets. It portrays a God who comes to this planet as a human baby. He chooses a bunch of fickle, dense men to follow Him, and He spends most of His time with prostitutes, tax collectors, and outcasts. He tells them the kingdom of God is reserved for those who are by every cultural standard less successful. Finally, He suffers and dies at the hands of the political and religious elite. I don't think the Bible qualifies as propaganda for some political or religious agenda. In fact, if someone were to write a "holy" book for his or her personal worldview, I suspect they wouldn't use the Bible as a template because the Bible represents reality and not the illusory utopian dreams of human pretensions to divinity. The Bible is powerful because it explains what we already know; man is sinful and incapable of fixing himself, but then in a surprise twist, it catches us off guard by offering a solution we could never have predicted: a God willing to sacrifice all and die for the sins of a corrupt people.

Grace Rolls Downhill

> Behold, I am doing a new thing; now it springs forth,
> do you not perceive it? I will make a way in the
> wilderness and rivers in the desert.
> The wild beasts will honor me, the jackals and the
> ostriches, for I give water in the wilderness, rivers in
> the desert, to give drink to my chosen people,
> the people whom I formed for myself that they might
> declare my praise. (Isa. 43:19–21)

Under the influence of the inviolable law of love gravity, God's grace, like a river, waterfall, or a rainstorm, flows downhill, pooling in the low points of our lives. Jesus often spoke of those blessed puddles of pooled grace—the poor, the suffering, and the grieving. He made it clear the people in the greatest danger were not those whose homes were under divine water but those who had built their homes upstream, content to admire the view and occasionally stick their toes in its soothing water. They didn't dare jump into God's treacherous but good current because they feared they would be swept away and lose illusory control of their lives.

While the men I work with at the Union Gospel Mission splash around in the healing water of God's pooled grace, they can't help but laugh at those upstream who foolishly spend all their time trying to divert it or dam it up instead of letting His life-giving water reach the obviously parched areas of their lives. Astonishingly, we humans attempt to micromanage God's overwhelming love and grace.

Little Italy

One of the most interesting aspects of the kingdom that Jesus has inaugurated is that it has already begun but is not complete. Theologians speak of this transition as the "already and not yet." This tension should make every Christian antsy. The church has been given God's vision of shalom, the vision of God's true intention for the world, but it has left the job unfinished, and while Jesus' physical presence may be gone, His body lives on in the church. The church therefore cannot rest because the baton of the work of Christ has been passed on; it must bring to fruition that which Jesus Christ made possible.

We have signed up for citizenship in a kingdom to come, and as we find out how wonderful it will be in the future, "not yet," we feel like pilgrims, strangers, and foreigners in the "already." We have two choices: retreat to enclaves of like-minded wanderers content to separate themselves from the strange, dysfunctional world around them, or infiltrate ourselves everywhere as participants in

God's shalom transformation project. We cannot isolate ourselves in the "Little Christianity" section of the big secular city; we must let our lamps shine on every metropolitan, ethnic, and cultural lamp stand. We will find that once our citizenship papers have been stamped with the Lamb's blood seal, we will no longer accept the reigning power paradigms of this world. Our response should not be retreat but engagement. Our battlefield strategy should be "shock and awe." The world will be shocked as we attack it head-on, brandishing only a wooden, cross- shaped sword, and it will be awed as we breach their frontline, ignore their generals, and enter the trenches to attend to the wounded enemy troops hit by the friendly fire of their own confused worldview artillery. It's unacceptable for the Church to sit in the pews of the "already" because raging outside the stained glass windows is the war for the "not yet," and we are called to "spiritual" battle.

Antique Road Show

You are a creation art expert. You understand the work of the Artist. You know His technique, His use of texture and color, and the objects He is fond of painting. You can recognize His original work miles away. Now it's time to take your expertise on the road because there are millions of people out there who have some of His finest pieces hanging on their life walls but don't know it. They're pretty sure they possess something of value but don't know its actual worth. They carefully pack it up and bring it to your Ancient of Days road show. You can barely contain your excitement as they slowly tell the story of how they acquired it, because you instantly recognize that this is an original work created by the Master Painter Himself. You know they have no idea that what they brought in is of inestimable value, and you can't wait to see the looks on their faces when you tell them its true worth.

In true road show fashion, you begin with the old story of the Painter and point out the distinguishing features of His work. You ask the owners if they know how much it's worth, and you get the usual response, "I'm not sure that's why I brought it to you." You then tell them that it's an original painted during His joyful garden phase and that it's worth millions, that it's the "pearl of great price." They're stunned and can't wipe the smiles off their faces. You wrap up the segment by thanking them for bringing in this exquisite piece of art and watch them as they tenderly pack it up and head home.

Unfortunately, just as with the real Antique Road Show, once they leave the studio, you never find out what these people did with their newly discovered treasure, but you can't help but wonder, did they sell it for large quantities of Mammon or insure it with the blood of the Lamb?

"Your Mission, Jim, Should You Choose to Accept It ..."

Aren't you tired of living in a two-storied home in which the floors don't connect? Doesn't it seem silly to put on a parka or strip down to shorts every time you want to visit Jesus just so you can acclimate to the ever-changing cultural seasons outside? Why not take the bold step of popping a hole through your pristine pride ceiling and constructing a stairway into the Holy of Holies? Jesus is waiting! Once you do, everyone in your neighborhood will see a holy light emanating from your windows and will be attracted like bugs to a porch light. Your personal remodeling project may then become a show home for the radical kingdom housing development, a place where others can safely experience what it would be like to build in that neighborhood.

> No one after lighting a lamp covers it with a jar or puts it under a bed, but puts it on a stand, so that those who enter may see the light. (Luke 8:16)

If you are seeking God, I hope this book has helped you recognize that you live in God's world, a world best understood as a story with a set, props, and characters. It's a story everyone agrees has a conflict that when carefully analyzed has only one possible Jesus solution.

If you already accept Jesus Christ as your Lord and Savior, I hope I've made you feel more comfortable in your Christian skin because now it's time for you to boldly let others in on the best news ever. I will leave you with one warning—always check to see what kind of wind fills your missionary sails; is it the glorious Holy Spirit breeze or your own hot air? Many a good evangelistic effort has been blown off course by an untimely human squall.

The church should be God's physical presence in this world, the body of Christ roaming from East to West, to help the least and lost. Sadly, many of us live like couch potatoes, snacking on bread and wine on our comfy Christian sofa, scanning the cultural boob tube with our apologetic remote control, looking for alternative worldviews to ridicule. We yell at the screen, we laugh at their antics, but we never step outside the narthex of our personal Christian walk to personally engage them. We fear that our Christian clothing may be ridiculed, so instead, we lounge around in our spiritual jammies, vowing that tomorrow we'll take a shower, comb our hair, and leave the house.

I hope I've made it clear that the Christian suit you once felt so uncomfortable in fits perfectly and appropriately matches every occasion. So now, when you venture out into the world, you will begin to notice a very interesting thing; those who you feared would ridicule your Christian fashion choice are the ones in need of wardrobe makeovers. They're the ones who look like tourists wearing knee-high black socks and sandals to the world "beach," squinting their eyes because they're not used to the brightness of the Son. We can now walk up to them and tell them it's okay to go barefoot and wiggle their toes in the warm sand of God's creation, to comfortably sit in the lounge chair of life, and bask in the theatrical glow of the gloriously restored Director's Cut.

Chapter 1: Christian Couture

1. Ann Lee, "Lady Gaga defends meat dress by claiming she's no 'piece of meat." Online posting September 14, 2010, Metro, metro.co.uk/2010/09/14/lady-gaga-defends-meat-dress-by-claiming-shes-no-piece-of-meat-511375/.

2. Calvin Miller, *Into the Depths of God* (Bloomington, Minn.: Bethany House, 2000), 13.

3. Kathleen Norris, *Amazing Grace* (New York: Riverhead Books, 1998), 23.

4. Athenagoras, *A Plea Regarding Christians*, in *Early Christian Fathers*, ed. Cyril C. Richardson (New York: Touchstone, 1996), 310.

5. Ideas borrowed from Glen Sunshine, *Why You Think the Way You Do* (Grand Rapids: Zondervan, 2009), chapter 11.

6. Martin B. Copenhaver, *To Begin at the Beginning* (Cleveland: United Church Press, 1994), 254.

7. Frederick Buechner, *Now and Then* (San Francisco: Harper, 1983), 22.

8. John R. Stott, *Basic Christianity* (Grand Rapids, Mich.: Eerdmans, 1971), 134.

9. C. S. Lewis, quoted in *The Quotable C. S. Lewis*, Ed. Wayne Martindale and Jerry Root (Wheaton, Ill.: Tyndale, 1990), 55.

10. Richard Dawkins, *The God Delusion* (New York: Houghton Mifflin, 2006), 55.

11. Francis Schaeffer, *Trilogy* (Wheaton, Ill.: Crossway Books, 1990), 237.

12. Christopher Hitchens, *God Is not Great* (New York: Twelve Hachette Book Group, 2007), 1

13 Richard Dawkins, "Is Science Religion?" *The Humanist*, vol. 57, no. 1 (January/February) 1997.

14 Ravi Zacharias, *Can Man Live Without God?* (Nashville: W Publishing, 1994), 6–7.

15 Sam Harris, *Letter to a Christian Nation* (New York: Vintage, 2006), 91.

16 Douglas Adams, *The Ultimate Hitchhiker's Guide* (New York: Gramercy, 2005), 271.

17 Ibid., 273.

18 Malcolm Muggeridge, *Jesus: The Man Who Lives* (New York: Harper & Row, 1975), 37.

19 Quoted in Ravi Zacharias, *Can Man Live Without God?* (Nashville: W Publishing, 1994), 10.

20 C. S. Lewis, quoted in Philip Yancey, *Rumors of Another World,* Grand Rapids: Zondervan, 2003), 167.

21 Bill Cosby found on *BrainyQuote* at www.brainyquote.com/quotes/authors/b/bill_cosby.html

22 Kathleen Norris, *Amazing Grace* (New York: Riverhead Books, 1998), 4.

23 Winston Churchill, quoted at www.goodreads.com/quotes/33-men-occasionally-stumble-over-the-truth-but-most-of-them

24 G. K. Chesterton, *Orthodoxy* (Colorado Springs: 1994), 20.

25 Ravi Zacharias, *Beyond Opinion* (Nashville: Thomas Nelson, 2007), 318.

26 Samuel M. Shoemaker, quoted in *Conversions*, ed. Hugh T. Kerr and John M. Muller (Grand Rapids: Eerdmans, 1983), 198.

27 Simone Weil, *Waiting For God* (New York: G. P. Putnam Sons, 1951), 27.

28 Brennan Manning, *A Glimpse of Jesus* (New York: HarperCollins, 2003), 72.

Chapter 2: To the Unknown God

29 Douglas Adams, *The Ultimate Hitchhiker's Guide* (New York: Gramercy Books, 2005), 121.

30 Ibid., 122.

31 T. S. Eliot, *The Complete Poems and Plays: 1909–1950* (Orlando: HarcBrace), 145.

32 Vox Day, *The Irrational Atheist* (Dallas: Benbella Books, 2008), 62.

33 Frederick Buechner, *Telling the Truth* (New York: HarperCollins, 1977), 41.

34 Martin B. Copenhaver, *To Begin at the Beginning* (Cleveland: United Church Press, 1994), 274.

35 Phillip Yancey, *Soul Survivor* (Galilee/Doubleday: New York, 2001), 269.

36 G. K. Chesterton, *Orthodoxy* (Colorado Springs: Harold Shaw, 2001), 111.

Chapter 3: Improvisation or Grand Theater?

37 Eugene Peterson, *Eat This Book* (Grand Rapids: Eerdmans, 2006), 47–48.

38 Peter Whoriskey, "Instant-Messengers Really Are About Six Degrees from Kevin bacon." *Washington Post*, August 2, 2008, www.washingtonpost.com/wp-dyn/content/article/2008/08/01/AR2008080103718.html

39 Eugene Peterson, *Eat This Book* (Grand Rapids: Eerdmans, 2006), 42.

40 Frederick Buechner, *The Clown in the Belfry* (New York: HarperCollins, 1992), 133.

41 Frederick Buechner, quoted in Phillip Yancey, *Soul Survivor* (New York: Galilee/Doubleday, 2001), 247.

42 Eugene Peterson, *Reversed Thunder* (New York: HarperCollins, 1988), 13.

43 Kevin J. Vanhoozer, "Lost in Interpretation? Truth, Scripture, and Hermeneutics" in *Whatever Happened to Truth?* ed. Andreas Kostenberger (Wheaton, Ill.: Crossway Books, 2005), 110, 122.

44 Timothy Keller, *The Reason For God: Belief in an Age of Skepticism* (New York: Dutton/Penguin, 2008), 123.

45 Louie Giglio, *I am not but I know I AM* (Sisters, Ore.: Multnomah Publishers, 2005), 9.

46 Charles Colson and Harold Fickett, *The Faith* (Grand Rapids: Zondervan, 2008), 63.

47 Frederick Buechner, quoted in Phillip Yancey, *Soul Survivor* (New York: Galilee/Doubleday, 2001), 253.

Chapter 4: All the World's a Stage

48 Stephen Hawking, *A Brief History of Time* (New York: Bantam Books, 1988), 174.

49 Francis Crick, quoted in Nancy R. Pearcey and Charles B. Thaxton, *The Soul of Science* (Wheaton, Ill.: Crossway Books, 1994), 245.

50 Albert Einstein, quoted in Phillip Yancey, *Soul Survivor* (Galilee/Doubleday: New York, 2001), 47.

51 Abraham Joshua Heschel, *Man is Not Alone* (New York: Farrar, Straus and Giroux, 1951), 4–5, 8.

52 Ibid., 63.

53 William Paley, *Natural Theology* (1802).

54 Carl Becker, quoted in Nancy Pearce and Charles Thaxton, *The Soul of Science* (Wheaton, Ill.: Crossway Books, 1994), 219.

55 Sir James Jeans, Simple to Remember.com, www.simpletoremember. com/articles/a/science-quotes

56 Albert Einstein, quoted in John Lennox, *Beyond Opinion* (Nashville: Thomas Nelson, 2007), 119.

57 Guillermo Gonzalez and Jay W. Richards, *The Privileged Planet* (Washington D.C.: Regnery, 2004), xv.

58 Annie Dillard, quoted in Philip Yancey, *Soul Survivor* (New York: Galilee, 2001), 232.

59 Dennis and Adair, *Let's Get Away from it All,* 1941.

60 G. K. Chesterton, *Orthodoxy* (Colorado Springs: Harold Shaw, 2001)

61 Abraham Joshua Heschel, *Man is Not Alone* (New York: Farrar, Straus and Giroux, 1951), 26.

62 G. K. Chesterton, *Orthodoxy* (Colorado Springs: Harold Shaw, 2001), 84.

63 Ibid., 167.

64 Abraham Joshua Heschel, *Man is Not Alone* (New York: Farrar, Straus and Giroux, 1951), 147.

65 Simone Weil, *Waiting for God* (New York: HarperCollins, 2001), 76.

66 Douglas Adams, *The Ultimate Hitchhiker's Guide* (New York: Gramercy, 2005), 53.

67 Ibid., 187.

68 Ibid., 199.

69 Richard Dawkins, *The God Delusion* (Boston: Mariner Books, 2008), 157.

70 Annie Dillard, *Faith Interface,* www.faithinterface.com.au/ notable-quotes/teaching-a-stone-to-talk-annie-dillard

Chapter 5: Propped Up

71 Simone Weil, quoted in Phillip Yancey, *Soul Survivor* (New York: Galilee/Doubleday, 2001), 262.

72 Andy Crouch, *Culture Making* (Downers Grove, Ill.: InterVarsity Press, 2008), 109–110.

73 G. K. Chesterton, *The Everlasting Man* (San Francisco: Ignatius Press, 1993), 27.

Chapter 6: Meet the Cast

74 Saint Augustine, quoted in Malcolm Muggeridge, *Confessions of a Twentieth Century Pilgrim* (San Francisco: Harper & Row, 1988), 128

75 Charles Colson and Nancy Pearcey, *How Now Shall We Live?* (Wheaton, Ill.: Tyndale, 1999), 420.

76 G. K. Chesterton, *Orthodoxy* (Colorado Springs: WaterBrook Press, 1994), 217.

77 John Merrick, "The Elephant Man Quotes," *Rotten Tomatoes*, www.rottentomatoes.com/m/1006527-elephant_man/quotes

78 G. K. Chesterton, *The Everlasting Man* (San Francisco: Ignatius Press, 1993), 26.

79 Ingrid Newark, "Ingrid Newkirk," Wikiquote, en.wikiquote.org/wiki/Ingrid_Newkirk

80 G. K. Chesterton, *The Everlasting Man* (San Francisco: Ignatius Press, 1993), 38.

81 David Bentley Hart, *Atheist Delusions* (New Haven: Yale University Press, 2009), 230.

82 Walker Percy, *Lost in the Cosmos* (New York: Picador, 1983), 254.

83 Richard Dawkins, quoted in Ravi Zacharaias, *Beyond Opinion* (Nashville: Thomas Nelson, 2007), 192.

84 T. S. Eliot, *The Complete Poems and Plays* (Orlando, Fla.: Harcourt Brace, 1952), 96.

85 Leslie Newbigin, *The Gospel in a Pluralist Society* (Grand Rapids, Mich.: Eerdmans, 1989), 100.

86 Pierre Teilhard de Chardin, "Teilhard de Chardin Quotes," Thinkexist, thinkexist.com/quotes/teilhard_de_chardin/

87 Walker Percy, *Lost in the Cosmos* (New York: Picador, 1983), 124.

88 Abraham Joshua Heschel, *Man is Not Alone* (New York: Farrar, Straus and Giroux, 1951), 129.

89 Frederick Buechner, *The Eyes of the Heart* (New York: HarperSanFrancisco, 1999), 85.

90 D. E. Strandness, *My Life to Now* (Unpublished).

91 Mary C. Neal interviewed on the *Today* show. today.msnbc.msn.com/id/48242202/ns/today-books/t/i-was-home-former-skeptic-shares-glimpse-heaven/#.UBcgHxztitA

92 Walker Percy, *Lost in the Cosmos* (New York: Picador, 1983), 8.

93 Ernest Thayer, *Casey at the Bat: A Ballad of the Republic Sung in the Year 1888*, First published in the *San Francisco Examiner*, June 3, 1888.

Chapter 7: Houston, We Have a Problem

94 Douglas Adams, *The Ultimate Hitchhiker's Guide* (New York: Gramercy, 2005), 1.

95 Johann Wolfgang Von Goethe, Quotes Daddy, www.quotesdaddy.com/quote/1334873/johann-wolfgang-von-goethe/man-can-only-endure-a-certain-degree-of-unhappiness

96 Ravi Zacharias, *Jesus Among Other Gods* (Nashville: W Publishing, 2000), 137.

97 Keith Miller, *The Becomers* (Waco, Tex.: Word Books, 1973). 31–32.

98 N. T. Wright, *Simply Christian* (New York: HarperCollins, 2006), 20.

99 Katherine Whitehorn, quoted in *Christian Counter-Attack* (New Rochelle, N.Y.: Arlington House, 1969), 50.

100 G. K. Chesterton, quoted in Phillip Yancey, *Soul Survivor* (New York: Galilee/Doubleday, 2001), 58.

101 Kathleen Norris, *Amazing Grace* (New York: Riverhead Books, 1998), 165.

102 The Cure, "Where the Birds Always Sing," *Bloodflowers*, Rhino/Elektra, 2006.

103 Karl Rahner, quoted in Ronald Rolheiser, *Against an Infinite Horizon* (New York: Crossroads, 1995), 11.

104 David B. Hart, *Christ or Nothing*, www.firstthings.com/article/2007/12/christ-and-nothing-28

105 Jeff Bridges, "Funny How Fallin' Feels Like Flyin'." *Crazy Heart Original Motion Picture Soundtrack*, New West Records, 2010.

106 Timothy Keller, *The Reason For God: Belief in an Age of Skepticism* (New York: Dutton/Penguin, 2008), 46.

107 Dietrich Bonhoeffer, *The Cost of Discipleship* (New York: Macmillan, 1970).

108 Dag Hammarskjold, parkstepp.tumblr.com/post/1198854359/you-cannot-play-with-the-animal-in-you-without

109 Frederick Buechner, quoted by Philip Yancey in *Soul Survivor* (New York: Galilee-Doubleday, 2003), 264.

110 Flannery O'Connor, quoted by Kathleen Norris in *Amazing Grace* (New York: Riverhead Books, 1998), 270.

111 Benedict Groeschl, heard on EWTN radio.

112 Philip Yancey, *Soul Survivor* (New York: Galilee-Doubleday, 2003), 263.

113 Ravi Zacharias, *Jesus among Other Gods* (Nashville: W Publishing, 2000), 137.

114 Kathleen Norris, *The Cloister Walk* (New York: Riverhead Books, 1996), 127.

115 Francis Collins, *The Language of God* (New York: Free Press, 2006), 40.

116 Phillip Yancey, *Rumors of Another World* (Grand Rapids: Zondervan, 2003), 148.

117 Francis Schaeffer, *Trilogy* (Wheaton, Ill.: Crossway Books, 1990), 236.

118 Emmylou Harris, "Lost Unto This World," *Stumble into Grace*, Nonesuch Records, 2003.

119 Frederick Nietzsche, *Parable of the Madman*, quoted in Ravi Zacharias, *Can Man Live Without God* (Nashville, Tenn.: W Publishing, 1994), 18.

120 Ravi Zacharias, *Can Man Live Without God?* (Nashville, Tenn.: W Publishing, 1994), 24.

121 G. K. Chesterton, *Orthodoxy* (Colorado Springs: A Shaw Book, 2001), 139.

122 Morris West, quoted in Ronald Rolheiser, *Against an Infinite Horizon* (New York: Crossroad, 1995), 11.

Chapter 8: Pathology Report

123 Christopher Hitchens, *God Is Not Great* (New York: Twelve–Hatchet Book Group, 2007), 87.

124 Walter Brueggemann, *Theology of the Old Testament* (Minneapolis: Fortress Press, 1997), 453.

125 G. K. Chesterton, quoted in Philip Yancey, *Soul Survivor* (New York: Galilee-Doubleday, 2003), 51.

126 G. K. Chesterton, *Orthodoxy* (Colorado Springs: A Shaw Book, 2001), 11.

127 Henri Nouwen, *The Wounded Healer* (New York: An Image Book—Doubleday, 1979), 7.

128 Geisler and Brooks, quoted in Charles Colson and Nancy Pearcey, *How Now Shall We Live?* (Wheaton, Ill.: Tyndale House, 1999), 193.

129 C. S. Lewis, *The Weight of Glory* (New York: HarperOne, 2001), 46.

130 William Temple, quoted in John R. Stott, *The Cross of Christ* (Downers Grove, Ill.: InterVarsity Press, 1986), 197.

Chapter 9: Conflict Resolution

131 Lin Yutang, quoted in *Conversions*, ed. Hugh T. Kerr and John M. Muller (Grand Rapids: Eerdmans, 1983), 207.

[132] Pascal, quoted in quoted in C John Collins, *Genesis 1–4* (Phillipsburg, N.J.: P&R Publishing, 2006), 258–59.

[133] Stephen Turner poem *Creed*, quoted in Ravi Zacharias, *Can Man Live Without God?* (Nashville, Tenn.: W Publishing, 1994), 44.

[134] Ravi Zacharias, *Can Man Live Without God?* (Nashville, Tenn.: W Publishing, 1994), 32.

[135] Ibid., paraphrase.

[136] Albert Schweitzer, quoted in Phillip Yancey, *Rumors of Another World*, (Grand Rapids, Mich.: Zondervan, 2003), 225.

[137] Timothy Keller, *The Reason for God: Belief in an Age of Skepticism* (New York: Dutton/Penguin, 2008), 49–50.

[138] Ignatius of Antioch, *Early Christian Fathers,* ed. Cyril C. Richardson (New York: Touchstone, 1996), 100.

[139] C. S. Lewis, *Mere Christianity* (Nashville, Tenn.: Broadman & Holman, 1996), 56.

[140] Carl Sagan, *Cosmos* (New York: Random House, 1980), 4.

[141] Stone Temple Pilots, "A Song for Sleeping." *Shangri-La Dee Da*, Atlantic, 2001.

[142] Staind, "Zoe Jane," *14 Shades of Grey*, Elektra, 2003.

Chapter 10: Cruci"fix"

[143] Dominic Frontiere and Alan Alch, "Branded." *STLyrics,* www.stlyrics.com/lyrics/televisiontvthemelyrics-sciencefictionwesterns/branded.htm

[144] Malcolm Muggeridge, *Jesus: The Man Who Lives* (New York: Harper & Row, 1975), 19

[145] Gerald Sittser, *Water from a Deep Well* (Downers Grove, Ill.: InterVarsity Press, 2007), 120.

[146] John R. Stott, *The Cross of Christ* (Downers Grove, Ill.: InterVarsity Press, 1986), 160.

[147] Frederick Buechner and Lee Boltin, *The Faces of Jesus* (New York: Riverwood Publishers, 1974), 150.

[148] Calvin Miller, *Into the Depths of God* (Minneapolis, Minn.: Bethany House, 2000), 32–33.

[149] John R. Stott, *The Cross of Christ* (Downers Grove, Ill.: InterVarsity Press, 1986), 157–58.

[150] Paul Johnson, *The Quest for God* (New York: HarperCollins, 1996), 170, 171.

151 Frederick Buechner and Lee Boltin, *The Faces of Jesus* (New York: Riverwood Publishers, 1974), 150

152 Keith Miller, *The Becomers* (Waco, Tex.: Word Books, 1973), 42.

153 Brennan Manning, *A Glimpse of Jesus* (New York: HarperSanFrancisco, 2003), 69.

154 Timothy Keller, *The Reason for God* (New York: Dutton/Penguin, 2008), 32.

155 Brian Welch, *Save Me from Myself* (New York: HarperOne, 2007), 213.

156 Philip Yancey, *Rumors of Another World* (Grand Rapids, Mich.: Zondervan, 2003), 156–57.

Chapter 11: The Cast Party

157 C. S. Lewis, *The Great Divorce* (New York: HarperCollins), 105–7.

158 Jack Graham, comments heard on his radio broadcast.

159 Robert Jastrow, source unknown.

160 Jacques Choron, *Death and Modern Man* (New York: Collier, 1964), 164.

161 Albert Camus, quoted at www.iwise.com/rDmBv

162 Ideas from Dinesh D' Souza, *Life After Death: The Evidence* (Washington, D.C.: Regnery, 2009), 220.

163 Ravi Zacharias, *Jesus Among Other Gods*, (Nashville: W Publishing, 2000), 71.

164 Eben Alexander, *Proof of Heaven* (New York: Simon & Schuster, 2012), 10, 144.

165 Mary C. Neal, *To Heaven and Back* (Colorado Springs: WaterBrook Books, 2011, 2012), 71.

166 Ibid., 70.

167 Ibid., 73.

168 Carl Sagan, *Cosmos* (New York: Ballantine, 1980), 1–2.

169 Richard Dawkins, quoted in Ravi Zacharias, *Beyond Opinion* (Nashville: Thomas Nelson, 2007), 192.

170 Toad The Wet Sprocket, "Little Buddha," *Coil*, Sony, 1997.

171 Thousand Foot Crutch, "Be Somebody," *End is Where We Begin*, TFK Music, 2012.

172 John Donne, "Death Be Not Proud," Poem Hunter.com, www.poemhunter.com/poem/death-be-not-proud/

173 Eben Alexander, *Proof of Heaven* (New York: Simon & Schuster, 2012), 39.

174 Peter Kreeft, quoted in Gerald Sittser, *Water from a Deep Well* (Downers Grove, Ill.: InterVarsity Press, 2007), 137.
175 Eben Alexander, *Proof of Heaven* (New York: Simon & Schuster, 2012), 10, 144, 38.
176 The Eagles, "Hotel California," *Hotel California*, Elektra/Asylum, 1984.
177 Randy Alcorn, *Heaven* (Carol Stream, Ill.: Tyndale House, 2004), 313.

Chapter 12: Lingua Dei

178 Ingrid Newark, "Ingrid Newkirk," <u>Wikiquote,</u> en.wikiquote.org/wiki/Ingrid_Newkirk
179 Frederick Buechner, *The Clown in the Belfry* (New York: HarperSanFrancisco, 1992), 165.
180 Timothy Keller, *The Reason for God* (New York: Dutton, 2008), 54.
181 John R. Stott, *Basic Christianity* (Grand Rapids, Mich.: Eerdmans, 1971), 138.
182 Keith Miller, *The Becomers* (Waco, Tex.: Word Books, 1973), 128.

Printed in Great Britain
by Amazon

37392994R00219